The Internet and Higher Education

CHANDOS INTERNET SERIES

Chandos' new series of books are aimed at all those individuals interested in the internet. They have been specially commissioned to provide the reader with an authoritative view of current thinking. If you would like a full listing of current and forthcoming titles, please visit our web site **www.chandospublishing.com** or contact Hannah Grace-Williams on email info@chandospublishing.com or telephone number +44 (0) 1993 848726.

New authors: we are always pleased to receive ideas for new titles; if you would like to write a book for Chandos, please contact Dr Glyn Jones on email gjones@chandospublishing.com or telephone number +44 (0) 1993 848726.

Bulk orders: some organisations buy a number of copies of our books. If you are interested in doing this, we would be pleased to discuss a discount. Please contact Hannah Grace-Williams on email info@chandospublishing.com or telephone number +44 (0) 1993 848726.

The Internet and Higher Education

Achieving global reach

ALFRED P. ROVAI

Chandos Publishing

Oxford · England

Chandos Publishing (Oxford) Limited
TBAC Business Centre
Avenue 4
Station Lane
Witney
Oxford OX28 4BN
UK
Tel: +44 (0) 1993 848726 Fax: +44 (0) 1865 884448
Email: info@chandospublishing.com
www.chandospublishing.com

First published in Great Britain in 2009

ISBN:
978 1 84334 524 4 (paperback)
978 1 84334 525 1 (hardback)
1 84334 524 2 (paperback)
1 84334 525 0 (hardback)

© A. P. Rovai, 2009

Typeset by Domex e-Data Pvt. Ltd.
Printed in the UK and USA.

Contents

List of figures

Preface

An increasing number of traditional universities are transforming themselves from single to dual-mode universities as they acknowledge the importance of distance education and seek to become global institutions. This transformation has significant organisational, operational, cultural and economic implications. The purpose of this book is draw from the professional literature in order to provide a planning and operational framework for those universities intending to extend their reach globally through distance education using the internet.

The distance education literature is vast and runs the gamut from research and practitioner information on topics such as information and communication technology, computer-mediated communication, course design and pedagogy, to educational outcomes and costs. Moreover, this field is in a continuous state of change as technology advances and new innovations are implemented, necessitating further changes in online programmes and courses. These changes fuel the need for additional research.

This book is designed for educational administrators, faculty members, students and others who have an interest in the topic of distance education using the internet. Its goal is to make accessible, in a clear and concise form, a body of current evidence-based knowledge on online distance learning in higher education to increase understanding of the major theories, issues, challenges and solutions. The book does not aim to offer an exhaustive treatment of the topic, but rather to provide a straightforward perspective of online distance education with a focus on global and international universities. Consequently, the implications of a culturally diverse study body are explored in each chapter.

The term *online learning* is used synonymously with *web-based learning* and *internet-based learning*. The term does not suggest the entire learning experience must be online. Blended or hybrid programmes and courses that utilise a mix of traditional and new media are becoming increasingly popular. Thus, the amount of teaching and learning using online technologies can vary within any programme and/or course.

Existing books on distance education fall somewhere along a continuum anchored at one end by a strong research orientation with little, if any, practical advice. At the other end, the continuum is anchored by a strong practical orientation with few links to the theoretical and research-based underpinnings of the teaching and learning strategies presented. Moreover, research-oriented books are often difficult for practitioners to understand and apply, while practitioner-oriented books may be inconsequential for the experienced scholar. Without a theoretical basis, the practical advice lacks a conceptual framework for planning and implementing an effective teaching and learning strategy and may represent opinion rather than evidenced-based solutions.

This volume focuses on the middle space between these two extremes by balancing theory and research with practical advice so that readers are well prepared for the excitement and opportunities of designing and implementing distance education programmes and courses in a global higher education environment. Various aspects of online distance education, to include a discussion of challenges and solutions, are presented in seven chapters:

- *Chapter 1* covers key concepts of online higher education – historical and research perspectives, a profile of the online student, globalisation and internationalisation, constructivism, sense of community, self-directed learning and adult learning;

- *Chapter 2* covers global distance education issues – access to technology and higher education, multiculturalism and diversity in distance education, culturally-based online learning differences, online racial discrimination, and academic capitalism and consumerism;

- *Chapter 3* covers technology and the internet – generations of distance learning technologies, Web 1.0, 2.0, 3.0 and beyond, open education resources and computer-mediated communication;

- *Chapter 4* covers designing global online programmes and courses – single-mode online and blended designs, learning management systems, and synchronous and asynchronous learning activities;

- *Chapter 5* covers global online teaching and learning – computer-mediated communication, inquiry-based learning, facilitating and moderating online discussions effectively, and assessment of online student learning;

- *Chapter 6* covers quality assurance and institutional effectiveness – quality online programmes and red flags, programme evaluation, course evaluation and programme accreditation;
- *Chapter 7* provides a summary and conclusion.

These seven chapters are connected by six themes:

- the emergence of a global learning society and the role of online distance education to satisfy the higher educational needs of this society;
- transformational changes in higher education on a global scale as the result of advances in information and communication technology;
- changing patterns of learning to respond to evolving individual and societal needs;
- the impact of online delivery on course and programme design and instruction;
- the importance of a multicultural approach to higher education as the result of a globally diverse student body; and
- the incorporation of global learning themes across the curriculum.

About the author

Alfred (Fred) Rovai joined the faculty of Regent University, Virginia Beach, Virginia, in 2000, and teaches strategic planning, programme evaluation and statistics courses in the online education and philosophy doctorate programmes. He previously taught online courses for the University of California at Los Angeles online teaching programme.

Rovai is the lead editor of *Closing the African American Achievement Gap in Higher Education* (2007) and lead author of *Distance Learning in Higher Education: A Programmatic Approach to Planning, Design, Instruction, Evaluation, and Accreditation* (2008), both released by Teachers College Press. Since 2000, he has also written over 50 journal articles and book chapters that focus on distance learning, sense of community, and/or the roles of gender and culture in computer-mediated communication.

Rovai graduated from San Jose State University with a bachelor's degree in mathematics. He completed postgraduate work in systems management at the University of Southern California and received masters' degrees in public administration and education from the University of Northern Colorado and Old Dominion University, respectively. He also earned a doctor of philosophy degree with a concentration in academic leadership from Old Dominion University in 1996.

The author may be contacted at:

Regent University
1000 Regent University Drive
Virginia Beach
VA 23464-9800
USA
Tel: +1 757 352 4861
Fax: +1 757 352 4857
E-mail: *alfrrov@regent.edu*

Key concepts of global online higher education

Introduction

Worldwide enrolment in higher education is growing between 10 and 15 per cent per year (Heyneman, 2006) and some universities have become mega-universities with enrolments in the hundreds of thousands. Higher education participation rates of around 50 per cent are now the norm in developed nations, whereas in some nations in South Asia and Sub-Saharan Africa, participation rates remain below 10 per cent (Daniel, Kanwar and Uvaliæ-Trumbiæ, 2006). In developed nations, most universities offer some form of distance education, with the internet being the most popular mode of delivery.

Stephen Heyneman (2006) asserts that every country has three higher education ambitions, the first of which is to improve access. Accordingly, access to higher education is improving throughout the world, and the number of regions where it constitutes elite education, that is, where it reaches less than 15 per cent of the age cohort, is in decline. The second ambition is to improve the quality of higher education. Finally, the third ambition is to improve equity, that is, to offer scholarships and fellowships to able students from poor families or disadvantaged regions.

To help achieve these ambitions, educating and training students at a distance is a major and growing element of the mission of many universities as they respond to the needs of students beyond their traditional constituencies and to the massification of higher education. Online enrolments have been growing faster than overall higher education enrolments during the past several years in many nations, particularly in North America, Western Europe and in Australia and New Zealand. In 2006, for example, 23 per cent of all higher education enrolments in India were in distance education. The government's target is that by 2010, 40 per cent of all higher education participation will take place using distance education (Daniel, Kanwar and Uvaliæ-Trumbiæ, 2006). As a result of such expansion, online education is often referred to as a worldwide growth industry and it is likely to remain so for years to come.

A major contributor to this worldwide growth of online learning is the global spread of the internet. Internet growth and the concurrent increase in technological innovation for academic purposes provide increased opportunities for people to pursue advanced academic degrees. According to Lea and Blake (2004) and Perraton (2000), the expansion of online distance education in both industrialised and developing countries is influenced by the following:

- *the ideological goal* to widen access to higher education and to empower citizens in order to narrow the distance between privilege and poverty;

- *the economic goal* to expand higher education capacity at a relatively low cost in order to educate the workforce in response to labour market needs;

- *the technological goal* to use information and communication technologies to deliver education to remote areas and to people who cannot attend traditional on-campus programmes;

- *the political goal* to embrace distance education as a means to meet the demand for higher education.

Distance education broadly consists of any type of learning in which the components of a structured learning activity (i.e. learners, instructor and learning resources) are separated by time and/or geography (Rovai, Ponton and Baker, 2008). Barker, Frisbie and Patrick (1989) suggest that there are two forms of distance education. One is the traditional correspondence-based form, which is mostly based on independent study and can include mixed media, such as videocassettes and CD-ROM. The second is the telecommunications-based form of distance education that places emphasis on interactivity and collaboration.

The term *e-learning* is commonly used when electronic means, such as telecommunications technologies, are used to mediate learning. E-learning consists of synchronous tools, such as instructional television supplemented by two-way audio, and/or asynchronous tools, such as internet-based e-mail and online discussion boards. *Synchronous* refers to tools that permit the teacher and students to interact with each another in real time. Alternatively, *asynchronous* refers to tools that allow members of the learning community to receive instruction wherever and whenever they desire, as long as they have access to the internet and communicate with a time delay. Consequently, members of an asynchronous learning community have ample time for reflection before they respond to a communication, in contrast to a synchronous communication environment where the communication is in real time and is more likely to be characterised by spontaneity than by reflection.

The term *online learning* is used when the internet is used for e-learning. Online learning is also referred to as *borderless education*, as educational provision using the internet can easily cross geographical boundaries. Online learning also includes mobile learning (also called *m-learning*), which provides access to the mobile web using portable devices such as smart phones and ultra-portable computers. Asynchronous online learning is the most common form of distance learning in higher education. The anytime, anywhere delivery of online education and its power to bring people together for collaborative and reflective learning are widely recognised virtues of asynchronous learning networks.

Stansfield, McLellan and Connolly (2004) maintain that asynchronous learning networks provide:

- increased opportunities for reflecting on and refining ideas;
- a greater degree of learner control over instructional materials;
- flexibility permitted by unrestricted access to course materials; and
- richer levels of interaction both in relation to the materials and in the opportunities presented for active learning by means of conferencing and collaborative learning activities.

The purpose of this chapter is to describe the key concepts of global online higher education in order to provide a foundation for the discussions contained in subsequent chapters. The chapter starts by examining the historical roots of worldwide distance education followed by a description of the characteristics of distance education learners.

Historical roots

Early types of distance education were in the form of correspondence education. The nineteenth century saw the emergence of distance education institutions that specialised in correspondence education, such as the University Correspondence College in London in 1887 (Picciano, 2001). In 1886, H. S. Hermod's correspondence school in Sweden specialised in teaching English and became 'one of the largest distance learning organizations in the world' (Picciano, 2001: 8). In 1891, Thomas J. Foster created the International Correspondence School in the USA. By 1900, it had an enrolment of 225,000 students, increasing to over 2 million by 1920 (Simonson, Smaldino, Albright and Zvack, 2000). Today, the school goes by the name Thompson Publishing (Moore and Kearsley, 2005).

Technology-based distance education has its origins in the introduction of audiovisual devices in the early 1900s. One of the first catalogues of instructional films appeared in 1910 (Reiser, 1987). Shortly afterwards, instructional media in the form of slides and films were introduced into correspondence programmes.

During the 1920s and 1930s, broadcast radio became the instructional media and delivery tool preferred by educators in distance education (Picciano, 2001). As an example, radio was used to deliver educational programming in Australia and New Zealand by the Australian Broadcasting Company (ABC). In addition to broadcasts, the ABC provided financial assistance to schools for the purchase of radio receivers. However, the effectiveness of radio as an educational medium was limited. At the time, it was assumed that instruction intended for one medium (correspondence) could be directly applied to another (radio). The notion of adapting pedagogy to the medium was not conceived until later and even today some faculty members attempt to apply instruction developed for face-to-face learning to an online course without modification.

Starting in the 1950s, educational television usage began to grow. In the early 1960s, the use of educational television was promoted in several nations with governmental legal and financial support. However, the use of educational television declined by the 1970s (Reiser, 1987). Reasons given for this decline include teacher resistance to television in the classroom, the expense of the television systems, and the inability of broadcast television alone to meet all the requirements for student learning (Reiser, 1987).

In 1962, the University of South Africa declared it would operate entirely at a distance, offering correspondence, audio and television instruction (Moore and Kearsley, 2005). This declaration was an important milestone in the growth of technology-based distance education and soon other institutions followed suit.

During the 1960s, a commission formed in the UK identified ways of expanding the higher education system, especially by opening admission to working class adults (Cerych and Sabatier, 1986). The recommendations of this commission ultimately led to the establishment of the British Open University in 1969, using innovations such as the course development team method, first-come, first-served enrolment policy, and the use of mixed media to support distance learning. The first cohort of 25,000 students was admitted to the university in the summer of 1970.

The focus of the Open University is on student success rather than institutional profit. The original concept, which predates modern telecommunications advances, included carefully developed textbooks, audio and videocassettes supplemented by conventional broadcast radio and television, and a tutor who could be reached by telephone (Matthews, 1999). In the 1970s, the Open University implemented a successful interactive television programme (Picciano, 2001) and later entered the online learning market.

The intent of the Open University is to make learning available to all adults who want it, particularly working class adults and those who have been denied entry to formal higher education because of geographic location. The British Open University now has an international student body, enrolling more than 200,000 adult students with 20,000 students graduating each year (Moore and Kearsley, 2005).

This concept of an open university has been highly successful in terms of both quality and cost-effectiveness. Given the numerous contexts for education, all of which may have their distance learning and/or open learning components, distance learning and open learning have been merged into a single model with the label *open and distance learning*.

In the two decades following the establishment of the British Open University, four open universities were established in Europe and more than 20 were established in nations around the world, largely based on the UK model (Matthews, 1999). Many of these universities have become mega-universities, enrolling more than 100,000 students each. They include, along with year established, the University of South Africa (1973), the Korean National Open University (1982), the Anadolu University in Turkey (1982) and the Indira Gandhi National Open University in India (1985). More than 22 nations now have open universities with enrolments ranging from 100,000 to over 500,000 (Moore and Kearsley, 2005).

The USA is one of the few nations not to establish a national open university. The major reason cited is that responsibility for education in the USA is delegated to individual states (Moore, 2003). However, New York State's Empire State College commenced operation in 1971 to make higher education degrees more accessible to learners unable to attend traditional, campus-based programmes. Additionally, by the 1980s three US universities – Rutgers University (the state university of New Jersey), the University of Houston and the University of Maryland – were making use of course materials from the British Open University (Verduin and Clark, 1991).

During the 1970s, with advances in microwave technology and the use of direct broadcast by satellite, distance learning systems utilising these synchronous technologies were able to reach regional campuses and remote sites via a closed circuit television concept. Such systems typically employ audio systems using telephone technology for interactivity.

By the 1980s and 1990s, the advent of personal computers and the world wide web revolutionised the delivery options available to institutions and students for learning at a distance. The expansion of the internet resulted in a decline in the use of television as a medium for distance education. Online learning started as an important and growing part of traditional instruction as many courses were web-facilitated. Students attending face-to-face courses were able to access the internet between class meetings, obtain course materials and interact publicly with other members of the classroom community using a group discussion board, or interact privately, by e-mail. This model of employing both face-to-face and online components in a single course or a single programme is known as *blended learning* and remains a popular model today at many universities.

During the 1990s, distance learning and teaching moved from the periphery to the centre of university life. Single-mode universities were established, offering distance learning programmes through the internet. In the USA, successful examples, along with year established, include Western Governors University (1995) and Capella University (1993). Additionally, the University of Phoenix is a for-profit mega-university owned by the Apollo Group, Inc. and includes physical campuses in 38 states as well as in Canada and Puerto Rico. While the focus is on online delivery using mostly asynchronous tools, the physical campuses are used for supplementary services, such as workshops, computer access, study rooms and tutoring.

The expansion of online distance learning also led to the development of support systems for online learning management by companies like Blackboard, Inc. These companies develop and market learning management systems, such as the Blackboard Academic Suite. This system, for example, consists of learning, community, portfolio, content and outcomes subsystems. It facilitates e-learning by providing online access to numerous integrated tools that enable faculty to bring course materials online and manage learning and students to access these materials and interact with the teacher and other students using personal computers and portable wireless devices, such as personal digital assistants.

The establishment of the concept of open and distance learning and the emergence of online technologies using the internet changed the face of distance learning permanently, and the subsequent worldwide adoption of distance learning gave impetus to the field as we know it today. The concept of distance education and the advances in telecommunication technologies provide the means, but the phenomenal growth in online learning stems largely from the need for universities to meet the educational demands of non-traditional students who have family and work commitments that limit their access to a campus and/or a fixed class schedule. Online education has become the new answer to meeting the continuing and lifelong education needs of the busy adult. Moreover, the old industrial jobs are declining in number worldwide while Information Age jobs that require a more educated workforce are on the rise.

The distance education student

As higher education has expanded, the student body has become much larger and diverse in terms of age, ethnicity, cultural background and academic preparation. Compared with students on traditional programmes, distance education students tend to be older and are more likely to work full-time and attend school part-time. They are also more likely to be married, have greater family responsibilities and have greater average incomes (e.g. see Ashby, 2002). Additionally, many individuals with disabilities find that distance education courses improve their access to higher education by making in-person contact less necessary.

Consequently, distance education students have different educational and personal needs compared with more traditional university students. In particular, distance education students tend to be more mature and are thus better able to work independently. Mupinga, Nora and Yaw (2006) report the top needs of online students as:

- technical help;
- flexible and understanding teachers;
- advance course information;
- sample assignments;
- grading standards, e.g. a rubric;
- timely instructor feedback;
- interpersonal interaction;
- the same learning management system used in a consistent manner by all courses and teachers;
- additional reference materials; and
- equal recognition with on-campus students.

Unlike their on-campus peers, students enrolled in distance education programmes most often participate in coursework from off-campus locations using computer technology and the internet to access course materials and communicate with their teacher and other students. Unless required to attend on-campus orientations or residencies, they may never visit the university campus and typically access student support services at a distance, either by personal computer or by telephone.

An increasing proportion of college students are members of the 'Net Generation' (i.e. were born during or after the 1980s) who grew up using information technology with sensory-rich interactive environments, entertainment-style communication and immediate feedback, and who prefer experiential activities, whether virtual or real (Rovai, Ponton and Baker, 2008). Many of these new students rely more on the internet for information than on libraries. Moreover, they are accustomed to using the internet for multi-user online activities, such as participation in virtual worlds, like Second Life, as well as social networking. These changes suggest students from the Net Generation and beyond may be more motivated in immersive and authentic learning environments and engaging in flexible and convenient learning activities. For example, instead of reading course materials, many Net Generation students may prefer the convenience of listening to a podcast on an iPod while exercising. Edwards and Usher (2008: 129) identify the following characteristics shared by most members of the Net Generation:

- the hours spent online appear to have affected not so much what but *how* they think;
- they have a highly developed level of visual literacy and are able to weave together texts, images and audio;
- they are oriented to fast and multi-tasking;
- they make no distinction between physical and virtual reality and can move quickly between these worlds;
- as learners, the Net Generation clearly perceive the open space of the internet and the world wide web, of Google and Wikipedia, as their information universe and they prefer these as ways of researching;
- they have hypertext minds in the sense that they can leap around, piecing together information from multiple sources;
- they are not into careful investigation, placing more value on speed than accuracy;
- they thrive on interactivity, e.g. online short message service (SMS) and instant messaging. They tend to have poor listening skills but they do like to learn with others.

Consequently, many students of today expect their educational experiences to incorporate and reflect their extensive experiences with information and communication technologies.

Online virtual classrooms are less aimed at the traditional market of young college people, but rather are meant to serve disciplined adult learners. Additionally, by the late 1990s another market appeared: students already enrolled in traditional classes desiring to ease their schedules by taking one or more courses online. A report by the American Council on Education, Center for Policy Analysis and EDUCAUSE (Oblinger, Barone and Hawkins, 2001) cites seven distinct audiences for distance learning:

- corporate learners;
- professional enhancement learners;
- degree-completion adult learners;
- college experience learners (or the traditional student);
- pre-college learners;
- remediation and test-preparation learners; and
- recreational learners.

Oblinger (2003) argues that there is, in effect, a new breed of student – one with different needs as well as skills. These students, in turn, require different educational experiences.

The remainder of this chapter is devoted to addressing globalisation and internationalisation, multicultural education, constructivism, sense of community, self-directed learning and adult learning. These areas are foundational to an understanding of online distance education in a global context.

Copyright and intellectual property rights

Distance education presents complex copyright issues related to both ownership of newly-created course design and materials, such as recorded online lectures and written lecture notes, and the fair use of existing materials that are used in the course, such as journal articles and book extracts. There is no real difference regarding copyright based on the format in which the protected material is published. Works that are published in electronic format (e.g. CDs, online databases, webpages, computer files, podcasts, etc.) are protected in the same manner as their printed equivalents. In particular, information available on the internet has the same copyright protection as if it were in a printed book.

Each nation has its own copyright laws. Creators and users of copyrighted works should become aware of the copyright law of their own nation as well as differences in intellectual property law between nations if they are engaged in cross-border education. No international copyright law exists that will protect a work in every nation. There are, however, several important international treaties that protect works between and within member nations.

The Berne Convention for the Protection of Literary and Artistic Works, usually known as the Berne Convention, is the primary international copyright treaty designed to protect literary and artistic works. The convention is administered by the World Intellectual Property Organization (WIPO). Additionally, the Agreement on Trade-Related Aspects of Intellectual Property Rights (TRIPS), of which the 147 member nations of the World Trade Organization (WTO) are signatories, stipulates basic intellectual property rights largely in accordance with the terms of the Berne Convention. The Berne Convention and TRIPS require member nations to grant the following basic protection:

- the protection of literary and artistic works, such as books, pamphlets, journal articles, lectures, presentations and works of a similar nature that are likely to be used in an online course; and

- provision that the author (or owner of the copyright) can authorise its reproduction in various forms.

Automatic copyright protection is a central feature of the Berne Convention, meaning that it is not essential to display a copyright notice in order to assert this fact. Nonetheless, it is advantageous to use such a notice as this prevents copiers from claiming that they are innocent infringers as no copyright notice was given. Any nation that has signed the Berne Convention must extend to the citizens of other member nations the same copyright protection and restrictions that it extends to its own citizens. However, if something is published in a Berne Convention nation but the person responsible for its intellectual content is not a citizen of a member nation, then the work is protected only to the extent covered by the copyright laws in that person's nation of origin.

Although the Berne Convention specifies that the copyright law of the nation where copyright is claimed shall be applied, the convention also stipulates that unless the legislation of that nation otherwise provides, the term shall not exceed the term fixed in the nation of origin of the work. Additionally, TRIPS requires that member nations must apply their criminal laws in cases of commercial piracy.

Certain types of use are, however, exempt from the control of copyright owners. In particular, Article 9(2) of the Berne Convention stipulates that nations can permit reproduction of copyright works without the permission of the copyright owner 'in certain special cases, provided that such reproduction does not conflict with a normal exploitation of the work and does not unreasonably prejudice the legitimate interests of the author' (Berne Convention, 1886/1979: 10). This provision has led to a wide variety of exceptions around the world that are especially relevant to distance education programmes.

One of these exceptions is exemplified by the 1961 US 'fair use' citation of the US Copyright Act (Copyright Act, title 17, US Code), which permits any use of copyright for free and without permission provided it is fair. According to this doctrine, it is fair to reproduce a particular work for teaching, scholarship and/or research purposes, provided the following four factors are taken into full consideration:

- the purpose and character of the use, including whether such use is of commercial nature or is for non-profit educational purposes;
- the nature of the copyrighted work;
- amount and substantiality of the portion used in relation to the copyrighted work as a whole; and
- the effect of the use upon the potential market for or value of the copyrighted work.

Another example of copyright exception for educational purposes can be found under the 'fair dealing' provisions of the Copyright Act of Canada 1985. Thus, in Canada, provided certain criteria are followed, using copyrighted materials in the pursuit of research and study without first obtaining consent from the creator or submitting payment is not considered a copyright infringement. Similar provisions are also found in many of the common law jurisdictions of the Commonwealth of Nations.

As Petrina, Volk and Soowook (2004: 193) point out, 'extension of copyright is one thing; protection is something entirely different'. Their concern is with the uncontainable nature of digital property and the ease of copying it. Proactive moves to protect owners and their copyrighted material come under the label of digital rights management (DRM). DRM is a set of technologies used to protect digital products from copyright infringement. Each method of technological protection varies in the nature of protection and degree of security. These methods include access control protection, cryptographic protection and copy-control protection. The effectiveness of access control technologies, in particular, depends on the behaviour of users, such as a student who should not share passwords with others. Notwithstanding the importance of DRM technologies, implementation of DRM by publishers of copyrighted materials poses a potential threat to distance education. It is important that DRM technologies do not prevent material being displayed in a quantity and quality similar to what is seen in the traditional classroom setting.

According to Rovai, Ponton and Baker (2008), one method of providing protected materials to students under the provision of fair use in an online course is through the supporting library's electronic reserve service. Typically, fair use of copyrighted material held on electronic reserve is limited to one article from a journal issue and one chapter or less than 10 per cent of the contents of a book. Copyright permission is required when an article is needed for more than one academic term, when multiple articles from the same journal are required, when one chapter of a book is needed for more than one academic term, or when multiple chapters of a book are needed. Additionally, teaching materials may incorporate no more than 30 seconds of music, lyrics or a music video under copyright.

Another popular method that allows students access to copyrighted material is to provide students with a durable link to the copyrighted document in the virtual classroom, assuming the material is available online. Obtaining the internet address of the copyrighted document and making it available to students as a hyperlink can accomplish this task. However, this procedure can be problematic under certain circumstances. Deep linking, especially inside a frame, may require the copyright owner's permission to access its websites (Rao, 2003).

As many of the provisions of copyright law focus on the behaviour of institutions, each institution must develop its own policy, impose restrictions on access and disseminate copyright information. It is beyond the scope of this book to provide such detailed information as well as detailed information on national laws. To avoid copyright infringement, faculty who teach distance education courses must therefore obtain such information directly from their institutions.

Globalisation and internationalisation

We live in an increasingly interconnected world. Values are becoming more oriented toward a global perspective and global and international institutions are playing more important roles in world societies. Additionally, international trade in services, manufacturing and agriculture are on the rise, information and money are flowing across borders more quickly, we are moving toward a global economy and cross-border education is expanding. This phenomenon is variously referred to as *globalisation* and *internationalisation*, and presents both opportunities and challenges for higher education.

Globalisation refers to the process of increasing international interdependence of economies and to liberalising trade and markets (Friedman and Ramonet, 1999). A globalised world is therefore one in which political, economic, social, cultural and educational events become increasingly interconnected and which events in one society affect the lives of people in other societies. Many problems that were once national are now global, and dangers that once came only from nations now also come from hostile individuals and organisations or from social trends, such as human-caused biodiversity loss and climate disruption (Richardson, 2007).

The professional literature has no agreed definition for globalisation, and the word is often used as a synonym for internationalisation. The various definitions described in the literature can generally be classified as adhering to one of the following five views (Scholte, 2005):

- *internationalisation*, where globalisation is viewed as another adjective to describe cross-border relations between nations;
- *liberalisation*, where globalisation refers to a process of removing government-imposed restrictions on movements between nations in order to create an open, borderless world economy;
- *universalisation*, where globalisation is the process of spreading various objects and experiences to people in all corners of the earth, using such media as television and the internet;
- *Westernisation or modernisation*, where globalisation is understood as a dynamic, whereby the social structures of modernity (e.g. capitalism, rationalism, industrialism, etc.) are spread the world over, normally destroying pre-existent cultures and local self-determination in the process;
- *deterritorialisation*, where globalisation entails a reconfiguration of geography, so that social space is no longer wholly mapped in terms of territorial places, territorial distances and territorial borders.

Global universities need to expand their strategic environmental scanning beyond the confines of national borders to include the political, economic, cultural, legal and technological changes occurring around the globe. Edwards and Usher (2008) summarise the professional literature regarding how globalisation influences education. They identify the following five factors:

- improving national economic performance requires tightening the connection between education, employment, productivity and international trade;

- addressing the criticism that education does not deliver what is needed requires student outcomes in employment-related skills to be improved;

- changing education without significant governmental financial support results in institutions attaining more direct control over curriculum and assessment;

- reducing the cost of education to governments results in the movement of education towards a business model with commercial and business-like ways;

- increasing accountability in education results in the increased use of community involvement in education decision making.

Green, Luu, Calderon and Eckel (2007) identify the opportunities and drivers of global education and attending a global university. They describe a 'push' that includes prestige/competition, advancement of globalisation, quality improvement and furthering of the institution's service mission. At the same time, they describe a 'pull' that includes increased demand for higher education, the appeal of receiving a foreign education while staying at home, the increase of governmental policies that attract foreign educators, and the rise of English-language education. Although cross-border distance education is a growing phenomenon in developed nations, its impact so far is limited in developing nations, which have the most to gain from cross-border provision (Daniel, Kanwar and Uvaliæ-Trumbiæ, 2005).

International universities enrol foreign students and faculty come from other nations to study, teach or conduct research while faculty from the home institution frequently go abroad. However, globalisation, as applied to higher education, refers to the global reach of the university into the functions of teaching, research and public service. A global university, in contrast to an international university, operates in multiple nations, either with a physical presence, such as satellite campuses or learning centres, and/or by cross-border distance education delivered by technology, and/or by forming alliances or partnerships with institutions in other nations.

Strategic alliances and partnerships are being established on a worldwide or regional basis. Distance education alliances and partnerships should focus on the specific needs of the target population in terms of the application of appropriate technology and delivery of relevant content at a competitive price in the receiving nation. These alliances allow universities seeking global reach to position themselves globally by taking advantage of opportunities too great to tackle on their own, to spread risk and to capitalise on each others' branding. Additionally, some nations are suspicious of external providers, while in other nations there is a government monopoly on higher education (Larsen, Martin and Morris, 2002). Cross-border alliances and partnerships with local providers help reduce or eliminate these obstacles.

A global university seeks and welcomes international students, who bring different cultures and values to the institution and the classroom. International students not only become a part of the fabric of university and classroom life, but the curriculum incorporates global learning themes across disciplines.

Global Learning

Thomas Friedman (2005) argues that an increasing number of nations and companies compete in global markets. The effects of globalisation are pervasive and are leading to new social, political and business models. This flattening of the world represents a fundamental change and requires that organisational leaders develop and use a global mindset. One way for universities to respond to globalisation and develop global mindsets is with global learning. Proponents of global learning identify it as a remedy for widespread cross-cultural misunderstanding, prejudice and global ignorance. If we are to become a truly global and educated world, we must explore issues of diversity and investigate how multicultural matters affect our society and us. We must also prepare leaders and a workforce who can succeed in a global environment.

Global learning involves the use of technology that enables global reach in a distance education environment and the acquisition of global perspectives and competencies, such as proficiency in cross-cultural communication. Drawing on Scholte's work, one can view global learning as the universalisation of education that is an emerging aspect of globalisation. The American Council on Education uses global learning as an umbrella term to cover three types of learning:

- *global learning*: understanding the systems and phenomena that transcend national borders;
- *international learning*: understanding nations and their relationships; and
- *intercultural learning*: understanding and navigating cultural differences.

Accordingly, in its Global Learning for All Project, the American Council on Education, defines global learning as:

> the knowledge, skills, and attitudes that students acquire through a variety of experiences that enable them to understand world cultures and events, analyze global systems, appreciate cultural differences, and apply this knowledge and appreciation to their lives as citizens and workers. (American Council on Education, 2006: ¶ 1)

Major themes related to the global learning movement include peace and conflict, human rights and social justice, cultural diversity, interdependence, environmental education, sustainable futures and the role of religion (e.g. Werner and Case, 1997). For example, Farideh Salili and Rumhahn Hoosain (2006) argue that global learning should include a critical analysis of the role of religion in constructing individual identity, group solidarity and power relations in a global, capitalist context. Themes such as these have constituted an attempt to broaden worldviews in the belief that:

> the problems, structural relationships, and emerging changes in the world ought to be represented from differing perspectives and with greater complexity. The obligation to do so is a matter of honesty, moral responsibility, and enlightened self-interest. (Werner and Case, 1996: 3)

Global competency

The purpose of global learning is to become globally competent by acquiring a global perspective and acting in a global and cross-cultural manner. Case (1993) describes global perspective as consisting of substantive and perceptual dimensions. He describes the substantive dimension as knowledge of various features of the world and how they work. This substantive dimension can therefore be viewed as the cognitive component of global learning. It provides a foundation upon which to build global competence. Case's perceptual dimension is 'an orientation of outlook [that] ... involves nurturing perspectives that are empathic, free of stereotypes, not predicated on naive or simplistic assumptions and not colored by prejudicial statements' (Case, 1993: 318). Thus, Case's perceptual dimension is related to the affective component of global learning.

Donald Cyr (2002) suggests that global competency can improve organisational performance by incorporating essential concepts from different cultures into organisational routines and thinking. According to Cyr, one can combine Eastern and Western values to become a more effective member of any community. Thus, one links the 'individual self' from the West and the 'civic self' from the East to emotional intelligence (i.e. the ability of individuals to understand their own emotions and those of the people with whom they work), leadership style, and institutional performance and effectiveness.

The professional literature includes numerous definitions of global competency, each focusing on different aspects of this multidimensional construct. Additionally, global competency varies by profession, although there is considerable overlap. For example, being globally competent in business does not mean that one will also be also globally competent in law, although some skills, knowledge and attitudes will be the same.

Below is a model of global competency that represents a synthesis of views from the professional literature (e.g. American Council on Education, 2006; American Council on International Intercultural Education, 1996; Case, 1993; Edwards and Usher, 2008; Werner and Case, 1996). A globally competent individual possesses the following characteristics:

- A globally diverse worldview with a global perspective
  - knowledge of global geography;
  - awareness of the diversity of cultures, religions, ideas, practices and values to be found in nations around the world;
  - comprehension of the foundational philosophical assumptions and resulting cultural norms of major cross-cultural worldviews, e.g. theism, pantheism, spiritism, naturalism and postmodernism;
  - awareness of the commonalities of nations;

- recognition of the geopolitical and economic interdependence of the world;
- understanding of the ways in which culture shapes worldviews including one's own worldview;
- recognition of how the ideas and practices of one's own culture might be viewed from the vantage points of other cultures;
- value and respect for the richness of diversity;
- commitment to lifelong learning.

■ Understanding of the major currents of global change and the issues they raise

- understanding of how human actions interact with global systems;
- ability to systematically acquire information from a variety of sources regarding diverse regions, nations, cultures and issues;
- ability to identify the cultural context of information sources.

■ Comprehension of the global dimensions of his or her profession

- possession of global professional skills and knowledge, e.g. for business this will include competence with e-commerce and the internet, global organising expertise and global business savvy;
- awareness of global forces that affect one's profession and their impact on theory and professional practice.

■ Working comfortably and effectively in global settings

- positive disposition towards cultural differences;
- capacity to think critically and creatively regarding the complexity of current global challenges;
- ability to work effectively in diverse teams;
- ability to identify and discuss global and cultural issues from multiple perspectives;
- possession of cross-cultural relationship skills, such as cultural literacy, social literacy, cross-cultural communication skills, conflict management skills, and cross-cultural sensitivity and adaptability skills.

These competencies include both cognitive and affective components. The cognitive component focuses on cultural knowledge and awareness, whereas the affective component addresses cultural sensitivity and the valuing of diversity.

Eduventures (2008) reports that many US universities incorporate similar curricular themes across global competency bachelor degree programmes in comparable areas of specialisation. For example, global/international business programmes require courses in accounting, finance, marketing and global management. International relations/ diplomacy programmes require courses in foreign affairs, foreign policy and diplomacy. General programmes in global/international studies incorporate a broad range of courses to include literature, politics, technology, economy, geography, media, environment, communications and business. A few universities also include foreign language and internship and/or foreign immersion requirements.

Global reach

Global reach is the extent to which an organisation can connect with its current and potential clients on a global level; such reach can be extended through the use of the internet (Haag, 2006). Although mostly related to international business, global reach can also apply to global education. Universities have the opportunity to extend their global reach through various strategies. The following list represents several possibilities:

- develop and/or expand cross-border operations through distance education programmes, to include internet-based delivery, formation of alliances and partnerships, and/or the establishment of satellite campuses or learning centres in other nations;
- increase international marketing;
- increase international enrolments;
- increase the cultural diversity of the faculty;
- increase international study programmes;
- make distance education friendlier to foreign students;
- expand open courseware;
- encourage university community participation in international conferences and symposia;
- invite foreign scholars to present at university symposia and colloquia;
- increase contacts and collaborative efforts with overseas universities;
- encourage partnerships with overseas universities;
- encourage collaborative international interdisciplinary research;
- outsource teaching of selected courses to distinguished foreign professors; and
- implement a visiting foreign scholars programme.

A major aim of global reach is to increase the diversity of the student body in order to promote global learning. In other words, it provides the diverse human resources needed to examine global issues from multiple perspectives within the university community. A culturally diverse university community becomes globally competent by facilitating cross-cultural awareness, creating a sense of inclusiveness for all students and permitting the authentic examination of various perspectives and worldviews on specific topics.

In such a globalised learning environment, the many national education systems are likely to evolve as they respond to globally diverse student needs and foster critical analyses of global conditions. The current need for educational interchange and interaction among institutions and countries requires the creation of institutional consortia, development of joint programmes of study and the establishment of regional or international education systems. An example of such a system is developing in Europe as many diverse national systems of education are moving toward a standardised system with regional quality assurance. This transformation, known as the Bologna Process, aims to create the European Higher Education Area (EHEA) by 2010. This process holds significant implications for international educational exchanges as well as global competition for students (Bell and Watkins, 2006).

Additionally, the European Community Action Scheme for the Mobility of University Students (the ERASMUS programme) is the operational framework for the European Commission's initiatives in higher education. The aim of the ERASMUS programme is to encourage and support the academic mobility of higher education students and teachers within the European Union, the European Economic Area nations of Iceland, Liechtenstein and Norway, as well as candidate nations such as Turkey. Already, the ERASMUS programme has generated numerous academic programmes in English. For example, Sweden now offers 450 degree programmes in English, while Germany offers around 350 English language programmes (Forrest, 2008).

The Andrés Bello Program in Latin America is another example of a regional programme. This programme's projects include a regional network of educational television programmes transmitted by satellite and the establishment of a regional school for training in public sector administration.

Major competitors in the international student market include Australia, Canada, the UK and the USA. In the future, Europe will offer an attractive alternative. The EHEA may end up challenging US dominance in international higher education, in much the same way as the European Union has become a counterweight to the USA and Japan in international trade.

However, the spread of technology and internet growth is not balanced worldwide and equal access to information technology does not exist. Thus, the extent of global reach is limited. The United Nations Development Programme's (1999) Human Development Report asks whether the information revolution is leading to globalisation or to polarisation between the haves and have-nots. According to this report, one-quarter of nations worldwide have not even achieved a teledensity of one telephone for every 100 people (the commonly accepted measure of basic access to telecommunications). Moreover:

> Beyond basic landline connections, the disparities are even more stark. In mid-1998 industrial nations – home to less than 15% of people – had 88% of internet users. North America alone – with less than 5% of all people – had more than 50% of internet users. By contrast, South Asia is home to over 20% of all people but had less than 1% of the world's internet users… The United States has more computers than the rest of the world combined and more computers per capita then any other nation. Just 55 nations account for 99% of global spending on information technology. (United Nations Development Programme, 1999: 62).

Gandhe (1998) reports that because of the information access gap in India, there has been no significant impact among the rural poor, marginalised communities and women, despite some 50 or 60 providers of open and distance learning.

Additional obstacles to global reach include:

- absence of high-level political support for distance education (Darkwa and Mazibuko, 2000);
- degree compatibility – some nations do not recognise degree-level qualifications gained through distance education as suitable or compatible with domestic degrees;
- non-localised programme content (Owston, 1997);
- translation of course materials;
- differences in culture – the content of the educational materials, the values implicit in the materials and the underlying assumptions about educational processes need to be reviewed and possibly transformed (Hall, 1996);

- employer recognition – some employers do not recognise distance learning when assessing the qualifications of potential employees (e.g. see Darkwa and Mazibuko, 2000);
- the perception of cultural contamination by foreign providers;
- relatively high tuition fees – tuition charged by providers in developed nations may be prohibitively high in less developed nations, necessitating financial support from agencies such as the World Bank, the US Agency for International Development (USAID) and institutional donors such as churches and employers (Darkwa and Mazibuko, 2000); and
- quality control and accreditation varies by nation and/or region.

Political changes also represent an element of risk to expanding global reach. For example, Media Lab Asia, the collaborative effort between the Massachusetts Institute of Technology and India's Information Technology Ministry, fell apart after the appointment of a new minister in India (Rai, 2003).

Nonetheless, collaboration is an essential component of cross-border provision, as it will strengthen the partner's ability to operate a distance learning system. One day, the partner may no longer require the partnership, in which case new directions may be explored. In the case of successful partnerships in developing nations, the partnership will have strengthened the nation's intellectual independence.

The Commonwealth of Learning is an example of a successful intergovernmental organisation created by 53 British Commonwealth heads of government to encourage the development and sharing of knowledge, resources and technologies associated with open and distance learning through collaboration and partnerships. Its international network of partner organisations has been fully operational since 1989 and is financially supported by Commonwealth governments on a voluntary basis. It responds to Commonwealth needs through national and regional programmes and initiatives, as well as fee-for-service consulting for international agencies and national governments.

In the coming decades, according to Daniel, Kanwar and Uvaliæ-Trumbiæ (2006), higher education will expand significantly in the countries of the global south, where the large majority of people under the age of 25 live. As cross-border higher education expands, governments need to protect their citizens against fraudulent providers. The challenge for international organisations such as the United Nations Educational, Scientific and Cultural Organization (UNESCO) is to provide support to national and regional efforts in this area.

Multicultural education

Values, beliefs, meanings and norms define a culture. These may vary according to national, organisational, regional, ethnic, religious or linguistic affiliation, as well as by gender, age and social class. Additionally, there is a strong relationship between culture and communication as demonstrated by the following quote:

> When I landed at a hospital for narcotics addicts in the late sixties, I watched a young Black addict from one city meet an older White addict from another city, watched them meet for the first time and talk immediately about several things in a way I couldn't make any sense out of. Here were native speakers of American English I couldn't understand, and the difference between me and them, I knew right away, had something to do with culture. (Agar, 2002: 118)

Individuals who have been exposed to only one culture typically have access only to their own cultural worldview and are unable to discern differences between their own perceptions of events and those of people who are culturally different. As Bhawuk and Brislin (1992: 416) write, 'to be effective in another culture, people must be interested in other cultures, be sensitive enough to notice cultural differences and then also be willing to modify their behavior as an indication of respect for the people of other cultures'.

Intercultural competence is central to increase understanding, improve relations and work effectively in a culturally diverse environment. In the case of global and international universities, cultural diversity not only occurs between the various cultural groups of the host nation represented on campus, but also between the national cultures represented by international students.

In a review of the international education literature, Darla Deardorff (2006: 247–8) reports that intercultural competence has many definitions, with the most popular being 'the ability to communicate effectively and appropriately in intercultural situations based on one's intercultural knowledge, skills and attitudes'. She suggests that other descriptions of intercultural competence include the ability to shift one's frame of reference appropriately and to behave appropriately and effectively in intercultural situations. Intellectual competencies regarding the global environment are also required in order to think and act in globally competent ways.

Within a national setting, most schools reinforce the nation's cultural values and accept the beliefs of the dominant culture as the truth, thereby marginalising the values and beliefs of other cultures. In contrast, multiculturalism is an ideology that advocates the presence of distinct cultural groups with equal status, notwithstanding a variety of differences between cultures that ultimately tend to hinder communication and comprehension.

Ewalt, Freeman, Kirk and Poole (1996: xi) define multiculturalism as 'the professional disposition to acknowledge, appreciate and understand cultural diversity ... [which includes] various racial, ethnic, cultural and religious groups'. Becoming multicultural is defined as a process whereby an individual develops competencies of perceiving, evaluating, believing and doing in multiple ways (Banks, 1988). However, there is a need to understand one's own cultural self before it is possible to fully comprehend the cultures of others (e.g. see Banks, 1988).

Global reach and global learning imply the need for a multicultural approach to education. Banks and Banks (1995) describe multicultural education in a national environment as:

> a field of study ... whose major aim is to create equal educational opportunities for students from diverse racial, ethnic, social-class, and cultural groups. One of its important goals is to help all students to acquire the knowledge, attitudes, and skills needed to function effectively in a pluralistic democratic society and to interact, negotiate, and communicate with peoples from diverse groups in order to create a civic and moral community that works for the common good. (Banks and Banks, 1995: xi)

Many scholars studying multicultural education advocate restructuring education within the areas of teaching styles, techniques, curriculum and interpersonal interactions in order to accommodate different cultural groups (Marshall, 2002). Applied to an international environment, an important goal of multicultural education is to prepare students to become global citizens by becoming globally competent. Without global competence, students will lack the skills to address national security needs and will be unable to compete successfully in the global marketplace.

Multicultural education has two major assumptions. The first is that exposure to cultural diversity is a positive and enriching experience that helps people learn about each other's cultures and become better and more fulfilled human beings (Banks, 1988). The second is that teaching is a cross-cultural encounter in which teachers and students have their own cultural backgrounds, values, customs, perceptions and prejudices (Hernandez, 1989).

Multicultural education employs a mostly multiculturalist model that accepts the legitimacy of the cultural distinctiveness of different students. This model assumes that students with different cultural backgrounds can retain their cultural characteristics and preferences without being denied full participation in the learning experience. This multiculturalist model is in contrast to the assimilationist model of integration in which all students are expected to conform to the dominant institutional culture and abandon the characteristics of their heritage. The assimilationist model is based on the assumption that an institution cannot be stable and cohesive unless all its members share a common culture, including common values, ideals of excellence, moral beliefs, social practices and so forth (Parekh, 1998). Therefore, assimilation involves relinquishing cultural heritage and adopting the values, beliefs and behaviours of the new culture. The assimilationist and multiculturalist models are at opposite ends of a continuum (see Figure 1.1), each with its own strengths and weaknesses. Stan Gaede (1993) argues that although the multiculturalist model has many positive features, its outcomes are cooperation and harmony rather than truth and justice.

While the assimilationist model tends toward intolerance and elitism, the pure multiculturalist model elevates the risk of cultural separation that maintains each group's heritage culture without positive intergroup relations. In such a situation, the intergroup sense of community remains low, students have low trust of other cultural groups, and interpersonal interactions suffer as an atmosphere of intergroup competition often emerges. Splintering can also occur as the most powerful cultural group

Figure 1.1   The assimilationist-multiculturalist continuum

Assimilationist
Model

Multiculturalist
Model

Potential Weaknesses

Cultural hegemony
Intolerance
Elitism
Academic imperialism
Devaluation of different cultures
Relinquishing cultural heritage
Assumes homogeneous culture

Cultural separation
Intergroup competition
Exclusive focus on culture
Ignores cultural heterogeneity
Denigrates majority culture
Overlooks cultural weaknesses
Ignores univeral norms/values
Moral relativism

excludes those groups that are most different from it. Another potential weakness is the danger of uncritical reliance on the multiplicity of perspectives, such as giving equal weight to the notion that the Holocaust never occurred. Salili and Hoosain (2001: 8) suggest that when using such an uncritical approach, 'the curriculum may be reduced to a variety of contesting folklore'.

The major issue is how to overcome the weaknesses of multiculturalism without creating the conditions for cultural hegemony. Institutions must find their own level of comfort along the assimilationist–multiculturalist continuum. In so doing, they must guard against relativism and the concept that all beliefs and values are equal. On the other hand, they must avoid policies that promote the maintenance of one group's cultural values while merely tolerating the values of others. The imperative is to create a proper balance between the need to treat all cultures as equal and the need to recognise universal truths that everyone must follow, regardless of cultural heritage. The institution must focus on dealing with diverse cultures without creating new boundaries or reinforcing old ones between cultural groups.

Consequently, some accommodations will be necessary in using a multiculturalist model, e.g. some students will be required to communicate using a language that is not their primary language and communicate in culturally different ways. However, culture is dynamic and one's cultural identity is subject to change (Wlodkowski and Ginsberg, 1996) and in today's globally interconnected world it is becoming increasingly difficult to find a stable independent culture. Thus, even using a multiculturalist model, global learning entails some change in values and beliefs. As such, multicultural education may require some students to maintain their cultural heritage while adopting a new cultural identity – that of the institution – and acquiring a global worldview. Such identities can remain independent of each other and the activation of each is context-dependent (Hong, Morris, Chiu and Benet-Martinez, 2000). As an example, W. E. B. Du Bois (1989: 5) describes the African American experience as 'movement back and forth between two souls, two thoughts, two un-reconciled strivings, two warring ideals'.

Many multiculturally competent individuals report that internalised cultures take turns in guiding their thoughts and feelings (LaFromboise, Coleman and Gerton, 1993), which suggests that (a) internalised cultures are not necessarily blended, and (b) absorbing a second culture does not always involve replacing the original culture with the new one. Tadmor and Tetlock (2006) suggest that individuals who cope with social and cultural conflict situations by internalising the values of multiple groups (i.e. become multicultural) will respond in reliably more complex ways than those who choose to adhere to the values of only one cultural group (i.e. become separated or assimilated).

Students need to account for their behaviour in the multicultural virtual classroom. This accountability is rooted in their fundamental need for social approval, whether as an end in itself or as a way to bolster their self-worth (Tetlock, 2002). According to Tadmor and Tetlock (2006), if individuals become accountable to a single audience, solely composed of members from their heritage culture, they will likely adopt a separatist strategy. In contrast, if individuals become accountable to a mixed audience composed of members from multiple cultures, they will more likely adopt a multicultural strategy.

As various cultures come together in the classroom, online teachers must mediate the learning diversity present in the multicultural classroom and promote a multicultural teaching and learning strategy. Culture influences online communication, which, in turn, affects social presence, cognitive presence and sense of community, which ultimately influences learner satisfaction, persistence and achievement (see Figure 1.2).

Gay (2000) defines culturally responsive teaching as using the cultural knowledge, prior experiences and performance styles of diverse students to make learning more appropriate and effective for them. He also describes culturally responsive teaching as having the following characteristics:

- it acknowledges the legitimacy of the cultural heritages of different ethnic groups, both as legacies that affect students' dispositions,

Figure 1.2 Relationship of culture to student outcomes

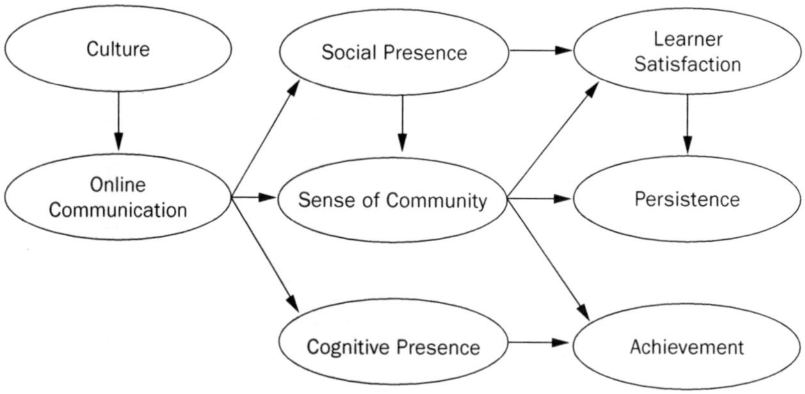

27

attitudes and approaches to learning, and as worthy content to be taught in the formal curriculum;

- it builds bridges of meaningfulness between home and school experiences as well as between academic abstractions and lived sociocultural realities;

- it uses a wide variety of instructional strategies that are connected to different learning styles;

- it teaches students to know and praise their own and each others' cultural heritages;

- it incorporates multicultural information, resources and materials in all the subjects and skills routinely taught in schools (Gay, 2000: 29).

To explain how people move from an ethnocentric to an ethnorelative orientation as they become globally competent, M. J. Bennett (1993) developed the developmental model of intercultural sensitivity (Figure 1.3). The basic assumption of this model is that as one's experiences with cultural differences become more complex, one's intercultural sensitivity

Figure 1.3 Developmental model of intercultural sensitivity (adapted from M. J. Bennett, 1993)

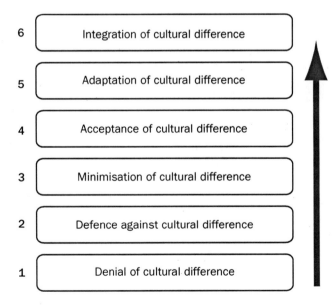

Ethnorelative

6 Integration of cultural difference

5 Adaptation of cultural difference

4 Acceptance of cultural difference

3 Minimisation of cultural difference

2 Defence against cultural difference

1 Denial of cultural difference

Ethnocentric

increases. Consequently, development of intercultural competence is based on experiencing cultural differences in complex ways. The six stages of this transition as theorised by Bennett (1993) are as follows:

1. Denial of cultural difference is the state in which one's own worldview is experienced as the only valid way in which to perceive events. Differences in cultures are not perceived.
2. Defence against cultural difference is the state in which differences between cultures are perceived, but one's own culture is viewed as possessing the only valid worldview.
3. Minimisation of cultural difference is the state in which elements of one's own cultural worldview are viewed as universal.
4. Acceptance of cultural difference is the state in which one's own culture is viewed as one of a number of equally complex worldviews.
5. Adaptation to cultural difference is the state in which the experience with other cultures results in perceptions and behaviour appropriate to that culture.
6. Integration of cultural difference is the state in which one's view of self is expanded to include the movement in and out of different cultural worldviews.

According to Hammer, Bennett and Wiseman:

> the more ethnocentric orientations can be seen as ways of avoiding cultural difference, either by denying its existence, by raising defenses against it, or by minimizing its importance. The more ethnorelative worldviews are ways of seeking cultural difference, either by accepting its importance, by adapting perspective to take it into account, or by integrating the whole concept into a definition of identity. (Hammer, Bennett and Wiseman, 2003: 426)

Each movement to a new stage generates new and more complex issues to be resolved in intercultural encounters. The resolution of these issues helps one move to the next stage of development.

For multicultural education to be effective, it must permeate the entire curriculum, not merely a single course. Culturally responsive teaching also requires a partnership in the classroom. Students must assume responsibility for their learning, but teachers must also accept responsibility for the effectiveness of the delivery of the curriculum to a diverse audience and for facilitating cognitive and social construction of knowledge in accordance with the philosophy of constructivism discussed below.

Constructivism

Constructivism is a philosophy of learning based on the premise that the individual, through his or her interactions with the environment, constructs knowledge (Rovai, 2004). It is closely related to self-directed learning because it emphasises the combined characteristics of active inquiry, independence and individuality in a learning environment (Shank and Sitze, 2004). Constructivism has its roots in the constructivist movement of cognitive psychology, which posits that individuals gradually build their own understanding of the world through experience, maturation and interaction with the environment, to include other individuals. Thus, from the constructivist viewpoint, the learner is an active processor of information. This is in contrast to direct instruction and the principles of instructivism and objectivism where the learner is viewed as a passive recipient of information – a receptacle, if you will, waiting to be filled with knowledge dispensed by the teacher.

Constructivism is the preferred educational philosophy for most online instructional designers and teachers whose goals are to simulate reality and assist students construct knowledge. It focuses attention on how people learn and the recognition that students come to class with different cultural backgrounds and different ways of learning. Each student possesses a collection of experiences constructed over time and stored in their memory that makes them who they are and influences how they learn. These experiences include cultural values and culturally-patterned ways of thinking, interacting and responding to the environment. This is particularly relevant to a distance education setting in which students are likely to be nationally and culturally diverse. Consequently, teaching in a constructivist learning environment should account for culturally-related learning differences.

David Jonassen (1995) maintains that learning occurs when students internalise the construction of meaning in their long-term memory, which in turn builds and reshapes their knowledge through experience and interaction with the world. He suggests that all constructivist learning environments have the following characteristics in common:

- they provide multiple representations of reality;
- they avoid oversimplification and represent the complexity of the real world;
- they emphasise knowledge construction instead of knowledge reproduction;

- they emphasise authentic tasks in a meaningful context rather than abstract instruction out of context;
- they provide learning environments such as real-world settings or case-based learning instead of predetermined sequences of instruction;
- they encourage thoughtful reflection on experience;
- they enable context and content-dependent knowledge construction; and
- they support construction of knowledge through social negotiation.

As a philosophy, constructivism comes in several flavours: radical constructivism, social constructivism and cognitive constructivism. Each is different from the other mostly in terms of emphasis, as they all share the common characteristics identified above. Radical constructivism, which was founded by Ernst von Glasersfeld (1987), posits that all knowledge is constructed in the mind and does not necessarily reflect the world. All human knowledge is evaluated according to its cognitive viability in the minds of individuals. Adherents often use this philosophy to argue against testing, as they claim that tests of cognitive knowledge are evaluated based on the reality of the evaluator, which may or may not reflect objective reality. The major emphasis of radical constructivism is that constructed knowledge is not an accurate representation of external reality.

Social constructivism is closely associated with many learning theories, most notably the developmental theories of Lev Vygotsky and Jerome Bruner, and Albert Bandura's social cognitive theory. It emphasises the importance of culture, context and social interaction in constructing knowledge. Instruction based on this perspective stresses the need for collaboration among learners and with practitioners. Social constructivism represents the flavour of constructivism most used in online learning environments.

Because of the social constructivist emphasis on interaction, effective communication is an important prerequisite to effective learning, and effective online communication requires the elimination of technical, psychological and semantic barriers. This is especially important in a global learning environment where multiple national and ethnic cultures are likely to be represented.

Anna Sfard (1998) characterises two major metaphors for learning: the participation metaphor and the acquisition metaphor. While social constructivism is closely related to the former, the acquisition metaphor is typical of many traditional university courses and is associated with direct instruction. Using this metaphor, knowledge can be considered as something that one can 'get', with learning being the process of 'getting it'. Sfard employs this metaphor to encompass not only the notion of transmission of concepts, but also construction of knowledge within the individual's mind. This view of cognition assumes the mind is the processor of knowledge and the world outside the mind is the source of stimuli.

The 'participation metaphor', on the other hand, suggests that important aspects of learning and cognition are related to interactions between individuals and with their environment. Sfard, however, does not rank one metaphor over the other. Instead, she suggests that there is a complementary relationship between the metaphors, where the different perspectives complement each other rather than compete for preeminence. This supports the view that there is a role for direct instruction in a constructivist learning environment.

Finally, cognitive constructivism, based on the work of Jean Piaget, holds that an individual's ability to learn is based on their age-related state of cognitive development. This flavour of constructivism emphasises the view that people actively construct new knowledge and they learn best when engaged in constructing personally meaningful knowledge. Whereas social constructivism emphasises learning as extending beyond the bounds of the mind into the social environment, cognitive constructivism emphasises the mind in terms of the individual, restricting its domain to the individual's brain. Therefore, cognitive constructivism approaches learning and knowing from the perspective of the individual. The emphasis is on self-regulation and self-awareness.

Sense of community

Glasser (1986) describes the need for belonging as one of the five basic needs written into the human genetic structure. Sense of community provides a sense of identity, emotional connection and wellbeing that underpins a productive social constructivist environment and satisfies the basic need for belonging. Synthesising much of the early literature on community, McMillan and Chavis (1986: 9) define the generalised sense of community as 'a feeling that members have of belonging, a feeling that members matter to one another and to the group and a shared faith that members' needs will be met through their commitment to be together'. McMillan (1996: 315) views sense of community as 'a spirit of belonging together, a feeling that there is an authority structure that can be trusted, an awareness that trade and mutual benefit come from being together and a spirit that comes from shared experiences that are preserved as art'.

He describes trade as the benefit community members derive from one another and from the community. In a classroom community, trade involves the exchange of information that supports learning.

Based on the general descriptions of community derived from the professional literature, Rovai, Wighting and Lucking (2004) theorise that members of classroom communities should feel that they belong and feel safe in the classroom, that they trust others, have ready access to others in the classroom, and that the class supports them. They should also believe that they matter to other students and to the class; that they have duties and obligations to each other and to the class; and that they possess a shared faith that their educational needs will be met through their commitment to the shared goals and values of other students in the class.

Studies of online environments provide evidence that one can create a sense of community and sustain strong ties through electronic media (e.g. Rovai, 2002a, 2002b). These studies show that when one views community as activities people do together, rather than *where* they do them, a sense of community can exist independently from campuses. Members of such communities exhibit behaviours that are associated with the traditional concept of community.

Research evidence shows that increasing the ethnic diversity of students while neglecting to attend to the sense of community can result in difficulties for all students (Hurtado, Milem, Clayton-Pedersen and Allen, 1999). Building and nurturing a strong sense of community in the virtual classroom are not easy and require faculty with the knowledge and skills to 'weave a complex web of connections among themselves, their subjects and their students so that students can learn to weave a world for themselves ... The connections made by good teachers are held not in their methods but in their heart' (Palmer, 1998: 11). This cannot be done without the teacher's full commitment to the process. There is a need to recognise that socialisation is as important as instruction in online school environments. In the context of online distance education, pedagogy is needed that brings students and faculty together in pursuit of a common cause and in so doing closes the psychological distance between members of the learning community.

Self-directed learning

Nell Noddings (1996: 252) suggests that higher education's preoccupation with creating the autonomous, self-directed individual with individual rights, combined with the concurrent neglect of alternative values associated with social responsibility and community, have eroded 'our understanding of human sociality'. Merriam and Caffarella (1999) suggest one view of promoting self-directed, autonomous individuals that stresses the social construction of knowledge and the social context of learning. The issue is not whether producing self-directed learners is an appropriate goal, but rather how best to achieve this goal in terms of course design and pedagogy without eroding community and increasing social isolation. In Caffarella's (1993: 32) view, being self-directed is 'to be primarily responsible and in control of what, where and how one learns'. This does not imply social independence.

To promote self-directed learning in students, Rovai, Ponton and Baker (2008) suggest involving students in decisions concerning what is to be learned, when and how it should be learned, and how it should be evaluated. In addition, learners should be allowed to pursue their own interests so that learning becomes more meaningful. However, the research on the role of self-direction in online learning is mixed. The image of the capable and autonomous adult distance learner may not be accurate. Many part-time, adult distance learners require all the support they can get to succeed (Paul, 1988).

Paul (1988: 50) maintains that 'distance education institutions bear considerable responsibility for helping ... students to cope with the difficulty inherent in this model of education'. Moreover, some studies characterise the successful distance student as an autonomous, independent learner (e.g. Tucker, 2000), but others have found no relationship between learning style and learning outcomes. There is a growing belief that self-directed learning is situational, that it is not always the best approach of instruction for all adults, and that there are times, places and circumstances when it should not be used at all (Grow, 1996). Such a belief supports the view that online courses should support multiple learning styles.

Adult learning

Adult learning theory and constructivism have the same goal: the construction of meaningful and authentic knowledge (Huang, 2002). Malcolm Knowles (1989) maintains that the customary characteristics of childhood teaching and learning (i.e. pedagogy) do not take into account the adult learner's age, lifelong experiences and practical approach to learning, and that adult learners are more self-directed than children.

Consequently, he has proposed a model of adult teaching and learning called *andragogy* (derived from the Greek for 'adult'), based on the following six assumptions that differentiate adult learning from that of children: need to know, self-concept, experience, readiness, orientation to learn and motivation (Knowles, Holton and Swanson, 2005). While the term 'adult' can be used to categorise a person of a given age, legal or social status, Knowles, Holton and Swanson (2005: 64) emphasise the importance of the 'psychological definition' of an adult as an individual who has reached a realisation of personal responsibility for his/her life that is characterised by self-direction. They continue:

> While adults are responsive to some external motivators (better jobs, promotions, higher salaries, and the like), the most potent motivators are internal pressures (the desire for increased job satisfaction, self-esteem, quality of life, and the like). (Knowles, Holton and Swanson, 2005: 68)

This perspective suggests that adults are primarily intrinsically motivated to learn. Consequently, to maximise motivation, the adult educator should relate expected learning outcomes to the learners' personal forms of self-satisfaction rather than solely emphasising extrinsic motivation, such as the employment benefits of higher education.

Drawing on the work of Malcolm Knowles and others, Betty Collis (1998) has developed the following six principles of adult education applied to the online learning environment:

- both learner and educator play an active and unique role in the educational process;
- the process of constructing knowledge involves human interaction and learner competence that are developed and evaluated within a communication-oriented education model;
- adult learners learn best in a learner-centred environment that encourages self-assessment, personal reflection and articulation of the learner's own ideas;
- the learning environment should maximise meaningful and reflective interaction while providing a variety of opportunities for feedback;
- educators need to monitor the work of their students in order to promote learner self-regulation and student responsibility for their learning;

- educators recognise that students want to move efficiently through their studies, in both time and energy, and that students do not necessarily have good study skills or motivation.

Meaning-making in adult learning is related to the spiritual quest of adults. Vella (2000) suggests that attending to the spiritual dimension of adult learning is part of honouring the learner as 'subject', and thus the author of their own life in the quest for meaning-making. Spirituality is not the same as religion; it is more about an individual's personal belief and experience of a higher power or higher purpose. Dirkx (1997: 83) indicates that our interest is less on addressing spirituality directly, although there may be legitimate reasons to do so, but rather to nurture soul, 'to recognize what is already inherent within our relationships and experiences, to acknowledge its presence with the teaching and learning environment, to respect its sacred message'. Lerner (2000: 174) presents an approach to spirituality that he calls 'emancipatory spirituality', which recognises the value of pluralism and the many manifestations of spirit within different cultures, religions and traditions. One of the ways adults construct knowledge is through spirituality. To ignore it is to ignore an important aspect of human experience in adult learning (Tisdell, 2001).

Some of the assumptions and models of adult distance education may not apply to nations with different cultures and educational traditions. Guy makes this point as follows:

> Theories and practices in distance education have emanated from industrialized nations and the metaphors that are used signify the attitudes and values, and the modes of thinking which are highly representative of those nations. Terms such as individual learning, personal work ... a plurality of scholarly positions ... individualisation, self-pacing, evaluation, apartness and autonomy ... represent much of the thinking about distance education in the developed world at present, and contain specific ideologies which may not be consistent or appropriate in third-world cultures. (Guy, 1990: 58)

It is therefore important that online teachers respond to diversity in the learning needs of students, especially if the class includes globally diverse students. Online learners should be encouraged to embrace the principles of adult learning and constructivism and behave as collegial partners in the learning process – not as teacher and student. Moreover, adult learning can and should be used to promote a greater sense of community and understanding across cultural and ethnic divisions.

Conclusion

The face of higher education has changed over the past century and various forces are moving higher education in new directions. These forces include the continued move toward open and distance learning, global competition, the massification of higher education, the need for a more educated workforce, and rapid changes in technology that empower further expansion of e-learning. Added to this mix are the formation of institutional alliances, outsourcing, globalisation and internationalisation. In particular, the expansion of the global economy and the global challenges faced by our planet necessitate cooperation on a global level. Moreover, the global reach of distance education permits institutions to reach and serve a new and potentially global constituency.

Educators concerned about educating the next generation of citizens and leaders need to consider carefully how best to teach the necessary skills, insights and understandings to foster global citizenship. Higher education institutions need to respond to this challenge if they expect to remain relevant and competitive.

Gary E. Miller (2008), Executive Director Emeritus of the Penn State World Campus, describes a recent keynote address by Stemenka Uvalic, from UNESCO, who has projected that cross-border distance education may become the most significant development in the years ahead. She notes that there are 132 million university students worldwide and that nations are having trouble funding capacity to handle demand. This has stimulated three trends:

- *the rise of new private (for-profit and not-for-profit) institutions that do not receive government funds*: for example, 80 per cent of university students in Japan are now in private institutions;
- *the increase in student mobility*: 2.4 million students went abroad in 2004, with 1 in 16 university students from Africa going abroad; and
- *the growth in open and distance learning*: for example, the number of open universities has doubled in Commonwealth nations, the number of for-profit online providers is growing globally, and one-third of all international students enrolled in Australian universities studied from their home country in 2004.

Some educators predict that the globalised world will be a highly differentiated society with a tolerance for diversity (Waters, 1995). Others predict that globalised education will contribute to the rise of 'imperialist attitudes, loss of indigenous cultures and the relentless imposition of Western values' (Mason, 1998: 10). Although each prediction for globalisation has some merit, educational leaders have a choice in how they prepare students to face the multidimensional challenges of globalisation. The diversity of learners in the online community requires an inclusive approach that respects differences and promotes understanding.

Global distance education issues

Introduction

The previous chapter provides summaries of the historical roots and theoretical underpinnings of distance education. It also provides a profile of distance education students and discusses some of the key concepts that affect global online higher education, including copyright and intellectual property rights, globalisation and internationalism, constructivism, sense of community, self-directed learning and adult learning.

This chapter builds on this foundation as it examines the major issues associated with universities reaching out globally using online distance education. The first topic deals with student outcomes in the form of lower student persistence rates and the perceived lower quality of learning attainment for distance education students when compared with their traditional on-campus peers. These issues have generated interest among educators concerning the nature of distance learning environments and the learning outcomes achievable through technology. Knowing the challenges and overcoming them is crucial to successful implementation of distance education programmes.

Student outcomes

Open and distance learning recognises that education is a human right, which, in turn, implies open access. Many people assume that one cannot have quality education without restricting access or differentiating curricula and instruction based on student abilities. However, as noted by John Daniel (2004), former UNESCO Assistant Director-General for Education, the intelligent use of technology allows institutions to increase access, raise quality and decrease costs, all at the same time.

Research evidence suggests that for many students, online or blended programmes provide a high level of satisfaction, particularly regarding flexibility of time and place for learning and the emphasis on interpersonal interaction (e.g. Collis and Moonen, 2001). Two issues that receive attention in the professional literature are the higher dropout rates for distance education over traditional programmes (e.g. see Carr, 2000) and the lower quality of learning attainment that some individuals perceive (e.g. see Abrami and Bures, 1996).

Student persistence

Although there are no comprehensive international statistics for course and programme completion rates for distance education students, studies of individual institutions suggest dropout rates are generally higher in distance education courses. Some accounts report the dropout rate for online courses is 10 to 20 per cent higher than for face-to-face courses (e.g. Carr 2000; Frankola 2001), while other reports for specific institutions reveal much higher dropout rates. However, as distance education programme students tend to be different from face-to-face programme students, it is difficult to draw conclusions regarding differences in student outcomes between the two groups. The different outcomes could be due to differences in the two groups of students as described in the previous chapter rather than to differences in the two types of educational delivery. What the research makes clear is that attrition is caused by multiple factors and no single profile exists for a typical student dropout.

Increased dropouts in distance education are often explained by personal, institutional and circumstantial variables, and interactions between these variables. Variables outside the influence of the institution, such as pressures on the student's life related to employment and family responsibilities, and the inability of the student to balance these pressures with stress arising from pursuing an academic programme, appear to be common reasons for explaining dropouts. Other factors frequently cited in the literature include a mismatch between the student's preferred learning style and the teaching style used in specific online courses, the inability of the student to organise his or her time adequately, feelings of detachment from the university, lack of adequate preparation or skills to engage in advanced academic work, and inadequate student support services (e.g. Frankola, 2001; Rovai, 2002a, 2003a). These factors can adversely influence student learning and satisfaction with online programmes and, in turn, result in student attrition.

Vincent Tinto (1987, 1993) theorises that the primary determinants of successful persistence can be broken down into factors that are drawn from student characteristics and skills upon entering the university, and internal and external factors that are drawn from experiences while the student is at the university. Figure 2.1 uses this model to identify factors that are relevant to a distance education context. Prior experiences and student characteristics are input variables that cannot be directly affected by schools. However, student experiences subsequent to admission, which Tinto refers to as 'integration' variables, are influenced by school policies and practices, as well as by school and classroom cultures. Tinto (1987: 123) suggests that 'the more central one's membership is to the mainstream of institutional life the more likely, other things being equal, one is to persist'.

Typically, higher education persistence studies find that academic integration has an important impact on persistence (Pascarella and

Figure 2.1   Persistence model (adapted from Rovai, 2003a)

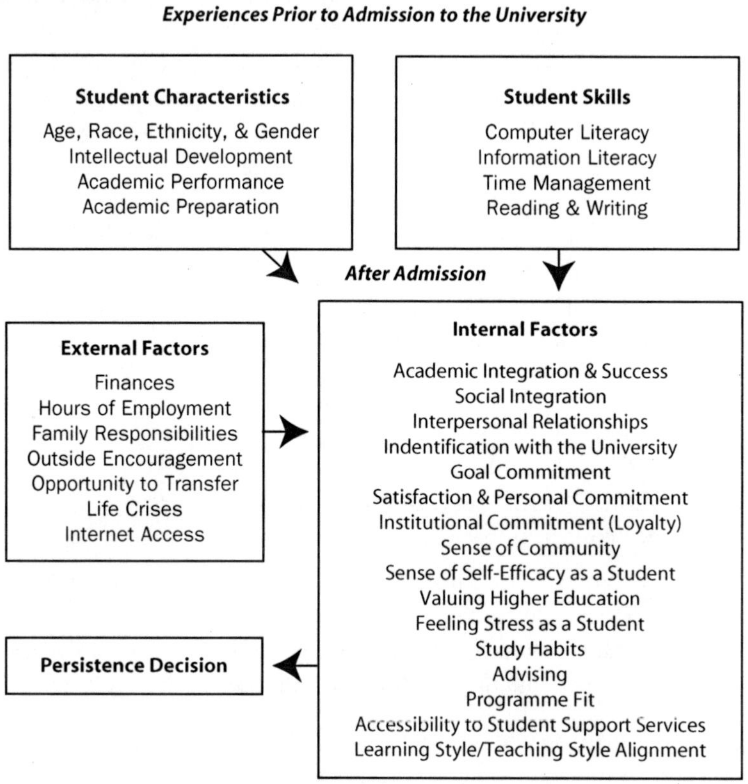

Experiences Prior to Admission to the University

Student Characteristics

Age, Race, Ethnicity, & Gender
Intellectual Development
Academic Performance
Academic Preparation

Student Skills

Computer Literacy
Information Literacy
Time Management
Reading & Writing

After Admission

External Factors

Finances
Hours of Employment
Family Responsibilities
Outside Encouragement
Opportunity to Transfer
Life Crises
Internet Access

Internal Factors

Academic Integration & Success
Social Integration
Interpersonal Relationships
Indentification with the University
Goal Commitment
Satisfaction & Personal Commitment
Institutional Commitment (Loyalty)
Sense of Community
Sense of Self-Efficacy as a Student
Valuing Higher Education
Feeling Stress as a Student
Study Habits
Advising
Programme Fit
Accessibility to Student Support Services
Learning Style/Teaching Style Alignment

Persistence Decision

Terenzini, 1991). Consequently, persistence is often viewed as a measure of how well students integrate into a particular university. Because of the physical separation of students from the university campus, integration in distance education requires the institution to be especially proactive in integrating students in both school and classroom communities. Research also provides evidence that strong feelings of community can increase persistence in online courses and can also increase commitment to group goals, cooperation among members, satisfaction with group efforts and motivation to learn (e.g. Rovai, 2002a). Nurturing a sense of school and classroom community is, therefore, one method of increasing institutional fit (Rovai, 2003b).

Student learning

Perceptions of the quality of online programmes vary based on the region, the institution, the observer and his or her interests, biases, politics and interpretations. Distance education is regarded by some people as the 'poor and often unwelcome stepchild within the academic community' (Merisotis and Phipps, 1999: 4). It is also considered by some as lower-quality education, or a poor replica of campus education (Allen and Seaman, 2004). One reason that some people view distance education as being of a lesser quality than traditional education is the presence of a growing market for distance higher education that includes dubious providers, phoney institutions and degree mills offering fake or low-quality diplomas. Another reason is the relatively high student attrition rates experienced by some institutions.

For example, Ibrahim, Rwegasira and Taher (2007) note the following two obstacles hindering the growth of distance education in the Arab region:

- The majority of Arab societies are sceptical about the merits of distance education and view distance education as a second-class form of education. This image is reinforced by higher student attrition rates in distance education programmes.

- Some Arab countries do not recognise distance education institutions and, therefore, do not grant licences to graduates or officially recognise their qualifications. This practice influences people's perceptions of the quality of distance education.

Most of the many media comparison studies result in a finding of 'no significant difference' (e.g. Russell, 1999). Nonetheless, Lockee, Moore and Burton (2001: 62) assert that 'a finding of no significant difference between face-to-face instruction and distance-delivered instruction does not mean they are equally good or bad'. Moreover, many such studies violate the assumption of ceteris paribus, that is, the assumption that all factors are the same except for the medium (e.g. Rovai, 2003b). The confounding factor is that the media and course combinations are not the same – the numerous uncontrolled characteristics can all vary, affecting learning outcomes accordingly.

Although successful learning in online and traditional courses requires similar student skills, they are not the same. Rowntree (1995: 207) observes that students enrolled in an online course require more advanced skills in computing, literacy, discussion, time management and interpersonal interaction. He also observes that the focus in online learning is often less on the content, as it is in traditional courses, and more on the cognitive process of 'offering up ideas, having them criticized or expanded on and getting the chance to reshape them (or abandon them) in the light of peer discussion'. Consequently, a major flaw in many media comparison studies is the uncontrolled mixing of instructional methods with the delivery medium.

A meta-analysis of 232 comparative studies conducted by Bernard et al. concludes that while there is no average difference in achievement between distance and classroom courses, there is wide variability. In other words:

> a substantial number of [distance education] applications provide better achievement results, are viewed more positively, and have higher retention rates than their classroom counterparts. On the other hand, a substantial number of [distance education] applications are far worse than classroom instruction. (Bernard et al., 2004: 406)

These findings suggest that quality assurance is an important issue in online distance education and that appropriate instructional design and good pedagogical practices, rather than the computer-mediating technology itself, are at the centre of effective online education. Moreover, results suggest that learning outcomes are improved by increased student cognitive engagement, particularly student–content, student–student and student–teacher interactions. Findings of the meta-analysis also suggest that strengthening student–student and student–teacher interactions also has a modest impact on student satisfaction.

The basic fact is that traditional education and distance education do not represent an 'either/or' proposition. Resident campuses and traditional programmes cannot meet the needs of the millions of students worldwide who are left out of higher education and for whom education via the internet may be their only course of action. The primary goal of distance education research should be to make online courses as effective as possible given the technologies that are available to use.

Student access to technology and higher education

High-quality open and distance higher education can be a valuable public good that contributes to economic development, globalisation and social equity. An important issue is the exclusion of some people from higher education and from the technology to participate in learning at a distance. The Organization for Economic Cooperation and Development (OECD, 2007) defines equity in education in terms of fairness, which implies that personal and social circumstances (e.g. gender, socioeconomic status and ethnic origin) should not be an obstacle to achieving educational potential. There is a worldwide need, particularly in developing nations, to substantially increase access and participation in higher education in order to advance social equity and economic prosperity. However, a major barrier in some cultures is the availability of time to participate in advanced education. Many nations have traditions of long working hours and although leisure time may be growing, there are also numerous competing opportunities for use of time (McGivney, 1993).

Expanding participation is most effective when it targets specific groups who are under-represented in higher education. These groups will vary from nation to nation, but often include individuals of low socioeconomic status, women, older individuals, individuals from rural or isolated areas, and ethnic minorities, including indigenous groups. Equity in education not only means equity in access, but also equity in success for students with equal intellectual capacity.

A major reason for the exclusion of some people from distance education is the digital divide – often referred to as inequitable access to information and communication technologies, both within and between nations. The digital divide between nations is usually measured in terms of differences between the number of telephones, computers and internet users. International Telecommunication Union (2007) indicators reveal that 30 nations in the world have less than one main telephone line per 100 inhabitants. Most of these nations are in Africa (24 nations). The remaining nations are in Asia (five nations) and North America (Haiti). Additionally, there are differences between regions on the same continent. Botswana, Tanzania and South Africa are far better placed in terms of information and communication technology resources than some other African nations like Kenya, Democratic Republic of Congo, Sudan, Angola, Ethiopia and Liberia; likewise, India is far better placed than Bangladesh and Nepal (Kumar and Bhattacharya, 2007).

Between groups of people within countries, the term *digital divide* describes inequalities in access to computers and the internet. It can also be used to address the inequalities in computer ownership and access to high-speed broadband digital services. Any discussion about the digital divide, particularly when related to digital inequality, also suggests a growing knowledge gap between individuals who have access to information and are able or unable to use it (Bonfadelli, 2002).

Numerous studies have consistently linked level of internet access and attitude toward internet technologies to gender (participation rates are lower for women in many areas), race, geographic location (including the rural/urban divide), education, income and age (e.g. see Katz and Aspden, 1997). These groups are broadly similar to those that have been historically denied access to higher education. Research studies also suggest that the character of the domestic digital divide varies from nation to nation. For example, the gender divide is more pronounced in India (where women account for less than 30 per cent of internet users) than South Africa (where internet users are evenly divided between women and men) (International Telecommunication Union, 2007).

Because access to the internet and to online distance education depends on having access to a telephone line and appropriate receiving devices, such as a personal computer and modem, there are substantial economic, technical and attitudinal barriers to universal at-home internet access and participation in online distance education. Technology must be affordable, accessible and relevant to all communities. Internationally, the digital divide tends to separate developed from developing nations. Closing the digital divide between nations promotes worldwide social equity and closing this gap may be the only way to achieve the full potential of globalisation. Closing this gap within a nation serves as a catalyst for broad-based and equitable national development (Rovai and Petchauer, 2008).

Modern approaches to distance education depend on the success with which technology is able to connect teachers and students. Effective implementation of information and communication technologies in individual nations is required if global reach of distance education is to be fully realised. Otherwise, there is a danger that the efforts of universities in more developed nations using advanced technologies and internet-based models to reach out to developing nations will be limited to the rich and elite in those nations. For example, internet connectivity is particularly important, but the proportion of people online is only 4 per cent in India, 1 per cent in Africa (half of them in South Africa) and 0.1 per cent in Bangladesh (Daniel, Kanwar and Uvaliæ-Trumbiæ, 2006).

DiMaggio, Celeste, Hargittai and Shafer (2004) suggest that as more individuals use the internet, it becomes less useful to discuss the digital divide in terms of access only. They claim that researchers also need to start looking at differences in people's digital competency, which they describe as the second-level digital divide. As Seiden argues:

> Addressing the digital divide is not simply a matter of running wire and providing public computers – it is also a matter of ensuring that people have the requisite skills to use the technology and that they see relevance of the technology to their lives. (Seiden, 2000: 329)

Consequently, looking at the digital divide exclusively in terms of technical access is insufficient. While economic, cultural and social factors have a greater role to play in narrowing the gap in the first-level digital divide, educational factors are more important in closing the gap in online skills.

Student global diversity

Ngai (2003: 157) asserts that 'the two D's – diversity and distance education – have been gathering momentum in higher and continuing education'. The increase in campus diversity is also reflected in the virtual classroom. Cultural diversity creates new possibilities, greater intercultural dialogue and improved understanding and cooperation. Culturally-diverse students bring to the university a mix of individualised characteristics representing their cultural heritage that can also result in tension and impede learning if not adequately considered by online course designers and teachers. Moreover, although the focus of the professional literature on diversity concentrates on student behaviour (Pincas, 2001), diversity also influences the behaviour and practices of teachers.

As constructivism is about situational sense-making, some educational researchers assert that all learning is context-specific. While new knowledge is associated with the context in which it is learned, transfer to another context can be more difficult for students whose culturally-related experiences differ substantially from the context in which new information is presented.

Universities have been struggling with how to cope with cultural differences on campus and in online programmes, but few scholars have delved deeply into how the learning environments of such schools are affected by student diversity. Fabos and Young (1999: 237) assert that although 'the internet holds the potential to link classrooms to exchange cultural information and critically address various problems ... [it may instead] encourage students to see the world through an Imperialist lens'. They provide evidence that illustrates how the use of electronic technologies by some educators misrepresents other cultures because teachers do not provide substantive background knowledge of the contexts of other cultures, question dominant culture assumptions, or examine the impact of global economic and political systems. While new information is associated with cues from the environment in which it was learned, online course design and instruction that promotes effective student–content engagement in a multicultural environment can result in transfer to other contexts (Anderson, Greeno, Reder and Simon, 2000), if properly presented.

In addition to student–content engagement, a cultural aspect also applies to computer-mediated student–student and student–teacher engagements. Knowing the identity of the individual with whom one is interacting along with his or her cultural characteristics can often be crucial to knowing how to communicate.

Culture can be defined as the norms, values, beliefs and patterns that provide particular rules for behaviour (Moll, 2005). It is a multidimensional construct and no single dimension can capture its essence. Understanding how students' personal characteristics may aid or hinder learning is an important pedagogical concern. One framework that is useful for considering the culturally-related characteristics of globally diverse students is Geert Hofstede's (2004) five-dimension model of national culture, represented by the first five dimensions shown in Figure 2.2. Hofstede (1991: 21) defines national culture as 'the collective programming of the mind which distinguishes the members in one human group from another'. His multi-dimension framework serves as a useful model for teachers and institutions to better understand the personal and cultural dynamics within the student population and thus enable the development of better-suited online learning environments.

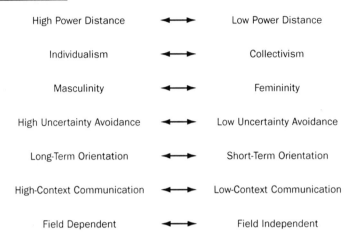

Figure 2.2 Dimensions of cultural diversity

In addition to Hofstede's five dimensions of national culture, Figure 2.2 also depicts high and low-context communication orientation and field dependency, which are widely viewed as additional dimensions of cultural diversity. One's relative positions along these dimensions guide one's behaviour through life. Consequently, one's relative positions can also be viewed as identity markers or ways in which people and cultures define themselves. They may sometimes conflict, but this is not a necessary feature of multiple identities, except when the forces behind any of these markers demand loyalty, as nations, religions and families often do.

Hofstede's work is highly influential, primarily because his research has been confirmed by hundreds of independent studies across different disciplines (Sondergaard, 1994). His model does have its critics, however. The characterisation of various cultures, while illuminating, is close to racial stereotyping (Ellsworth, 1994). Additionally, the research on acculturation and racial/ethnic identity views the acculturative and racial/ethnic identity process as different for each racial/ethnic person (e.g. see Carter, 2005). As a result of these distinctions, it is important for teachers to realise that there are individual differences within racial/ethnic groups and that similar groups can be culturally and linguistically diverse. Notwithstanding intra-cultural dissimilarities, it is useful for designing and presenting online instruction to understand how individuals in a globally diverse learning community can differ, although it is difficult to accurately predict the culturally-related behaviour of any single student based on national origin alone.

High and low power distances

The first dimension of Hofstede's model (power distance) represents the extent to which members of a culture accept that power is distributed unequally. Power distance focuses on relationships between people of different status within a society. People in high power distance societies accept a division between the powerful and less powerful members of society as a fact of life. Hofstede (1984) reports the highest power distance nations (from highest to less extreme) are the Philippines, Mexico, Venezuela, India, Singapore, Brazil, France, Turkey, Belgium, Peru, Thailand, Chile and Portugal; the lowest power distance nations (from lowest to less extreme) are Austria, Israel, Denmark, New Zealand, Ireland, Sweden, Norway, Finland, Great Britain, Germany, Canada and the USA. Power distance is mostly relevant within a national setting, but can also influence communication within the multicultural virtual classroom. In this setting, power distance is akin to what Matsumoto (2007) refers to as status differentiation or the degree to which different cultures maintain status differences among their members.

Within a classroom context, organisation theory predicts that uncertain tasks are performed more productively when students work laterally and interact with each other (Perrow, 1967). Expectation states theory predicts that students with relatively low status with their peers will interact with classmates less frequently and will learn less than high status students (Berger, Cohen and Zelditch, 1966). Elizabeth Cohen (1994) asserts that high status individuals are expected to be more competent than low status individuals across a wide range of tasks that are viewed as important.

Cohen (1994: 35–6) also reports that low status students engaged in group work 'often don't have access to the task … and don't talk as much as other students. Often when they do talk, their ideas are ignored by the rest of the group'. She concludes that low status students participate less in inquiry-based discussions than high status students, although some can make meaningful contributions.

Consequently, Cohen (1994) suggests instructors must pay particular attention to unequal participation of students in classroom activities and employ strategies to address status problems through complex instruction. Cohen (1997) describes complex instruction as a classroom management system where instructors delegate authority to students, through norms and roles, to generate student interactions. The instructor intervenes indirectly to equalise students' status by raising the status of those students with lower status. The premise is that when status is equalised, all students in the group will interact equitably and all will learn.

Individualism and collectivism

The second dimension of Hoftstede's (2004) model is individualism-collectivism. Members of individualistic cultures tend to be candid and task-related issues take priority over relationship-related issues. Individualism implies that social behaviour is established by personal goals and does not take precedence over the goals of the group. During discussions between members of an individualistic culture, views are expressed frankly and individuals, regardless of status, resist attempts by others to influence them. Individualistic learners support individual identity and believe that they should be self-sufficient (Hofstede, 2004). The task for them is more important than the relationship as they tend to define self as an autonomous entity.

Collectivistic learners, on the other hand, are more group-oriented and support group identity over individual identity (Hofstede, 2004). The group is more important than the individual, and members of the group are ready to cooperate in order to achieve group goals. Consequently, they are more likely than individualists to be driven by social norms, duties and obligations. Collectivistic learners rely not only on verbal communication, but also use nonverbal language, like gestures, timing and facial expressions (Francesco and Gold, 2004), which can create frustrations in the 'low context/high content' communication medium of text-based, computer-mediated communication. Although collectivistic learners are not task-oriented, they can still do well in online courses as they can collaborate easily with other members of the learning community. However, students with a collectivistic orientation may be less involved and perform less well in large lecture courses (Hwang, Francesco and Kessler, 2003) and in online courses with a low sense of community. Moreover, students with a stronger collectivist orientation may perceive themselves to be poorer students, to have less control over their learning, and to be less likely to overcome learning barriers.

Western nations tend to be more individualistic while Eastern cultures tend to be more collectivist. Hofstede (1984) reports the most individualistic nations (from highest to less extreme) to be the USA, Australia, Great Britain, Canada, the Netherlands, New Zealand, Italy, Belgium, Denmark, Sweden and France, while the most collectivistic nations (from highest to less extreme) are Venezuela, Colombia, Pakistan, Peru, Taiwan, Thailand, Singapore, Chile, Portugal and Mexico.

Masculinity and femininity

Hofstede's third dimension is masculinity/femininity. Gender roles are sharply differentiated in masculine cultures and masculinity leads to a preference for achievement, heroism, assertiveness, material success and the belief that men and women have different roles in society (Hofstede, 2004). Many collectivist cultures are masculine cultures, but not all. Germany, for example, scores high on both the individualistic and masculinity scales (Hofstede, 1984).

In high masculinity cultures the focus is on clearly-defined, hierarchical relationships where males assume a more authoritative role. The exaggerated difficulties likely to be experienced by males from a masculine culture, for example, in a multi-gender online course, include losing face to a female member of the learning community, earning poor grades, or being taught by a female teacher. Hofstede (1984) reports the strongest nations with the masculinity characteristic (from highest to less extreme) are Japan, Austria, Venezuela, Italy, Switzerland, Mexico, Great Britain, Germany, the Philippines, Columbia, South Africa and the USA.

In feminine cultures, gender roles are less sharply distinguished and little differentiation is made between men and women in the same job. Women in feminine nations have the same modest, caring values as the men; in masculine nations they are somewhat assertive and competitive, but not as much as the men (Hofstede, 2004). The strongest nations with the femininity characteristic (from highest to less extreme) are Sweden, Norway, the Netherlands, Denmark, Finland, Chile, Thailand, Peru, Spain, France, Iran and Taiwan (Hofstede, 2004).

Belenky, Clinchy, Goldberger and Tarule (1997) have theorised two paths of normal development in adult learning, resulting in two different gender-related communication patterns:

- *independent voice*: the independent, autonomous, or independent path, which is typical of the majority of men (and some women); and
- *connected voice*: the relational, connected, or interdependent path, which reflects the majority of women (and some men).

This model suggests that many female students place emphasis on relationships and prefer to learn in an environment where cooperation is stressed over competition. The connected voice nurtures classroom community building while the independent voice does not.

Computer-mediated communication reflects the inherent communication patterns of the users. In support of this view, Rovai (2001) reports the results of a case study in which an equal number of male and female students were enrolled in an asynchronous online course. Discussion board postings reveal the male voice tended to be impersonal and assertive, that is, it possessed an authoritative tone. The female voice, on the other hand, was generally supportive and helpful without being assertive. In particular, Rovai reports that the majority of men (and some women) exhibited an independent voice and the majority of women (and some men) used a connected voice. These differences were related to sense of community. Those with the highest sense of community (mostly female students) were more likely to write messages using a connected voice, while those with the lowest sense of community (mostly male students) tended to write messages using the independent voice.

High and low uncertainty avoidance

The fourth dimension is uncertainty avoidance. This dimension represents the degree of tolerance for deviation from the norm and ambiguity. Cultures with strong uncertainty avoidance have low tolerance for ambiguous situations and are more likely to be emotional, security-seeking, intolerant of ambiguity, and view difference as dangerous (Hofstede, 1984). If members of high uncertainty avoidance cultures are enrolled in a distance education programme, they expect the course design and all assignments to be clearly organised. Formal structure provides greater stability; less structure introduces uncertainty and anxiety. According to Gudykunst and Matsumoto:

> There is a strong desire for consensus in cultures high in uncertainty avoidance; deviant behavior is therefore not acceptable. Members of high uncertainty avoidance cultures also tend to display emotions more than do members of low uncertainty avoidance cultures. (Gudykunst and Matsumoto, 1996: 42)

Nations with the highest uncertainty avoidance (from strongest to less extreme) are Greece, Portugal, Belgium, Japan, Peru, France, Chile, Spain and Argentina (Hofstede, 2004).

Low uncertainty avoidance nations tend to be less emotional and more tolerant of unpredictable situations (Hofstede, 2004). Gudykunst and Matsumoto (1996: 42) assert that 'members of low uncertainty avoidance cultures have lower stress levels and lower superegos, and accept dissent and taking risks more than do members of high uncertainty avoidance cultures'.

In general, compared with high uncertainty avoidance cultures, innovations and new ideas are more appreciated by low uncertainty avoidance cultures where there are fewer rules. Additionally, members of low uncertainty cultures are more tolerant of opinions that differ from what they are used to and are comfortable with open-ended situations. Nations with the lowest uncertainty avoidance (from lowest to less extreme) are Singapore, Denmark, Sweden, Ireland, Great Britain, India, the Philippines and the USA (Hofstede, 2004).

Strangers in an unfamiliar group environment often experience anxiety and uncertainty and do not know how to behave (Griffin, 2008), leading to intercultural misunderstandings. Moreover, conflict and/or stress result when members of different cultures choose solutions that are incompatible with each other's basic cultural values (Kim, 1988). For example, how much harmony must someone from a collectivist culture give up to demonstrate assertiveness in a classroom dominated by members of an individualistic culture?

When perceived dissonance is low, people will prefer information that supports their opinion or values that are aligned with their cultural orientation; correspondingly, they will ignore information that favours a different opinion or requires a change in cultural values (Mills, 1999). In other words, one likely adopts the course of action that reinforces one's cultural values and denies the opposing values. However, when the perceived dissonance is high, more cognitively complex solutions must be used. When each constituency associated with differing positions possesses strong arguments in defence of its own view and counter arguments cannot simply be ignored, resolution may require some individuals to choose preemptive self-criticism, carefully weighing the merits of the alternative perspectives and forming connections and reasonable trade-offs among them (Tetlock, 2002). This course of action requires each individual to acknowledge the legitimacy of both sides and respond to criticism from both sides. It also requires the use of more effort-intensive solutions such as differentiation and integration (Tetlock, 2002). Under such circumstances, 'people will turn to "conceptually integrated" strategies that specify when, why and to what degree, one value should prevail over another' (Tetlock, Peterson and Lerner, 1996: 28).

William Gudykunst's (1995) anxiety/uncertainty management theory posits the reduction of uncertainty and anxiety as necessary and sufficient conditions for intercultural adaptation. Moreover, this theory can be used to understand inexperienced users' contact with technology as such contact might generate similar stresses that can interfere with effective communication. Accordingly, computer anxiety can be explained in terms low levels of knowledge about computers and limited experience using this technology.

Experiencing initial anxiety and uncertainty is normal during intercultural interactions. Such anxiety and uncertainty can however be managed by knowing Gudykunst's theory. According to this theory, efforts at adapting to unfamiliar environments and people involve cyclical patterns of behaviours to reduce tension and seek information.

Tension reduction is oriented toward reducing the anxiety or fear individuals feel when interacting with people from other cultures in unfamiliar situations or when interacting with people in unfamiliar environments, such as the virtual classroom. Anxiety is often the result of the initial tension and insecurity associated with contact with strangers. When the initial encounter is over, anxiety reduction may no longer exert a strong influence on adaptation. Reduction in anxiety and uncertainty toward people can, therefore, be reduced, in part, through increasing social presence. Similarly, reduction in anxiety and uncertainty toward technology can be reduced through increasing knowledge and experience using technology.

Information seeking is directed toward individuals increasing their ability to explain and predict behaviour (i.e. reduce uncertainty). Knowledge of the host culture is an important aspect of uncertainty reduction. Consequently, gaining knowledge about the culture and customs of other individuals in the learning community and of the technology used to communicate with others, can reduce anxiety and uncertainty.

Long and short-term orientations

Finally, Hofstede's fifth dimension is long/short-term orientation (also referred to as Confucianism), which he describes as the extent to which a culture exhibits a pragmatic future-oriented perspective rather than a more traditional or short-term perspective. Hofstede (2004) defines long-term orientation as the fostering of virtues oriented towards future rewards. Values associated with this orientation are thrift, perseverance, patience and willingness to subordinate oneself. Short-term orientation deals with a static, past–present orientation. Values associated with short-term orientation are respect for tradition, fulfilling social obligations, protecting one's 'face', concern with the possession of truth, and desire to obtain quick results.

Nations with the strongest long-term orientation (from strongest to less extreme) are China, Taiwan, Japan, South Korea, Brazil, India,

Thailand, Singapore and the Netherlands; nations with the strongest short-term orientation (from strongest to less extreme) are Pakistan, Nigeria, the Philippines, Canada, Zimbabwe, Great Britain, the USA, New Zealand and Australia (Hofstede, 2004).

High and low-context communications

In addition to the five dimensions of national culture identified by Hofstede (2004), it is also useful to discuss two additional culturally-related factors that influence interpersonal relations in a virtual classroom: high/low-context and field dependency. The first factor is Edward Hall's theory of high and low-context cultures (Hall and Hall, 1990), which addresses the manner in which individuals communicate within the same setting.

Robert Ibarra (2001) explains this theory as follows. 'Low context/ high content' cultures make little use of nonverbal signals, value direct communication with explicit verbal messages and depersonalise disagreements. They also use language with great precision and economy. 'High context/low content' cultures, on the other hand, rely extensively on nonverbal signals, see communication as an art form in which indirect, implicit and informal verbal messages are valued and personalise disagreements. They also use language more loosely as words have relatively less value.

Researchers have identified a variety of national origin cultures that can be described as either low-context or high-context. Nations with low-context tendencies include Germany, Switzerland, the USA, Sweden, Norway, Finland, Denmark and Canada, whereas high-context tendencies are associated with China, Japan, South Korea, Taiwan, Arab nations, people from other Middle Eastern and Mediterranean-based nations, Africans, Latin Americans and native North American Indian groups. As an example, Falicov provides the following description of the high-context interactive style of Mexican students:

> Indirect, implicit, or covert communication is consistent with Mexicans' emphasis on family harmony, on 'getting along' and not making others uncomfortable. Conversely, assertiveness, open differences in opinion, and demands for clarification are seen as rude or insensitive to others' feelings. The use of third-person ('One could be proud of...') rather than first-person ('I am proud of...') pronouns is a common pattern of indirectness, and is viewed as

a way of being selfless as opposed to self-serving. Thus Mexican [students] sometimes are left guessing rather than asking about the other's intentions; they often make use of allusions, proverbs, and parables to convey their viewpoints, which may leave an impression of guardedness, vagueness, obscurity, or excessive embellishment, obsequiousness, and politeness. (Falicov, 1996: 176)

Consequently, online classroom interactions that involve competition, emphasise individual accomplishments, or promote excessive directness are likely to silence Mexican students in particular and students from other high-context cultures in general.

The US population exhibits varying degrees of low and high context based on individuals' cultural heritages. However, mainstream American culture, including higher education, is primarily low-context and North American men generally, but not always, show lower context than North American women. According to Ibarra (2006), research among Latino graduate students and faculty attending American universities in the 1990s, found they were multi-contextual – a learned ability to survive in low-context academic environments while maintaining high-context characteristics in other aspects of life. Though academically successful, the consequences of this dual-world existence lead to conflicts, compromises and even underperformance in academic life. According to Ibarra, universities need to develop a truly multi-contextual system that accommodates both high and low-context styles into the fabric of the school's academic culture.

According to Morse:

> low context individuals, acculturated toward environmentally related learning variables anticipate that their role in learning is to attain some minimum level of competence which to some extent sees these individuals competing on an individual basis against a standard that may grow or change rapidly over time, and perhaps to a lesser degree, with their peers as well. On the other hand, those from high context cultures might expect formal communication to prevail, expect a single definitive or information specific form of assessment and expect to be directed where to obtain supplemental information, which would then be integrated into the body of knowledge for them. (Morse, 2003: 43)

When a nation delivering online programmes to a global clientele uses low-context communication in accordance with its own culture, those students whose cultural background relies on high-context communication may be at a disadvantage (Morse, 2003). Cross-cultural interactions can result in miscommunication. Because of the global reach of distance education, different cultures within the same nation as well as cross-border cultural differences must be considered. Cues needed by some students to determine how to interact in a given communication situation may be missing in an online environment. As a result, these students may feel uncomfortable, frustrated or reserved because, without context cues, they cannot determine how to react in a specific communication situation. Therefore, they may become silent or reserved in order to avoid offending other participants in an exchange.

This situation suggests the need for online course designers and teachers to adopt a multicultural education strategy that promotes an equitable learning environment. Robert Ibarra (2006) suggests reframing is the response. Reframing suggests expanding rather than necessarily eliminating or reforming the ways institutions presently deliver instruction. It means accommodating more than one cultural context. This does not mean that universities should change from low to high-context institutions or vice versa, but that they must become multi-contextual in order to educate culturally diverse learners effectively.

Field dependency

Field dependence/independence also accounts for differences in a multicultural classroom. Field theory explains the degree to which the surrounding contextual field affects a person's perception of information (Witkin and Goodenough, 1981). According to this theory, there is a continuum between extreme field dependence and extreme field independence, with individuals between these extremes often referred to as field-intermediate or field-neutral (Mancy and Reid, 2004). Field dependence/independence is viewed as a personality trait that is set early in life.

Field-dependent individuals have a tendency to rely on the surrounding field (i.e. others and the environment) as a primary referent for their behaviour. Such people are usually less autonomous and are likely to align themselves with the field (i.e. given situations and circumstances). They also tend to be more interpersonally oriented, pay more attention to and use more social cues, favour situations that bring them into contact with others over isolation, show more social behaviours and attributes important for effective interpersonal relations, and are better able to get along with others (Witkin and Goodenough, 1981). They also prefer working in groups, are externally directed, more pragmatic and accept ideas as presented. Field-dependent learners benefit from examples and contextual and cooperative learning environments that relate learning materials to students' personal experiences rather than casting them in an abstract, decontextualised manner (Ibarra, 2001).

Field-independent individuals, on the other hand, are more likely to rely on themselves as the primary referent instead of the local field. Consequently, they are more likely to have been socialised with an emphasis on autonomy over conformity, are more internally directed, and accept ideas through analysis. They demonstrate success in individualistic, competitive and more decontextualised learning environments (Ibarra, 2001). Field-independent learners approach learning more as an independent activity rather than a social or communal activity. Consequently, they may be inattentive to relational and affective aspects of the learning environment and their strength often lies in abstraction (C. I. Bennett, 2006). Men, on average, tend to be more field-independent than women, which accounts for differences in how men and women approach learning tasks in the virtual classroom. However, online learning environments tend to favour learners who are field independent and are accustomed to learning independently.

The following account from Simone Conceição is a good example how culture can affect students in a multicultural learning environment:

> Even though immigrating to the United States freed me somewhat from traditional female roles, it challenged my assumptions about my learning. I came from a culture where group cooperation was emphasized, time was relative, thinking was holistic, affective expression was evident, extended family was the norm, the worldviews of other cultures were generally accepted, and interactions were socially oriented. In Brazilian culture, I displayed a field-dependent cognitive learning style, which is relational, holistic, and highly affective... Moving to the United States and joining its higher education system required that I adapt and expand my learning style to accommodate the independent cognitive style of my new environment. (Conceição, 2002: 38)

Ignorance of a student's cultural values can lead to misunderstandings and conflicts. The professional literature suggests that these cultural values influence the way in which individuals learn. To promote learning equity, it is important that online course designers and teachers attend to student–content, student–student and student–teacher interactions and provide an array of learning opportunities that can variously assist diverse learners. Providing the student with a measure of freedom regarding the ways in which his or her learning takes place also develops learner self-direction.

Racial and cultural discrimination

People's ways of defining themselves vary depending on context and their various racial and cultural identities. For example, a student might identify himself or herself as a Muslim or Christian if the context is religious beliefs or by national origin if the context is national affiliation. Culturally-diverse students bring to the university a mix of individualised characteristics representing their cultural heritage and identities that can result in racial or cultural discrimination.

Both the preamble of the Charter of the United Nations and the 1948 Universal Declaration of Human Rights proclaim the right of everyone to enjoy all human rights and fundamental freedoms, without distinction to race, colour or national origin. Nonetheless, discrimination is a persistent feature of social interaction. The International Convention on the Elimination of all Forms of Racial Discrimination defines racial discrimination as:

> any distinction, exclusion, restriction or preference based on race, colour, descent or national or ethnic origin which has the purpose or effect of nullifying or impairing the recognition, enjoyment or exercise, on an equal footing, of human rights and fundamental freedoms in the political, economic, social, cultural or any other field of public life. (United Nations, 1965: Article 1 (I))

Cultural discrimination can be viewed as the power of one group or individual to define cultural values and the form those values should take, while maintaining dominance over other groups by rewarding those whose values correspond to its views and punishing those whose values do not. Racial and cultural discrimination is, therefore, based on behaviour.

Manifestation of racial and cultural discrimination varies in different contexts. In a classroom setting, it can reflect an 'us' versus 'them' outlook with positive self-presentation of one group and negative presentation of other groups. These attitudes lead to the ability of the dominant group to control the flow of communication and to influence the behaviour and thought processes of others. Such a racial and cultural climate in the classroom can hinder the contribution of minority students to classroom discussions and other activities fostered by intellectual engagement. The resulting sense of alienation can create a classroom climate for minorities where inter-cultural social connections are limited or do not exist.

Teachers are not exempt from biased attitudes and negative racial stereotyping. Some teachers are vulnerable to using stereotypical perceptions of student characteristics for which they hold lower expectations. In educational settings, racial stereotypes are often used to justify:

- having low educational and occupational expectations for minority students;
- placing minority students in separate tracks or classrooms;
- dumbing down the curriculum and pedagogy for minority students; and
- expecting minority students to one day occupy lower status and levels of occupations (Solorzano and Yosso, 2001).

Such low expectations are often blamed on the minority students themselves and/or their culture, rather than on the dominant society and its institutions.

The challenge for institutions that achieve global reach and possess a multicultural student body is to foster learning communities that are validating and supportive of all groups of students, especially minority students who are at risk of poor academic performance and/or dropping out of the institution because they are unable to adjust to the intellectual and social environments found in the virtual classroom. To assist minority and international students in overcoming the barriers that prevent some from successfully integrating into school and classroom culture, faculty and students representing the dominant culture at the university must fully embrace cultural diversity in the learning community and validate minority students. According to Rendon (1994: 45), validation entails the following tenets:

- validation is an enabling, confirming and supportive process initiated by in and out-of-class agents that foster academic and interpersonal development;

- when validation is present, students feel capable of learning – they experience a feeling of self-worth and feel that they and everything that they bring to the college experience, are accepted and recognised as valuable;
- like involvement, validation is a prerequisite to student development;
- validation can occur both in and out-of-class;
- validation suggests a developmental process, rather than an end in itself – the more validation students receive, the richer the academic and interpersonal experience;
- validation is most effective when offered early on in the student's college experience.

In a global distance education programme, in-class validation is the most practical approach, and the most important validating agent in this environment is the online teacher. Therefore, faculty members should be trained in techniques to create a validating classroom environment. Such training should orient faculty to the needs, concerns and strengths of minority students (Rendon, 1994). Teachers trained to validate students show genuine concern for all their students when teaching.

While desired learning outcomes may be the same for all students, many students require variation in how these outcomes are achieved. There is consequently a pressing need for enhancing learners' cross-cultural awareness and considering cross-cultural issues in online course design, instruction and dialogue. Teachers who treat all students the same show their lack of preparation for teaching in multicultural classrooms. Being treated equally does not mean being treated the same. When all students are treated the same, teachers are, albeit unintentionally, racist in their practices (J. E. King, 1991).

Academic capitalism and consumerism

The final issues described in this chapter are academic capitalism and consumerism. Eli Noam (1995) identifies three major functions of scholarly activity that historically give rise to universities: the creation of knowledge and information, the preservation of knowledge and information, and the transmission of knowledge and information. He points out that all three functions are based on technologies and economics. Changes in technologies and economics lead to changes in the university. Consequently, Noam and others believe that the institution of the university is in transition. Peter Drucker, economist and futurist, goes so far as to assert that universities 30 years from now will be 'relics' and will not survive as we know them today (Lenzer and Johnson, 1997: 127).

There is a new and growing international competition in higher education based on economics rather than the political, cultural and academic rationales that were the main driving forces until recently (Kälvermark and van der Wende, 1997). The economic potential of the international higher education markets has attracted new higher education providers, e.g. for-profit universities, operating on a purely commercial basis. According to Vugt (2004), the significance of these developments is illustrated by data on the three leading nations in this area – the USA, the UK and Australia.

In the USA, the education and training services sector ranks among the top five in services exports for the USA, accounting for 4 per cent of the total services revenue in 1999 and over US$14 billion of export receipts in 2000. In the UK, this sector also accounts for approximately 4 per cent of services revenues. The UK's share in the global market for international students is presently 16 per cent. The government's aim is to increase this to 25 per cent. In Australia, this sector ranks fifth in general exports (US$3.2 billion). In the year 2000, 150,000 foreign students were enrolled in Australian universities.

Public universities in the USA now receive only 15–20 per cent of their recurrent budgets from the government; the university itself is responsible for raising the remainder, hence making high-quality public and private universities similar in their management objectives and strategies (Heyneman, 2006). Consequently, in addition to drawing from their endowments, Heyneman (2006: 54) suggests that universities have options for funding:

- they can raise revenue from traditional sources (such as by raising fees, charging rent for facilities and increasing overheads);
- they can diversify into new sources of revenue (such as by establishing copyrights on inventions or investing in equity markets);
- they can allocate current resources more efficiently (for instance, by shifting from line item to block funding, differentiating faculty salaries and so forth); or
- they can eliminate outdated programmes or services.

Notwithstanding the massification of higher education, competition among universities for students has intensified as the result of the global reach of distance education and the emergence of a market structure as a means of regulation (Rovai, Ponton and Baker, 2008). The primary market areas of universities are no longer limited to the geographical areas in proximity to their campuses as universities are placing greater emphasis on strategic marketing and recruiting students nationally and internationally. This global reach can raise concerns in receiving nations regarding the contamination of local cultures and values, and create competitive friction between domestic and foreign education providers. Moreover, as accreditation is typically a national responsibility, global reach raises issues regarding cross-border accreditation.

In the highly-competitive environment for market share, many universities are embracing consumerism and assuming the role of educational vendors as they pursue a demand-led approach to student recruitment where education is largely viewed as a commodity shaped by consumer demand. Students are increasingly viewed as customers and institutions are using mass media, such as television and the internet, to market higher education directly to them. Much of this marketing strategy implies that customer satisfaction is of paramount importance and one result of this strategy is to intensify competitive pressures among institutions. Mary Cayton writes:

> many for-profit universities are driving down the cost of instruction by outsourcing it to part-time workers, often with lesser qualifications than those of faculty members at more traditional four-year degree-granting institutions. In so doing, those universities are forcing a reconsideration everywhere of how to cut labor costs in order to compete. (Cayton, 2007: B16)

Consumerism, in its pure form, assumes the consumer student knows best what must be learned and how best it should be taught, notwithstanding the fact that the student, by definition, is not the expert in either area, although it can be argued that students do know some of the things they need to learn to be successful in their chosen field. Additionally, the economic model that is typically aligned with consumerism values market-oriented decision-making, efficiency, product standardisation and tight control of the workforce in order to achieve cost-effectiveness and productivity gains. Applied to an academic institution, tight control of the workforce equates to constraining academic freedom. These values are in sharp contrast to the traditional values of higher education.

According to Rovai, Ponton and Baker (2008), the risk is that higher education institutions will become retailers of instructional commodities and will take care of some of their customers by tailoring academic rigour and standards to their customers' demands. Moreover, attempting to satisfy some students may become synonymous with lowering the degree of challenge, refraining from intellectually stretching students beyond their comfort zones during the educational process, awarding higher grades and placing more emphasis on entertaining rather than educating students.

The danger is that in responding to diminished funding support and increased competition, the ethos of academic altruism will give way to academic capitalism (Slaughter and Leslie, 1997). According to Rhoades:

> Academic capitalism is not simply a matter of entrepreneurial colleges and universities seeking to generate more revenues in tight financial times. It's a matter of these not-for-profit institutions behaving more like private enterprises, as the relationship between public and private entities shifts. (Rhoades, 2006: 385)

The risk with unfettered academic capitalism is that academic quality may become undermined when business becomes the prevailing model of distance programmes. While a market approach to distance education may allow institutions to secure funding and increase revenues, it may also bypass academic controls and practices in favour of supply-and-demand opportunities, if unchecked (Larreamendy-Joerns and Leinhardt, 2006). Business models may lessen faculty control of the curriculum in the name of efficiency, productivity and standardisation. The danger is that too much emphasis on the business model could create a cult of efficiency and undermine the academic integrity of the institution. Moreover, universities increasingly see faculty work as possible intellectual property, being valuable in global markets as a product or commodity rather than as a free contribution to an international community of scholars. Traditional faculty community service and scholarship will diminish, unless it provides an economic benefit to the institution. Consequently, the continued support of higher education to the public good may erode, given emphasis on the business model and the rise of for-profit institutions. The purpose of for-profit institutions is to create private benefits for providers and their customers, whereas the historic purpose of not-for-profit institutions is to create both public and private benefits. As Guy Neave (1998: 274), writing about European nations puts it, 'education is less part of social policy but is increasingly viewed as a subsector of economic policy'.

However, academic capitalism is not an unopposed trend in not-for-profit institutions. Organised challenges to rebalance the academy exist (e.g. see Rhoades, 2006). Many stakeholders are challenging the trend of higher education to adopt big business practices and are critiquing what academic capitalism does to the traditional areas of teaching, scholarship and service. Other stakeholders are celebrating the entrepreneurial efforts of higher education and consider these efforts to be a natural outcome of modernity (e.g. see Breneman, 2005).

Conclusion

Differences in culture and teaching methods may turn out to be the greatest barrier to global and international distance education (Hanna, 2000). Adding global themes to a curriculum does not change teaching methods, and it is precisely the teaching methods that need to be transformed if a university is to become truly global. As noted above, all cultures have their unique values and norms as well as perceptions of reality. Universities aspiring to become global need to heed the warnings of Edward Goldsmith (1993), who asserts that there is no surer way of destroying a culture than through a formal education system. Moreover, nations with a history of colonialism or fear of hegemony will reject educational methods they view as paternalistic or culturally imperialistic. Thamen makes this point regarding the Pacific islands area:

> Recent and future advances in their electronic media would mean that in our region multiculturality, people's sense of situational geography will become disoriented and it is possible that where people are physically will no longer determine who and where they are socially ... This trend may have serious implications for Pacific people's sense of identity. (Thamen, 1997: 31)

As discussed in Chapter 1, open and distance learning often results in a culturally diverse student body, mostly along the dimensions of age, ethnicity, cultural background and academic preparation. A global or international university will also have a nationally diverse student body. Although cultural backgrounds often differ with respect to students from the same nation, most of these students have been acculturated to some degree in the national culture of the university's host nation. However, achieving global reach results in an additional international dimension of diversity related to language and cultural backgrounds. Consequently, global online teachers as well as other learners need to acquire the ability to view the world through multiple pairs of eyes (Spronk, 1998).

Online learning materials and instruction should include resources and activities that respond to different learning style preferences, so that learners can select appropriate activities based on their preferred styles. There are several ways to conceptualise learning style preferences, based on information processing, personality, social interaction and multidimensional and instructional models. Personality models include field theory, which was discussed in this chapter and identifies the global, field-dependent preference of some students and the field-independent, analytical tendency of others.

Multidimensional instructional models address the student's environmental preference for learning and include Howard Gardner's (1999) theory of multiple intelligences. Gardner suggests that there are at least eight modalities (or intelligences) that can be used either singly or in combination to describe one's learning style preference. These intelligences are:

- *linguistic*: the ability to use language proficiently;
- *logical-mathematical*: the ability to reason deductively and think logically;
- *spatial*: the ability to create mental images;
- *bodily-kinaesthetic*: the use of mental abilities to coordinate bodily movements;
- *musical*: the facility to be familiar with and compose musical pitches, tones and rhythms;
- *interpersonal*: the ability to understand the intentions of others;
- *intrapersonal*: the ability to understand one's own feelings, motivation and intrapersonal feelings; and
- *naturalist*: the ability to discriminate among living things and to be sensitive to the natural world.

Although Gardner theorises eight intelligences, he emphasises that people will develop those that are most valued by their particular culture. If a teacher has difficulty reaching a student in the more traditional linguistic method (e.g. online lecture), Gardner's theory suggests the teacher might also address the topic drawing from other types of intelligence, e.g. interpersonal (i.e. collaborative discussion and/or projects), intrapersonal (independent study and reflection) and spatial (i.e. using pictures and/or video). The benefit of teaching to diverse learning styles opens teaching to more than one approach to complex intellectual work and learning (e.g. see James and Gardner, 1995).

Teachers can improve the quality of learning in a multicultural student environment if they adapt their teaching styles to accommodate multiple learning styles. Although the prospect of addressing multiple learning styles simultaneously in a single course might seem daunting, this approach is not to determine each student's learning style and subsequently individualise teaching to each student's preference. The idea is to design courses and to adapt teaching to address multiple learning style preferences at least some of the time and to provide students with a degree of choice whenever possible, e.g. providing students with text-based lecture notes for each major topic in addition to video or audio podcasts. If this balance can be achieved, students will be taught in a manner that sometimes matches their learning styles, thereby promoting effective learning and positive attitudes toward learning, while at other times compelling them to exercise and strengthen their less-developed abilities, ultimately making them better scholars.

Online teachers must reassess their teaching styles and philosophies and be open to change in order to better match the diversity of their students. The teaching styles and philosophies of a teacher often reflect the teacher's preferred learning style. Teachers should consider their teaching styles in this light and provide multiple approaches to teaching the same material in order to be inclusive of students from diverse cultural backgrounds who may possess different learning style preferences. However, teachers also need to teach students in ways that are authentic to the content area or vocation or profession being taught. For example, if the content area requires the graduate to engage in substantial hands-on activities, the teaching style should emphasise concrete (literal, actual, hands-on) content as opposed to abstract (theoretical, conceptual, symbolic) content. Teachers should obtain the skills needed to translate knowledge into effective instruction and enriched curriculum. If teachers are to increase learning opportunities for all students, they must be knowledgeable about the social and cultural context of teaching and learning.

3

Technology and the internet

Introduction

A few decades ago, the concept of distance education conjured up images of videocassettes with pre-recorded lectures and piles of do-it-yourself workbooks and programmed texts. However, the widespread use of the internet has revolutionised distance education, and advances in technology and new innovations fuel the need for additional changes. Consequently, distance education is in a continuous state of transformation as technology advances. Reviewing the potential impact of technology and the internet on higher education, Katz and Oblinger (2000: xvi) point out that 'the dominant issues facing the leaders of today's colleges and universities are what aspects to change and how fast can they be changed?' Information and communication technology has reached the point where the major challenges are related to course design and pedagogy.

If we envision a large part of a university education as education in the conduct and strategy of inquiry itself, then the university becomes society's site where students learn how to think, learn, construct and evaluate knowledge, providing the basis for lifelong, independent learning (Rury, 1996). An important implication of this vision is the need for a recommitment to the creation of an ideal learning environment for students with new pedagogies and technologies, as appropriate. According to Michael Privateer (1999: 72), 'Opportunities for real change lie in creating new types of professors, new uses of instructional technology and new kinds of institutions whose continual intellectual self-capitalization continually assures their status as learning organizations'. We must be wary of distance education schemes that simply call for placing handouts on the web. Old pedagogy delivered with new technology does not work. Advances in information and communication technology have a significant impact on the way teachers teach and the way students learn, and for technology to result in quality learning requires fundamental changes to traditional higher education pedagogy. Moreover, the connective power of the internet and the use of wireless technologies have made distance education a growth industry that enables schools to reach wider, more diverse audiences. Many schools see these technological advances as an opportunity to reach out and serve students in a wide area, even stretching to achieve global reach, without the constraints of the traditional classroom. Consequently, universities also need to become more inclusive, more relevant and more responsive to the needs of culturally diverse students. Intelligent use of technology has a major role to play.

Arguably, the biggest benefit of online learning is that it eliminates the expense and inconvenience of getting the teacher and students together at the same place and at the same time. However, the technologies used in online distance education possess a strong cultural component, suggesting that their use is influenced by cultural factors. This conclusion is consistent with the professional literature on information and communication technology, which describes technology as a 'culturally embedded, value-laden activity' (Nelson and Clark, 1994: 20).

Using information and communication technology and the internet to develop a competitive advantage is a big draw for universities seeking to achieve global reach via distance education. Moreover, the rapidly changing technology of distance education requires universities to cope with and keep pace not only with periodic upgrading of hardware and software, but also with the changes to course design and online pedagogy necessitated by these changes. In implementing change, one reality seems clear: universities will face more competition to attract quality-conscious students and thus cannot afford to underestimate the depth and speed of the changes necessary to remain competitive.

Thus, one of the greatest challenges in higher education today is keeping up with the rapid speed at which educational technology is advancing, particularly as it applies to distance education. The five generations of distance education technologies depicted in Figure 3.1 and discussed below clearly reveal the rapidity of changes and how changes to technology fuel changes to the very nature of distance education itself. These generations of modern distance education have been adapted from the work of Tony Bates (1995) and extended based on recent technological advances.

- The first generation is characterised by one technology, e.g. print, radio or television, to deliver education and is decidedly teacher-centred. It covers early modern distance education and continues until approximately 1960.

Figure 3.1 Generations of distance education technologies

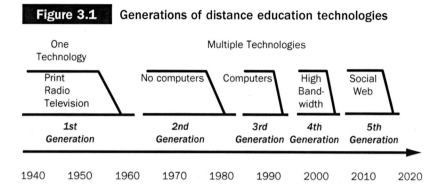

- The second generation makes use of multiple technologies, without the use of computers, and goes from the 1960s to the mid-1980s. Media primarily consist of audiocassettes, videocassettes, television, fax and print. Like the first generation, communication is still primarily one-way.

- The third generation also makes use of multiple technologies, but now also includes computers and computer networking. It spans the period from the mid-1980s to the mid-1990s. A major change from previous generations is the expansion of two-way interactive capabilities, to include two-way audio conferencing.

- The fourth generation includes multiple technologies plus higher bandwidth internet connectivity. This generation goes from the mid-1990s to approximately 2004. The major change from previous generations is the use of high bandwidth transmissions for individualised, customised and live video via the internet.

- The fifth generation of distance learning technologies starts with the introduction of Web 2.0 technologies and the advent of the social web to further empower discourse and allow members of the learning community to extend their social reach using a variety of technological tools.

The purpose of this chapter is to describe present and emerging distance education technologies, to identify and discuss the tools available for designing, teaching and managing online courses, and to examine the strengths and weaknesses of relying on computer-mediated communication for interpersonal interactions and engaging online content. Changes needed in course design as a result of new technologies are discussed in the next chapter.

Generations of web technologies

Web technologies have advanced rapidly during the past two decades. One popular way to conceptualise the advances in this technology and to distinguish between the first three generations of web technologies is to use the labels Web 1.0, Web 2.0 and Web 3.0 (see Figure 3.2). Reed Hastings, founder and CEO of Netflix, is quoted as saying, 'Web 1.0 was dial-up, 50K average bandwidth, Web 2.0 is an average 1 megabit of bandwidth and Web 3.0 will be 10 megabits of bandwidth all the time, which will be the full video web, and that will feel like Web 3.0' (Paczkowski, 2007, ¶ 3). However, there is no clear boundary or dividing line between Web 1.0 and Web 2.0, and Web 3.0 is not yet here. Web 3.0 is a designation to describe the next generation of web technology, whatever that might entail. Use of these labels presumes a hard distinction that is not easily drawn. Furthermore, many people view these terms as jargon with no clearly-defined or agreed meanings. Nonetheless, there is widespread use of these terms in the professional literature. Consequently, it is useful to discuss web technologies in terms of this framework.

Concurrent with advances in web technologies that improve online learning, advances in wireless technologies are also being achieved to support mobile learning. The first generation of wireless (1G) was analogue cellular; the second generation (2G) is digital cellular with integrated voice and data communications. Third-generation (3G) wireless networks provide faster data transfer rates and enable new wireless applications such as streaming media (Sun Certified Mobile Applications Developer Center, 2005).

Wireless technologies are used to complement web technologies, to reach new distance education learners and to extend the benefits of digital technology and e-learning to previously unreachable populations. Portable computing/communication devices, such as smart phones and portable

Figure 3.2 Generations of web technologies

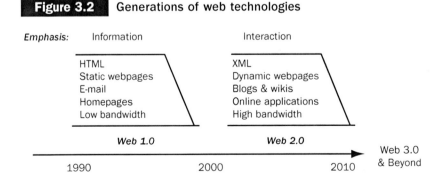

Emphasis:	Information	Interaction

HTML
Static webpages
E-mail
Homepages
Low bandwidth

XML
Dynamic webpages
Blogs & wikis
Online applications
High bandwidth

Web 1.0   *Web 2.0*

Web 3.0
& Beyond

1990   2000   2010

digital assistants, connected to wireless networks, enable mobility and facilitate mobile learning. Mobility allows teaching and learning to extend beyond the home computer. Portable computing/communication devices give teachers and students increased flexibility and provide new opportunities for interaction in a distance learning environment.

Web 1.0

The first generation of web technologies, e.g. HyperText Markup Language (HTML) and static webpages, text-based searches and e-mail with document attachments, using low bandwidth is known as Web 1.0. Simply, everything on the web before approximately 2004 is one way to think of Web 1.0. The aim of these technologies is to provide information that internet users can access and view. Only the creator of a Web 1.0 site can modify the information provided on the webpages that make up the site, resulting in a read-only medium. Web 1.0 is, therefore, aimed at the independent learner who desires to access information, much like a library user. From a social perspective, creating static personal webpages and communicating via e-mail and instant messaging are common occurrences using Web 1.0 technologies.

Web 2.0

Internet users, in particular younger users, have a strong desire for community, and this desire fuelled the Web 2.0 movement. The second generation of web technologies, referred to as Web 2.0, builds on Web 1.0 by increasing bandwidth and allowing internet users to incorporate user-generated content on webpages and to run software applications using their internet browser.

Web 2.0 is still young; most websites still rely exclusively on Web 1.0 technologies. Using online applications instead of programs installed on personal computers is a hallmark of Web 2.0. This feature has become so popular that it has acquired its own name – cloud computing – where the internet is referred to as the cloud.

Using advanced web technologies, e.g. Javascript and Asynchronous JavaScript and XML (AJAX), or web application frameworks like Ruby and Rails, Web 2.0 programmers create websites consisting of dynamic webpages that allow users to modify webpages, add to the information that is already presented, or to interact dynamically with the site in some way. For example, YouTube and MySpace rely on user submissions. In implementing Web 2.0, programmers shift much of the processing load from the server to the client, making the web faster and more efficient.

Web 2.0 technologies continue to expand. For example, the New Media Consortium (NMC) is an international not-for-profit consortium of over 260 learning organisations (i.e. universities and technology companies) located throughout the USA, Canada, Europe, Asia and Australia. It is dedicated to the exploration and use of new media and new technologies. The annual NMC Horizon Report describes the continuing research-oriented effort that seeks to identify and describe emerging technologies likely to have considerable impact on teaching, learning and creative expression within higher education. The technologies featured in the 2008 Horizon Report include:

- *Grassroots video and collaboration webs*: Video-sharing sites continue to grow on the internet; it is very common to find news clips, tutorials and informative videos listed alongside music videos. The newest tools for collaborative work are small, flexible and free. Colleagues simply open their web browsers and edit group documents, hold online meetings, swap information and data, and collaborate in any number of ways.

- *Mobile broadband and data mashups*: New devices and interfaces make it possible to use mobile devices to access almost any internet content that can be delivered over either a broadband cellular network or a local wireless network. Mashups are custom applications where combinations of data from different sources are 'mashed' together using a single tool.

- *Collective intelligence and social operating systems*: The kind of knowledge and understanding that emerges from large groups of people is collective intelligence. Social operating systems will be the essential ingredient of the next generation of social networking; they will base the organisation of the network around people instead of content. (New Media Consortium and the EDUCAUSE Learning Initiative, 2008: 3–7)

Web 1.0 and Web 2.0 technologies exist side-by-side and complement each other. Most existing websites use Web 1.0 technologies exclusively, as the purpose of these sites is to provide information. However, if the purpose of the site includes user interaction, Web 2.0 technologies are also used, as appropriate. Consequently, the internet, using Web 1.0 technologies, is a place where users can interact impersonally with the medium in order to obtain information, much like a virtual library. However, Web 2.0 is transforming the internet into a place where users can interact with each other as well as with the medium. It becomes much more than a virtual library; it also becomes a gathering place for people around the globe to come together as part of a single global community. It also offers other capabilities. Instead of keeping track of internet addresses and checking websites for updated information, users are able to subscribe to feeds that push the updated information to them directly via their personal computer or mobile device.

The implications of Web 2.0 are enormous. Online journals and other traditional online publications have yet to fully implement the concept, but Web 2.0 thinking and technologies applied to library services and collections have been framed as Library 2.0. Jack Maness (2006: ¶ 8) conceptualises Library 2.0 as follows:

- *it is user-centred and socially rich*: users participate in the creation of the content and services they view within the library's web presence;

- *it provides a multimedia experience*: both the collections and services of Library 2.0 contain video and audio components;

- *it is communally innovative*: it rests on the foundation of libraries as a community service, but understands that as communities change, libraries must not only change with them, they must allow users to change the library. It seeks to continually change its services, to find new ways to allow communities, not just individuals, to seek, find and utilise information.

Web 2.0 provides the tools to change the way teachers interact with students and how students interact among themselves in online courses. Advantages accrued from the enhanced communication and collaboration abilities include the ability to communicate rapidly, to distribute information and documents efficiently, to reach many different people worldwide simultaneously, and to record interactions by leaving a 'paper trail'. Consequently, Web 2.0 affects every online distance education programme. We have only begun to see and effectively use what the internet can deliver.

The emergence of a highly interactive and collaborative global community using the internet entails risks regarding unintentional miscommunication. Successful communication is the correct and complete exchange of information between sender and recipient. The culturally-related issues that can result in intercultural miscommunication described in Chapter 2 still exist. Moreover, although communication can be successful, Web 2.0 technologies also present the possibility for the exchange of intentional inflammatory information.

Web 2.0 provides enhanced tools for internet users to communicate on a global basis; how they choose to communicate is up to them. Moodiness, quickness to become angry and to take risks, prejudice, territoriality and disrespectful language can all be manifest through Web 2.0 technologies. Angry individuals can find themselves transferring that anger to the nation, race, or culture of the offending person. Issues of miscommunication are discussed in the section on computer-mediated communication.

Web 3.0

Although Web 3.0 is not yet here, there is already speculation regarding what the future holds for the internet above and beyond Web 2.0 advances. The most popular speculation so far is that Web 3.0 will implement artificial intelligence as it creates a semantic web. Nova Spivack, founder and CEO of Radar Networks, defines the semantic web thus:

> The semantic web is a set of technologies which are designed to enable a particular vision for the future of the web – a future in which all knowledge exists on the web in a format that software applications can understand and reason about. By making knowledge more accessible to software, software will essentially become able to understand knowledge, think about knowledge, and create new knowledge. In other words, software will be able to be more intelligent – not as intelligent as humans perhaps, but more intelligent than say, your word processor is today. (Spivack, 2006, ¶ 10)

According to Spivack, the semantic web will not be a separate new web, distinct from the existing web. Rather, it will simply add new metadata to the existing web. However, this view is not universally held. Ross Mayfield, Chairman, President and Co-founder of Socialtext, visualises Web 3.0 as more of a high-capacity social web than a semantic web. He writes, 'Less semantic fuzz than social discovery. Less artificial intelligence than human intelligence. Less automation and more augmentation' (Mayfield, 2006, ¶ 4).

Web educational technology tools

The virtual classroom requires structure as well as the functionality to pursue educational processes effectively. Producing a quality course requires a web-based teaching and learning environment that:

- creates a user-friendly environment to include a single academic gateway providing a simple, central access to the virtual classroom, course content and management tools, online libraries and student information systems;

- organises and manages teaching and learning activities, including provision for tools to assist students in assuming responsibility for their own learning;
- provides capabilities to support multiple teaching and learning strategies;
- provides access to appropriate multimedia learning resources so that students can engage content effectively based on their learning style preferences;
- facilitates social networking where students have the ability to express themselves using multiple user-driven tools, e.g. e-mail, voice over internet protocol (VoIP), discussion boards, chat, blogs, wikis, video conferencing, etc.;
- assesses students' progress using a rich set of assessment tools;
- enables students and faculty to store and classify their web resources and share them with others;
- tracks student engagement; and
- allows faculty and administrators to benchmark outcomes in order to promote institutional effectiveness.

During the Web 1.0 era of distance learning, the discussion forum was the heart of online courses. However, the advent of Web 2.0 tools has made teaching online a qualitatively different experience for the teacher as well as for students. Below is a description of the major technology tools available that are appropriate for online teaching and learning and that can be used in combination to address the major requirements outlined above.

Learning management systems

A learning management system (LMS) is a web-based software solution that consists of an integrated set of technology tools offering multiple modes of learning that make up the virtual classroom. A robust LMS also supports and connects the academic and administrative assessment processes across the institution's many departments so that administrative and supervisory tasks can be made more efficient and the overall cost and impact of education can be tracked and quantified at the course, programme and institutional levels. A good LMS is a cost-effective solution and possesses the following characteristics:

- *reliability*: the system must respond to the aggregate demand of clients (i.e. students, teachers, administrators and staff) at all times, and mean time between failure (MTBF) must be very high;

- *maintainability*: when the system goes down, it must be easily restored to service, and mean time to repair (MTTR) must be very low;

- *availability*: the system must be accessible and usable upon demand by authorised system users, and the system should not appreciably slow down at times of peak demand (availability equals MTBF/(MTBF + MTTR));

- *usability*: the system must be easy to use for all users;

- *scalability*: the system must have the capacity to keep pace with changes and future growth;

- *security*: the system must selectively limit and control access to the virtual classroom and assessment data to authorised users; and

- *interoperability*: the system must be able to communicate and exchange information with other systems used by the institution.

There are many LMSs on the market, each with its own strengths and weaknesses. However, Blackboard (*http://www.blackboard.com*) and WebCT, which Blackboard acquired in 2005, are major players.

Although features of specific systems vary by vendor, most LMSs enable the teacher to organise learning resources and activities, create discussion forums, access a course roster, maintain a grade book, and track student participation. These systems provide teachers with a means to sequence content and create a manageable virtual classroom structure. Registered students log into the LMS with any web browser and enter the virtual classroom to access course content, participate in online discussions, manage learning activities and submit assignments for grading. Moreover, because of the ease with which students can organise asynchronous and synchronous communication activities, e.g. chat and discussions, LMSs enable teachers to facilitate dynamic learning communities consistent with the social constructivist perspective.

Two criticisms often heard regarding these systems are their inflexibility and sometimes confusing interface. The typical LMS is simply a management system and not a learning creation system. Most of the technology tools that come with the system are fixed and generally consist of simple content sequencing and asynchronous discussion forums, although some vendors are expanding available tools to include synchronous as well as asynchronous tools. The LMS determines what a teacher can do. However, teacher needs should drive the solution, not the other way around. The proper role of technology is that of an enabler and facilitator of learning, not the determiner of pedagogy. What is required is a student-centred, not teacher-centred or technology-centred, learning creation and management system.

LMSs often lack the modularised functionality that permits the addition of other tools, e.g. blogs and wikis, based on what the teachers and students want or need. However, additional technology tools can be used by the online teacher to complement the tools included in the LMS. The downside to this approach is that the additional tools will not be integrated into the learning system. However, having all social networking tools bundled with the LMS and locked inside the walls of the virtual classroom may not be a good idea either. What is needed is to find ways to allow a better handling of solutions inside and outside the firewall.

According to Rovai, Ponton and Baker (2008), one result of the open source software movement is the development of open source course and content management system software that anyone can use for their own purposes. For example, some schools that cannot afford commercial products or choose not to commit to a proprietary platform have turned to Moodle (*http://moodle.org*) or Sakai (*http://sakaiproject.org*) as an alternative. These platforms are open source and hence free to use (presuming, of course, that one has access to a web server on which to install them), thus making it possible for virtually anyone to develop and offer online courses without requiring the purchase of commercial LMS software. Similarly, numerous organisations have developed their websites on open source systems, making them easier to manage than using multiple flat-files developed with web publishing programs such as Adobe Dreamweaver or Microsoft Expression.

Any institution intending to acquire an LMS or change LMSs is under intense pressure to ensure that all the institution's needs are addressed and all stakeholders are onboard with the ultimate decision. Consequently, it is important that stakeholders are represented on the institution's LMS section committee. Although membership requirements will vary from institution to institution, the following committee composition seems reasonable:

- academic director (chair);
- colleges, schools or academic departments;
- information technology;

- finance;
- institutional effectiveness;
- student services;
- registrar/enrolment;
- faculty; and
- students.

Social web tools

Networking, in technical terms, refers to linking multiple electronic devices, such as computers. However, the social web refers to 'social networks', where people are linked rather than devices. Social networking sites are interactive websites designed to build online communities for individuals who have something in common and a desire to communicate with others who share common interests. These individuals interact with each other and with dynamic web content in a conversational manner. This concept is very much aligned with Web 2.0 technologies. Perhaps the two best examples of social web tools used on interactive websites are blogs and wikis.

A blog, short for 'web log', is a place where anyone or any organisation, such as a school or course, can post a running commentary on just about any topic they desire and add links to other webpages, as appropriate. 'Blogosphere' is a collective term encompassing all blogs and provides the perception that blogs exist together as a social network. Although most blogs are textual with the ability of adding multimedia content, blogs may be specialised with regard to specific media types, such as video blogs (vlogs) or photo blogs (photoblogs). Mobile blogging (moblogging) is a specialised type of blogging where the user publishes blog entries directly to the web from a mobile device, such as a cell phone.

The ability for blog readers to leave comments in an interactive format is an essential characteristic of a blog. Consequently, teachers can use blogs to share thoughts on current events, articles and activities with others in a learning community, as well as with a broader, even global, audience. Similarly, students can manage their own blogs and use them for reflective journals, course diaries, electronic notebooks, knowledge management, or a host of other learning efforts. According to Glenn (2003), what many scholars find most thrilling about blogging is knowing that anyone can read and comment on their discussions, and the immediacy of thoughtful responses they receive. In particular, most academic bloggers report that their blogging has brought them into contact with people of diverse persuasions from all around the globe, providing diverse views and commentary on the blog's topic.

There is even a search engine dedicated to blogs. Technorati (*http://www.technorati.com/*) is a blog search engine that claims, as of 2008, that it tracks 112.8 million blogs and over 250 million pieces of tagged social media, including MySpace blogs.

While a blog is primarily one person's online diary with visitor replies, a wiki is a website where anyone can quickly add or edit webpages without needing special administrative access rights (the name 'wiki' is derived from a Hawaiian word meaning 'quick'). This would be the equivalent of a large chalkboard on campus where anyone could add, edit, or remove content at will. Consequently, a wiki is a great online tool for collaborative writing. Once the author establishes the wiki website, it can be set to allow anyone to participate or only registered users. Either way, everyone who writes content for the wiki shares in its growth. In the meantime, wiki software tracks all changes as well as who made them. If some content is lost, it can be added back by reverting to a saved version. Through the combined efforts of a small group of people, or a great many, the wiki's content can grow.

The wiki is a powerful tool for online communication and collaboration and for teaching and learning. It allows a group of people to produce or work towards a final product. It is easy to learn and use, not requiring special software coding knowledge or software other than a standard web browser. Moreover, teachers and learners can use wikis to create searchable and reusable resources that extend beyond the duration of any individual course. For example, the teacher can create a wiki for each major discussion topic to serve as a consensus-based record of the discussion. A student can be designated to summarise class discussions on a teacher-assigned topic and other students can add their perspectives regarding the discussion.

Although there are numerous online wiki sites, with subjects ranging from technical support to classical music, Wikipedia (*http://www .wikipedia.org*) is perhaps the most extensive. Wikipedia is a remarkably fast-growing online encyclopaedia with increasingly robust articles on a vast variety of topics. Like a print encyclopaedia, Wikipedia is a collection of knowledge. Unlike a print encyclopaedia, it seemingly has no end to the extent of its entries because its depth and breadth go as far and as wide as the personal interests of the people who add to its content (Rovai, Ponton and Baker, 2008).

In addition to blogs and wikis, there are numerous proprietary applications available on the social web, such as Facebook and MySpace. The Facebook Company, with offices in California, New York and London, develops technologies that facilitate the sharing of information through the digital mapping of people's real-world social connections. The website's name refers to the paper facebooks depicting the members of a campus community that some universities give to incoming students as a community-building gesture. The company's free-access website, Facebook (*http://www.facebook.com*), was started in 2004.

Facebook is a social utility that connects people and consists of many networks, each based around a region or organisation, such as a school. It gives people tools to control the information they share and with whom they choose to share. As of 2008, the company claims 80 million users worldwide. Users can add friends and communicate with them and update their personal profile to notify friends about themselves.

MySpace (*http://www.myspace.com/*) is another popular social networking website. It offers an interactive, user-submitted network of personal profiles, blogs, photos, music and videos. It claims it is for everyone:

- friends who desire to communicate online;
- single people who want to meet other singles;
- matchmakers who want to connect their friends with other friends;
- families who want to keep in touch;
- business people and co-workers interested in networking;
- classmates and study partners; and
- anyone looking for lost friends.

Both Facebook and MySpace are planning to extend their reach beyond personal computers to cell phones.

Social bookmarking is yet another social web tool. It is used to store, organise, search and manage bookmarks of webpages, e.g. blogs and wikis. Most social bookmark services encourage users to organise their bookmarks with informal tags instead of the traditional browser-based system of bookmarking that employs a hierarchical system of filing using folders and subfolders. Del.icio.us (pronounced 'delicious', at *http://del .icio.us/*) is an example of a social bookmarking web service. Its users can:

- keep links to favourite articles, blogs, music, reviews, recipes and more, and access them from any computer connected to the web;
- share favourites with friends, family, coworkers and the del.icio.us community; and
- discover new things.

Other social booking systems, such as Furl (*http://www.furl.net/*), also exist. From a distance education perspective, social networking services can be used to keep track of all the source materials and commentary that one locates online for an educational project, such as a preparing a manuscript for publication or for organising a literature review for a thesis or dissertation, or simply to organise additional resources to complement a course textbook.

Describing social web technologies and their potential to support distance education is not complete without also mentioning cell phones and their potential role in mobile learning. Included here is the cell phone feature known as 'texting' – sending and receiving messages via the short message service (SMS). SMS is often referred to as microblogging. Twitter (*http://www.twitter.com*) is an example of a real-time SMS that works over multiple networks and devices. It allows an individual, such as a student, to receive another person's Twitter updates from their cell phone, personal computer or other mobile device, thereby becoming a 'follower'. Followers can then set notification preferences for each person they follow.

At the University of the Philippines Open University, SMS-based mobile courses are being offered in formal sector English, maths and science education (Librero, Ramos, Ranga, Triñona and Lambert, 2007). SMS messages involve asynchronous communication. One can therefore reply to an SMS message at any time. The big appeal of this tool in support of distance education is its massive worldwide use, making it particularly attractive in less developed nations where large segments of the population may not have access to computers and the internet. Even in developed nations, this technology can be used to complement internet-based tools.

Podcasting and feeds

Podcasting is the Web 2.0 technology that has received the most publicity. It is the automated delivery of pre-recorded digital audio files via the internet to individual computers and mobile devices. Many people have likened podcasting to creating an online radio programme. Dixon and Greeson (2006) identify the following three characteristics of podcasting:

- podcasts are file-based downloads and are not streamed, that is, podcast files must be downloaded in their entirety before they can be played;

- podcasts are often subscription-based and are 'pushed' to the user through a syndication process discussed below; and
- the podcast is played on the user's personal computer or portable device with MP3 or MP4 playback capabilities.

The recent expansion of podcasting to video format is sometimes described as vodcasting, vidcasting, or vlogging. The convergence of freely available software, mobile audio and video technology, such as Apple's iPod and iPhone, and available hosting sites on the internet, have contributed to the explosive growth of podcasting in particular and mobile learning in general.

Apple's iTunes, which runs on both Macintosh and Windows-based computers, is arguably the most significant player in the podcasting industry. It can be used to listen to (or watch) podcasts on one's computer or to transfer them to one's iPod or MP3 player. While anyone can host their podcast somewhere on the internet, in January 2006, Apple launched 'iTunes U[niversity]', an educational portal within the iTunes website for US universities to manage and deliver podcast materials. In June 2008, Apple expanded the reach of iTunes U, bringing in additional universities from Australia, Canada, Ireland, New Zealand and the UK (including the British Open University), all of which provide content via the iTunes U education portal free of charge (Nagel, 2008). Additionally, iTunes U has expanded its Beyond Campus content to include educational materials from sources beyond colleges and universities, including Smithsonian Global Sound, KQED educational television, the US Museum of Modern Art, and American Public Media, which is making its radio programming available free for educational purposes. iTunes U is based on the iTunes store and enables educational institutions to make audio and video files available to the public or just their enrolled students. Unlike the general iTunes store, iTunes U lets colleges and universities build their own branded sites where material is grouped by course.

Podcasting technology gives teachers a further instructional tool to communicate with their students and is especially useful for addressing the needs of students who prefer audio or visual learning over text-based learning. Auditory learning can add clarity and meaning because of the addition of voice inflection over written communication, and can increase teacher presence.

An increasing number of online teachers are turning to podcasting technology to record their lectures and send them to their students, a process increasingly known as coursecasting. The portability of coursecasting makes the technology ideal for students who fall behind in class or those for whom English is a second language. Faculty can post audio and video content, students can download podcasts, and online learning becomes highly mobile. For example, in the UK, first-year microbiology lectures at the University of Bradford have been exclusively delivered as audio podcasts (Stothart, 2006). Brock Read (2005) describes Purdue University's podcasting project, called BoilerCast. The project's website stores recordings for about 70 different courses. Students can download the podcasts individually or subscribe to have a whole semester's worth of lectures automatically transferred to their computers or portable players.

Research suggests teacher-encountered barriers to creating podcasts include unfamiliarity with the technology, lack of time to prepare podcasts and perceptions of low relevance for their content area (e.g. see Bull, Tyler and Eaton, 2007). Research evidence regarding optimum educational podcast duration based on student preference is mixed. Anzai (2007) reports that most students prefer a podcast duration of about 5 minutes. Chan and Lee (2005) report student preferences of 3–5 minutes (29 per cent), 6–8 minutes (25 per cent) and 9–10 minutes (45 per cent), whereas Muppala and Kong (2007) report student preferences ranging from 5 to 20 minutes.

In addition to being podcast consumers, students can also produce their own podcasts. When students are assigned the task of creating a podcast they are given the opportunity to engage in authentic, constructivist learning. The process of creating a podcast provides important learning experiences for students and builds on previous experiences, thus helping them develop their own understanding, create tangible products (that could potentially become reusable learning content), engage in problem solving, and work collaboratively with other classmates. Developing podcasts also appeals to a variety of learning styles, as well as providing an opportunity for developing increased proficiency in the use of technology.

A frequent companion to podcasting and blogging is the web feed, which provides users with frequently updated content. Really Simple Syndication (RSS) 2.0 and Atom 1.0 are the two feed formats. Most aggregators (i.e. feed readers) support both formats. These aggregators periodically check the feeds to which the user subscribes and then collect new content. The user then checks the aggregator and views all new content in a single place, rather than having to check multiple sites manually for updates. These aggregators make it possible for someone to create a newspaper-style website that pulls content from several individual blogs. Blogging plus RSS or Atom makes it possible for anyone to syndicate content that can be freely picked up by anyone for publication on their website. Suprglu (*http://www.suprglu.com/*) is a technology tool that permits multiple feeds on one webpage. Stead, Sharpe, Anderson, Cych and Philpott (2006: 37) suggest the following educational applications for this tool:

- aggregate all of a student's production on one page;
- bring a range of different search feeds together for easy viewing;
- create a class site that aggregates whatever content feeds you are providing for students;
- create a collaborative project site;
- bring teacher lesson plans or ideas together on one page.

While many existing LMSs enable one to upload digital content (including audio and video), there is a significant advantage to hosting one's audio or video on a podcast-friendly site. That advantage is the use of feeds. Just as blogs use RSS or Atom to publish headlines from one site to another, if an online teacher makes his or her podcasts available via feed, then students can subscribe to the podcasts and be alerted when new audio or video is available (Rovai, Ponton and Baker, 2008). From an educational perspective, this means that teachers can post new content to a course website, and any student who has subscribed to the corresponding feed will be immediately notified of the addition. Rather than having to log into a LMS to see whether an instructor has posted something new, students can have their own RSS subscription and be alerted anytime something new is added.

Streaming multimedia

Streaming multimedia is multimedia that is received by an individual via the internet while being delivered by a streaming provider. Whereas a podcast is a separate downloadable computer file that can be viewed and copied to a portable device, a streamed file is simultaneously downloaded and viewed, but leaves no physical file behind on the viewer's computer. Non-streamed multimedia files, e.g. podcasts, can be very large in size and take a long time to download before it is possible to access the content. Most streamed video comes in one of three formats: RealNetWorks RealMedia, Microsoft Windows Media, or Apple QuickTime. Some of the advantages of using streaming multimedia include:

- instant play,
- distributing live events,
- delivering long-forms of media,
- multicasting to multiple viewers, and
- easy creation of streamed files (Hartsell and Yuen, 2006).

For example, ReelGood.tv (*http://www.reelgood.tv*) is an internet television station that has the goal of providing quality streaming internet television programming, in addition to on demand video content, using streaming technology. It was founded by the Regent University School of Communication and the Arts and seeks to influence a postmodern popular culture through innovative mediated communication using streaming technology. The station provides an incubator environment in which student team members develop leadership and managerial skills to maximise their educational experience and prepare them for a postgraduate environment.

Virtual worlds

Until recently, online virtual worlds were largely text-based environments such as multiple user dimensions (MUDs), also known as multi-user dungeons on account of having roots in an online version of the Dungeons & Dragons game, and the variant, object-oriented MUDs (MOOs). MOOs are simply MUDs that are object or multi-object oriented using a user-accessible programming language within the MOO. This programming language allows users to create and manipulate their own virtual objects, to include rooms and their furnishings. MUD is now mostly used as a generic term that encompasses both MUDs and MOOs. MUDs are mostly used for role-playing adventure games and social networking, but can also be used for educational purposes.

When used for online learning, MUDs offer students the opportunity to learn in computer-generated virtual worlds customised for the online learning experience. Some MUDs have been created to simulate fictional settings that users can explore, such as C. S. Lewis's Narnia, while others simulate real settings, like the Massachusetts Institute of Technology (MIT) Media Lab MUD. Educational and research MUDs are used for such purposes as social interaction, exploration of simulated worlds, conferencing and computer-supported cooperative work.

A user usually connects to a MUD using a Telnet application instead of a web browser. Telnet applications come with most personal computers and basically create a separate text window that accesses the text-based virtual world. The oldest (founded in 1990) and the first public social MOO is LambdaMOO (*telnet://lambda.moo.mud .org:8888/*). LinguaMOO is an example of an educational MOO dedicated to general studies of arts and humanities.

Recent years have seen the emergence of graphical, three-dimensional virtual worlds, such as Second Life (*http://secondlife.com/*) and the concurrent decrease in the popularity of MUDs. Second Life was created by Linden Labs in 2003 and has grown significantly, with numerous commercial and governmental organisations establishing a presence. Essentially, it is a graphical world where participants customise their appearance via an avatar (i.e. a graphical image of the user), purchase land, construct buildings, socially interact and basically live in a virtual world. In 2008, an open beta trial was initiated for a Second Life mobile application that lets users travel and communicate in-world by logging in from a handset using an existing account. The service, introduced for free, requires downloading a thin client to a 3G or wi-fi enabled mobile device. From an educational perspective, Second Life provides a unique and flexible simulated environment that can be used for experiential learning, multi-person scenarios, simulations and a host of social networking options.

The *New York Times* has described one teacher's use of Second Life in her online composition course (Lagorio, 2007). The teacher does not use Second Life to impart textbook knowledge; instead, she sends her students out to interact with other inhabitants to get them thinking and writing about their own identity, respecting the identities of others and exploring the look of their own avatar. Each week, she requires students to complete a 500-word blog on their experiences.

However, a word of caution is required. Some individuals can become addicted, especially in virtual worlds dedicated to adventure games or social networking, spending hours in these simulations each day. The result can adversely affect learning if the user is a student who becomes distracted and mistakes pure entertainment for learning.

Open education resources

The availability of open education resources (OER) on the internet, e.g. on iTunes U or MIT's OpenCourseWare Project website (*http://ocw.mit .edu*), represents free knowledge. The term 'OER' refers to educational resources (e.g. lesson plans, syllabi, instructional lectures, simulations, podcasts, etc.) that are freely available for use, reuse, adaptation and sharing, as long as they are used for nonprofit purposes. OER has more recently come to cover not only educational content, but also learning and content management software and content development tools. According to Charles M. Vest, MIT's ex-president who oversaw the start OER at MIT, education can be advanced 'by constantly widening access to information and by inspiring others to participate' (MIT, 2001, ¶ 6).

MIT's efforts in this area have become the world's model for OER and have guided similar initiatives worldwide. For example, China Open Resource for Education (CORE) is a nonprofit organisation to promote closer interaction and open sharing of educational resources between Chinese and international universities. Together, MIT and CORE have brought OER to China. Similarly, the Japan Open Courseware Consortium was established in 2006.

Another noteworthy initiative in this area is the Open Learning Initiative (OLI) at Carnegie Mellon University (*http://www.cmu.edu/ oli/*), which began in 2002 with a grant from The William and Flora Hewlett Foundation. It represents a collaborative effort among cognitive scientists, experts in human–computer interaction and faculty to create web-based courses that are designed so students can learn effectively with minimal use of a teacher. OLI courses include innovative features such as intelligent tutoring systems, virtual laboratories, simulations and frequent opportunities for assessment and feedback (Lovett, Meyer and Thille, 2008). The OLI programme automatically generates reports for each course that the supervising teacher uses to select discussion topics and example problems that target the areas where students are struggling. Opportunities are then provided for the teacher and students to interact as they engage the content that requires additional explanation and dialogue.

Although OER represents a valuable resource, free knowledge is usually not the same thing as free learning. Placing course materials on the internet does not enable computer users everywhere to learn in the same manner as students who enrol at a university; a course of study consists of substantially more than just the supply of a set of materials (Larsen, Martin and Morris, 2002). However, Carnegie Mellon University's OLI programme may represent the exception. What is especially interesting and unique about this programme is that research results show that OLI statistics course students learned a full semester's worth of material in half as much time and performed as well or better than students learning from traditional instruction over a full semester

(Lovett, Meyer and Thille, 2008). Perhaps the OLI programme points to the future of online distance education technologies. The more an online course relies less on the direct involvement of a teacher, the more productive the institution becomes. The real question is then to define the point at which increased productivity begins to reduce institutional effectiveness regarding its core mission of promoting learning. Clearly, a research agenda is needed to address this issue.

Computer-mediated communication

Effective communication is the foundation upon which the success of classroom learning rests. Without the face-to-face interaction among teachers and students, effective communication, in general and learning, in particular, can become more difficult. Moreover, common interests lead to relationship-building and the formation of a sense of community, which can become more difficult to form in a virtual classroom where members never meet face to face. The relationships that develop within any community are dependent on the nature of communication (i.e. information exchange) within that community.

Computer-mediated communication (CMC) is communication that takes place using some form of computer technology. Consequently, CMC is an indirect means of interaction. Although this definition is broad in scope, the focus of CMC addressed in this book involves interpersonal communication using the internet. Such communication can be either asynchronous, e.g. discussion boards or e-mail, or synchronous, e.g. real-time audio and video or internet relay chat. Asynchronous communication is the dominant form of interpersonal CMC used in distance education.

Communication is widely regarded as one of the most critical components of learner success in a distance learning setting. Randy Garrison (2000: 12) claims that 'asynchronous collaborative learning may well be the defining technology of the postindustrial era of distance education'. However, research suggests that CMC is not neutral; it can cause changes in the way people communicate with one another as well as influence communication patterns and social networks (e.g. see Fulk and Collins-Jarvis, 2001).

Additionally, the expansion of distance education in many universities has resulted in a shift in their student populations from local and regional students towards the national and international. While such

CMC-based internationalisation has created opportunities for global learning and global reach, it is also fraught with difficulty.

There are many appealing features of CMC as well as weaknesses. However, the effects of CMC depend upon the type of CMC as well as on the communicators and their culturally-related communication style preferences. The biggest appeal of CMC is its ability to eliminate the physical distance between individuals and thus provide the means to facilitate online distance education at a relatively low cost. It can also reduce the social boundaries imposed by traditional norms and social rules because of the relative greater anonymity of CMC over face-to-face communication (e.g. see Vrasidas and McIsaac, 2000). In particular, high-status individuals may not dominate online discussion or exert as much influence as they do in face-to-face discussions. However, Postmes, Spears and Lea (1998) argue that CMC does not necessarily lead to increased equality or democratisation and may even increase intergroup discrimination and hostility under certain conditions, as discussed below.

Media richness theory (Daft and Lengel, 1986) posits that information is processed to reduce equivocality (i.e. ambiguity caused by conflicting interpretations) and uncertainty. Applied to a virtual classroom setting, when equivocality is high, students are not certain what questions to ask, and when equivocality is low and uncertainty is high, students know what questions to ask but lack the necessary information to accomplish a project or assignment. As information increases, equivocality and uncertainty decrease. Daft and Lengel (1986) conclude that written media are preferred for unequivocal messages while face-to-face interactions are preferred for messages where equivocality is an issue. Face-to-face communication is considered to be the richest medium, while other media are thought to be leaner as they have fewer contextual cues and slower feedback.

Two-way video conferencing gives users more awareness of their partners and is able to transmit more nonverbal cues than text-only communication. However, even the best video links are not as rich as face-to-face interaction (Bal and Teo, 2001). Text-based communication, which is the backbone of much internet-based e-learning, provides even more communication limitations due to the reduction of nonverbal cues such as body language or gestures, which can convey important meanings, and the absence of other visual and auditory cues (Vrasidas and McIsaac, 2000). When the communication medium is lean, communicators receive fewer cues and social presence becomes more difficult to attain; this adversely affects the development of a sense of community and satisfaction with the exchange, especially for individuals from high-context cultures. Consequently, the result of lean communication at a distance, particularly among members of an online learning community who may be meeting for the first time online, is often a less accurate representation of the participants and their messages.

Leaner communication can also affect the time taken to communicate and complete tasks in CMC. From a meta-analysis of 18 CMC versus face-to-face studies, Bordia (1992) reports that CMC groups took longer than face-to-face groups to complete the same tasks. Consequently, text-based asynchronous CMC can at times be overwhelming to students and teachers who are expected to read and/or respond to large numbers of messages or discussion board postings. Rice (1992) suggests using rich media, such as video conferencing, for difficult non-routine tasks, whereas leaner media may be more suitable for simple routine tasks. However, Dennis and Kinney (1998) argue that media per se do not affect outcomes. They report that richer media enable faster decision-making regardless of task equivocality and conclude that matching media richness and task equivocality does not improve performance.

Walther (1996) reports that participants in online discussions often fill in the blanks when it comes to forming perceptions of others, a concept he labels 'hyperpersonal interaction'. In such situations, members of an online learning community may develop idealistic or unrealistic images of other students and the teacher by projecting images. For example, if an online communicator believes he or she is communicating with a person of lower intelligence or status, perhaps as the result of racial stereotyping, interpersonal communication is likely to reflect this perception.

Additionally, text-based communication between individuals who are not well acquainted can create miscommunication. For example, a student can perceive the online communication of his or her teacher as sharp and acrimonious while the instructor attempts to be concise and to the point as a time-management tool. According to Walther (1996), such hyperpersonal interaction may influence perceptions of one's online communication partners and the quality of one's communication. Such perceptions can negatively influence trust and feelings of connectedness among members of the learning community, particularly in a multicultural context where members of the community may not all understand or appreciate cultural differences and where cultural bias may exist.

Cross-cultural interactions can also create miscommunication. Because of the global reach of distance education, different cultures within the same nation as well as cross-border cultural differences must be considered. Charles Ess (2001: 2) strongly disagrees with the often-heard claim that CMC technologies facilitate a democratising form of communication 'that flattens traditional hierarchies, expands freedom of individual expression and gives everyone a voice in a global society'. He argues that the image of a 'global village' is a bad myth. CMC technologies are far from culturally and morally neutral, he claims. The danger is that CMC technologies applied globally, as we see with the social web, will eliminate distinctive cultural values. In particular, Ess notes that contrasts can now be seen on a global continuum ranging from:

> the relatively modest clashes between culture and technology apparent within the US and Europe, to especially striking conflicts with the cultural values and communicative preferences of Middle-Eastern, Asian, and indigenous cultures, to the conscious rejection of the Net in light of perceived cultural conflicts. (Ess, 2001: 4)

Further to Chapter 2's discussion of Edward Hall's theory of high and low-context cultures (Hall and Hall, 1990), CMC is likely to be more problematic for members of 'high-context/low-content' cultures, like Japanese and Latin American cultures, than 'low-context/high-content' cultures, such as the USA, the UK and Australia. This situation is primarily due to the view that the communication tools used in most LMSs are text-based and consequently offer fewer social context cues. Such differences can have dire consequences in cross-cultural interactions within any multicultural online learning community and isolate students not fully acculturated in the majority culture.

However, the emergence of new social web tools, such as video podcasts, which provide a richer form of communication, can help level the communication playing field in a multicultural online learning environment. Moreover, richer forms of communication have the ability to assist all members of the learning community to improve social information processing.

Lorna Heaton (1999) provides an excellent example of the design of computer-supported cooperative work using CMC in Japan, with particular attention to the influence of culture on the design process. She points out that Japan is a 'high-context/low-content' communication culture and much of the communication in Japanese culture uses nonverbal components. Consequently, Japanese designers, when confronted with the low-context, text-based CMC tools designed by Western designers, designed their own group work environment using CMC tools that better capture the nonverbal communication cues important to Japanese culture. They used two-way video CMC tools to convey the proper body posture, distance, gaze and hand gestures. Moreover, according to Heaton, Japanese designers were also careful to provide support for traditional, paper-based forms of working and ways of integrating paper and electronic information. Consequently, they also found ways of using video tools to capture texts or drawings from paper sources and to allow people to draw using pen-based computing technology.

Heaton (1999) observes that Japanese designers have been criticised for simulating face-to-face reality as closely as possible in designing virtual group work environments and for neglecting to exploit the transformative potential of CMC, as is the strong tendency in Western cultures. However, she points out that rather than abdicating responsibility for the consequences of their designs, Japanese designers have adopted a more pragmatic, culturally-sensitive approach of designing for use as they understand it now and permitting these uses to evolve over time.

Other cultural conflicts are possible, such as cultural traditions of paternalism and communalism versus the manner in which CMC technologies are thought to promote individualism and independence (Ess, 2001). Consequently, a strong argument can be made that CMC technologies do favour particular cultural values and communicative preferences, and these may be transformed or resisted. In other words, CMC can homogenise distinctive cultural values and communication preferences into a single 'McWorld' (Ess, 2001).

The major challenge facing the global university is to determine how these cultural considerations influence the design and delivery of cross-border online distance education as well as the design and delivery of online education for minority subpopulations, with their distinctive cultures, within a national setting.

Labi (2005) reports on quality-assurance guidelines for cross-border higher education by the Organization for Economic Cooperation and Development (OECD) and the United Nations Educational, Scientific and Cultural Organization (UNESCO). These guidelines for institutions involved in cross-border higher education include ensuring their programmes take into account the cultural and linguistic sensitivities of the receiving nation.

There are obvious practical reasons for choosing English as the language of choice for cross-border online distance education. Manning and Mayor note that its development as a global language is regarded as natural, neutral and beneficial:

It is 'natural' in that, while the colonial imposition of English is clearly recognized, its more recent spread is seen as the product of 'inevitable [primarily economic] global forces'. [It] is 'neutral' because, as an international language, English has become detached from its earlier cultural contexts [e.g. the UK, the USA, Australia] ... it has become the lingua franca for communication across diverse groups for whom it is not a first language. English is 'beneficial' because it facilitates international communication across several important domains, such as commerce, science and technology. (Manning and Mayor, 1999: 3)

However, even using English as a common language in CMC, there is a potential to infringe on people's linguistic sensitivities. 'Because language encodes meanings derived from collective experience, very different meanings may be attached to a text across the range of different cultures and contexts of use' (Chambers, 2003: 252).

Physical presence in a face-to-face environment affords interacting individuals the opportunity to monitor external cues that can moderate communication in a manner that fosters cooperation and politeness. Such cues include environmental indicants of status, body language and voice quality. Unfortunately, with a reduction of such cues in the online environment, the reduction of social control coupled with few immediate consequences to inappropriate social interaction can create opportunities for negative behaviour, broadly described as disinhibition. Joinson (2006) defines disinhibition as behaviour characterised by a reduction in concerns for self-presentation and critical judgment of others.

The social identity model of deindividuation effects posits that disinhibition often results from deindividuation, which is a shift from a personal identity to a social identity, shared by members of a group, which can sometimes occur in the relatively impersonal medium of CMC (Postmes, Spears and Lea, 1998). This model predicts that relative anonymity can increase the social influence exerted by social identity and group norms. Theorised causes of deindividuation are also related to reductions of responsibility, arousal, sensory overload and a lack of context.

Writing about online disinhibition, Suler (2004: 321), describes how people communicating online may 'say and do things in cyberspace that they wouldn't ordinarily say and do in the face-to-face world'. He asserts that this effect can be either benign (e.g. personal disclosures, acts of kindness) or toxic (e.g. abusive or rude language, and excessive aggressiveness, often referred to as 'flaming').

Susan Herring (1996: 149) addresses the phenomenon of flaming, which she describes as the use of 'derogatory, obscene, or inappropriate language and personal insults' in CMC. She points out that it is almost exclusively males who engage in this type of online communication behaviour. She argues that women place a high value on consideration for the needs of others while men assign a 'greater value to freedom from censorship (many advocate absolute free speech), forthright and open expression and agonistic debate as a means to advance the pursuit of knowledge' (Herring, 1996: 150). Consequently, she concludes that:

> [men and women] constitute different discourse communities in cyberspace – different cultures, if you will – with differing communicative norms and practices. However, these cultures are not 'separate but equal' as recent popular writing on gender differences in communication has claimed. Rather, the norms and practices of masculine net culture ... conflict with those of the female culture in ways that render cyberspace – or at least many 'neighborhoods' in cyberspace – inhospitable to women. (Herring, 1996: 151–2)

Complete anonymity, a factor explaining deindividuation and disinhibition, is not typically present in course-related CMC (an exception is anonymous end-of-course student evaluations of teaching). However, CMC is relatively more anonymous than face-to-face communication. According to Suler (2004):

- invisibility precludes an awareness of disapproving nonverbal somatic cues;
- asynchronicity prevents immediate reactions to one's postings;
- solipsistic introjections infuse the characteristics of oneself into the personas of others;
- dissociating the online world from the real world reduces beliefs of responsibility for behaving appropriately in the cyberworld; and
- minimising status due to the lack of environmental cues that may define authority can impede healthy, positive social interactions.

One important way in which to minimise online disinhibition and to promote social norms is to nurture a strong sense of community in the online classroom and establish positive group norms, perhaps using a rubric that describes expectations regarding online discussions. Most importantly, moderators can serve the purposes of not only keeping discussion on track, but more relevantly, observing the behaviour of participants and enforcing social norms.

Conclusion

From the primarily one-way, one-lane information trail of early correspondence courses, distance learning has evolved as technologies have developed. Early technologies such as print, radio, television, audiocassettes and videocassettes, which resulted in a mostly one-way learning process, have been superseded by the internet and Web 1.0 technologies, leading to a mostly one-way information superhighway. Shank and Cunningham (1996: 39) describe pre-Web 2.0 technologies as 'a series of convenient off-ramps that allow discrete individuals essentially one-way access to the riches of the internet'. Reflecting on Web 1.0 technologies, Heather-Jane Robertson (1998) suggests that technology reduces learning to simple information transfer, or instrumental learning, rather than fostering common sense, critical thinking and the creative capacities necessary for meaningful democratic citizenship. Instrumental learning, in this sense, is viewed as:

> students reducing what is to be learnt to a series of unconnected facts, which have to be memorized or reproduced later, with the intention of meeting the assessment requirements with the minimum of effort. (Macfarlane and Ottewill, 2001: 23)

The movement toward Web 2.0 technologies changes this situation. This shift in technology parallels the paradigm shift from a teacher-centred environment to a learner-centred one. Web 2.0 technologies help expand internet-based learning from mostly instrumental learning using one-way transfer of information, to expressive learning, which supports self-fulfilment during the learning process and nurtures critical thinking skills. Expressive learning, therefore, supports a learning environment in which 'students aim to understand ideas and seek meanings. They have an intrinsic interest in the task and an expectation of enjoyment in carrying it out. They adopt strategies that help satisfy their curiosity' (Prosser and Trigwell, 1999: 3).

The social web offers exactly the right sort of technologies to embody the theory of discourse and 'ideal speech act' of Jürgen Habermas

(1987), where everyone is empowered to speak and to doubt the validity of other speakers' claims in the collective pursuit of consensus and truth. Thus, Web 2.0 technologies better align CMC with the social constructivist view of learning as 'conversation'. Using this view, the teaching/learning process is seen as a form of conversation, whether real or in the mind of the learner, which leads to an 'agreement' on the meaning of specific content. It can be argued that CMC, through the provision of real opportunities for conversation, is an appropriate medium for the pursuit of those types of learning objectives where a conversational approach is of particular importance, i.e. higher-order learning objectives associated with problem-solving and critical-thinking skills.

One must also keep in mind that 'while education is the great equalizer, technology appears to be a new engine of inequality' (Gladieux and Swail, 1999), particularly as it applies to developing nations. Rockenbach and Almagno elaborate this theme by arguing:

> yes, to be sure, technology costs are lowering. And, yes, the required skills are more easily attained. But for many, the dollars needed for the equipment and instruction are simply not there ... Here we are faced with an inequality which is the real digital divide between the information haves and have-nots ... a reality that is one of our most important economic civil (human) rights concerns. (Rockenbach and Almagno, 2000: 458)

While the rhetoric regarding the use of CMC is often highly inclusive, the reality is frequently that CMC excludes certain groups or individuals from full access to discourse. This is because some individuals are excluded from full use of technology because of the digital divide and equitable access to technology, in addition to the previously discussed problems associated with equitable opportunity for discourse in a multicultural virtual classroom. Based on the emergence of the social web, the real questions that arise do not deal with whether or not CMC is adequate to support higher education learning outcomes. The real questions deal with what technology tools are best to use in the virtual classroom in various learning situations, and how best to ensure culturally-related differences do not silence or disadvantage some learners in the social learning process. The aim of CMC should always be in the direction of ideal discourse and the ideal speech situation.

4

Designing global online programmes and courses

Introduction

Learning in any environment should never be based on a single technology tool or teaching method, and the number of complicating factors increases when designing online learning environments for a multicultural student population. Learners are not homogeneous and neither are their attitudes about learning nor their confidence to succeed; where one student may be self-motivated and persistent regardless of the structure of the programme, another may feel discouraged and disengage if his or her learning style preference is not well aligned with the dominant teaching style or learning context.

Because of the nature of the technology-mediated environment, designing distance education programmes requires more careful attention to aspects of the instructional design process than is generally afforded to traditional face-to-face programmes. Online courses should incorporate a wide variety of instructional methods, including opportunities for both asynchronous and synchronous communication and access to supporting learning resources that vary so that both high-context and low-context communicators will have resources that suit their communication preferences. Without careful attention to design, distance education courses can become disjointed, teacher-centred and user-unfriendly for some users. A fair and equitable learning environment:

- provides an equal opportunity for all students to learn;
- includes flexibility, as needed, to meet individual student preferences;
- maintains student accountability for his or her learning; and
- accurately matches grades to performance, even when students have a choice regarding how best to demonstrate their learning.

Most aspects of designing and delivering instruction are common to all methods and modes of delivery and many design considerations are universal. However, there may be tremendous differences in the amount of effort needed to design specific components of a course based on the mode of programme delivery. One of the first considerations online programme designers find different from those in more traditional instruction is the tremendous amount of time required 'up front' to design and develop course components such as learning objects, thought-provoking questions and projects that nurture critical thinking skills.

The capabilities of the internet and, in particular, the effects of Web 2.0, strongly influence how online programmes and courses are designed and developed, with some educators referring to the relationship between online courses and Web 2.0 as 'e-learning 2.0'. According to David Jonassen (2000), e-learning technologies are cognitive tools that assist learners to elaborate on what they are thinking and to engage in meaningful learning. Web 2.0 tools are ideally suited for this purpose.

Instructional design (also called *instructional systems design*) is the process, guided by learning theory, by which instruction is developed and improved through the analysis of learning needs and instructional goals. It also includes development of instructional materials to satisfy those needs and goals (Dick, Carey and Carey, 2005). Although this process places emphasis on structure, it should be flexible enough to provide a rich array of tools and resources for students to use in creating their own learning pathways.

Programme design

A proposed new or revised distance education programme must fit within the mission of the university and support a defined need. Moreover, the institution must have adequate resources to support a quality programme and provide student advising and other support services without diminishing support for existing programmes. Such a programme is most effective when it is carefully designed and due attention is given to providing students with the flexibility that they value. Flexibility is especially important for those students who are balancing work and family responsibilities with their studies and students whose culturally-related learning style preferences differ from the host nation's dominant culture.

Groen, Tworek and Soos-Gonczol (2008) identify four areas that are essential for any online programme: programme administration, technical support, teachers and students. Consequently, each of these areas must be addressed when designing an online programme. Programme administration is important because it provides the foundation and scaffolding necessary to support the programme. Technical support maintains the scaffold. Teachers build around the scaffold to give structure to learning. Finally, students use the structure for learning.

Programme design model

The purpose of distance education programme design is to determine the mode(s) of programme and course delivery, identify programme goals and desired learning outcomes, and provide structure and a framework for the programme using courses and support services as the major building blocks. In contrast, the purpose of the instructional design model is to give meaning to the design process by helping one visualise the design task and to break it down into discrete, manageable units. This top-down, modular approach begins with the 'big picture' and gradually adds details, ultimately identifying the course structure for the programme. This process also provides the institution with an opportunity to make the case for programme need and demand.

A model to design a distance education programme consists of the following six steps, which are typically conducted by a multidisciplinary programme design team:

1. Describe the programme in general terms (i.e. provide the big picture).
2. Determine the model of distance education that will be used to deliver the programme.
3. Conduct a market survey to determine the extent of programme need and then initiate development of a marketing plan.
4. Develop programme goals, features and admissions criteria, and identify desired student outcomes.
5. Identify themes that will link all courses and provide coherence to the programme.
6. Conduct job and context analyses to develop programme structure, authentic learning environments and course goals.

The first step consists of developing a general description of the proposed programme and its intended audience. The design team must also estimate the proposed programme's impact on and relationship to existing programmes at the institution and identify the anticipated impacts, positive or negative, on other programmes.

The second step in designing a programme is to determine the distance education model that is best suited for the programme based on institutional preferences and capabilities. Dick, Carey and Carey (2005) identify three models of distance learning:

- the academic model of distance learning that replicates the classroom experience using the internet (suitable for all learner independence levels);
- the open university model of distance learning that replicates the large lecture hall experience using the internet and broadcast television (suitable for fairly-independent learners); and
- the professional and technical training model of distance learning using the internet and computer-based training (suitable for highly-independent learners).

Each model identified above includes a technology component. This component can be entirely asynchronous, entirely synchronous, or a combination of the two. Additionally, the technology component can consist of web technologies for online learning using desktop computers, wireless technologies for mobile learning, or a combination of the two. Determining an appropriate model for the programme and ascertaining the learning management system used by the institution informs the programme design and helps identify the technology tools that can be used to facilitate learning.

The third step is to determine if there is a general need for the programme and to conduct a market survey to determine the extent of that need:

> The main task of the institution is to determine the needs and wants of target markets and to satisfy them through the design, communication, pricing and delivery of appropriate and competitively viable programs and services. (Kotler and Fox, 1995: 8)

The characteristics of adults who are likely to be interested in enrolling in distance education programmes are identified and discussed in Chapter 1. Even once the programme is developed and implemented, the extent of the enrolment will still need to be addressed. A market survey, supplemented with selective interviews and focus groups will help answer this question.

To be credible, the survey should sample potential students in the target population as well as potential employers and educators. Specific information to be obtained includes:

- degree of difficulty in locating qualified workers in the programme area;
- the number of full-time and part-time openings in the field;
- a forecast of changes in demand for personnel in the field over the short, mid and long terms;
- identification of critical skills required to perform the job satisfactorily; and
- identification of skills in which newly hired personnel are often weak.

An internet search should also be conducted to assess the competition. How many similar programmes do other institutions offer? What is the student enrolment? What is the duration and scope of the programmes? What are the programme entry requirements? What is the tuition? How will the proposed programme differ from those already offered elsewhere? At the conclusion of this step, the design team should have a better idea of the scope of the proposed programme, the need it satisfies and potential demand.

The fourth step in the programme design process is to develop programme goals, features and admissions criteria, and to determine desired student outcomes. A detailed needs assessment should be conducted to outline programme coursework and to identify the specific skills, knowledge and attitudes to develop programme goals. This needs assessment consists of identifying discrepancies between existing programmes and the levels of knowledge, skills and attitudes required for a specific job.

There are many possible models to conduct a needs assessment. Kosecoff and Fink (1982) describe the following model, developed by Dr David Satcher, former acting dean of the King-Drew Medical Center in Los Angeles:

1. *Identify potential goals*: Compile a comprehensive list of goals for the programme. Go to the experts, the literature, the results of the market survey and/or the community for examples and suggestions.

2. *Decide which goals are most important*: Select a sample of individuals and groups whose interests and views of the programme are important. Have them rate the goals and then synthesise the results.

3. *Assess the nature and type of currently available programmes*: This step is to analyse information about competing programmes offered at other institutions.

4. *Select final programme goals*: Here one must synthesise information in order to set priorities among goals.

The fifth step is identification of themes that will link all courses and provide coherence to the programme. The design team should develop a thematic framework for the programme at this time. Thematic instruction is based on the notion that individuals acquire knowledge best when learning in the context of a coherent whole and when they are able to connect what they are learning to the real world. Thematic instruction seeks to put the teaching of content in the context of a real-world subject that is both specific enough to be practical and broad enough to allow creative exploration. Thus, thematic instruction is highly compatible with constructivism and multicultural education.

Themes should be broad and often involve large, integrated systems (such as globalisation) or a broad concept (such as global learning). Programme designers should clearly define each theme and list its identifying characteristics and/or key concepts. Themes should relate to student experiences and interests and be relevant to programme content. Designers should then arrange the themes for spiralling.

Spiralling refers to the revisiting of themes at different levels according to students' previous mastery of prerequisite content. Spiralling could be applied at the programme level when sequencing courses or within specific courses when the teacher is sequencing lessons and learning objects. In other words, students revisit concepts and ideas several times during their programme at increasingly sophisticated levels. Figure 4.1 provides an example of spiralling applied to the theme of global learning.

The sixth and final step is conducting job and context analyses to determine programme structure, authentic learning environments and course goals. According to Dick, Carey and Carey (2005), a job analysis examines a particular job in order to develop an inventory of tasks that are believed to comprise the job. These tasks are then grouped according to common characteristics into categories. Subject matter experts, job incumbents and employers validate the categories and tasks, usually by means of surveys and/or focus groups. As a result of this analysis, programme and course goals are developed and courses are identified and sequenced.

A context analysis proceeds concurrently with the job analysis. The purpose of this analysis is to describe the environment in which

Figure 4.1   Global learning spiral

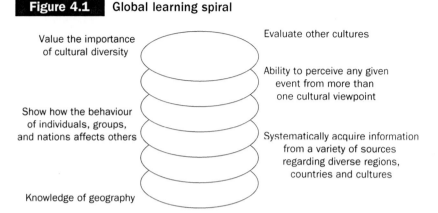

Value the importance of cultural diversity

Evaluate other cultures

Ability to perceive any given event from more than one cultural viewpoint

Show how the behaviour of individuals, groups, and nations affects others

Systematically acquire information from a variety of sources regarding diverse regions, countries and cultures

Knowledge of geography

graduates will use the knowledge and skills acquired in the programme. Course designers require this information in order to create authentic learning and assessment activities.

Programme designers should give due consideration to including a cornerstone course in the programme that introduces students to the institution and provides a solid foundation for students to build upon. Similarly, it is worth considering a capstone course that provides a capping to each student's experiences and to the programme. The cornerstone course is typically taken during the first term of study to prepare students to effectively engage the challenges of the programme and to develop a learning plan that identifies their educational goals and learning strategies. It also socialises students and introduces them to the discipline being studied by providing and discussing such topics as career information, the conceptual framework of the programme, major programme requirements, the skills and resources needed to succeed in the programme, student support services, and information about the technology used by the programme. For a blended programme, the cornerstone course could be in the form of an initial on-campus residency, which is discussed below.

The capstone course, normally offered during the final term of coursework, provides an opportunity for students to demonstrate their abilities to write, speak and use the skills, knowledge and attitudes acquired during the programme at professional levels. It encourages students to use what they have learned about themselves and to develop a plan for lifelong learning and development. The course should include a variety of experiences, such as an internship experience. It can also include a project that addresses the reflective integration of all programme coursework, perhaps in the form of a student portfolio. Alternatively, students can present original work that responds to the question or set of questions identified by each student at the beginning of the programme in the cornerstone course. As another example, a capstone course for an advanced programme could include creation of significant original research that demonstrates the student's proficiency as an independent thinker.

To support global learning outcomes, the programme designer must consider two dimensions: global learning at home and global learning abroad. The major goal of global learning at home is to provide all students with a global dimension to their learning, not merely the small percentage of students who study abroad. Content-based instruction integrates language with content and emphasises the integration of content and linguistic components at advanced levels of second language and culture instruction. Davison and Williams (2001: 53) believe that one justification for integrating content and language in the classroom is that it follows the 'current "communicative" trends in language teaching that emphasize the meaningful use of language in appropriate contexts in the language classroom'.

Immersion programmes can be established both at home and abroad for students to achieve an authentic exposure to a foreign language and/or culture. Immersion programmes in Canada and the USA have successfully employed this technique in university curricula, targeting foreign students, immigrants and others who have the desire to learn a second language and culture intensively.

A formal programme review usually takes place at this point to complete the formal programme design phase. This review has three possible outcomes:

- the programme is approved as proposed and responsibility for further work moves to the course design team, if one exists, or to the designated teachers to develop and implement the courses;
- the programme is revised and passed on for course development and implementation; or
- the programme is terminated or sent back to the programme design team for further analysis and programme development.

Blended programmes

There is a growing interest in combining distance education and face-to-face instruction into a blended learning model (sometimes called mixed-mode or hybrid learning). According to Collis and Moonen (2001), blended learning is a hybrid of traditional face-to-face and distance learning so that instruction occurs both in the classroom and at a distance, and where the distance component becomes an extension of traditional classroom learning. This concept introduces a flexible approach to programme and course design that supports the combining of different times and places for learning, offering some of the conveniences of distance courses without the complete loss of face-to-face contact. There are two models that are used for blended learning, with many variations possible for each model: the blended programme model and the blended course model.

Designers create a blended programme by adding face-to-face residencies to a distance education programme and/or including any mix of single-mode face-to-face, single-mode online and blended courses. Such a design helps to promote a sense of community and satisfy the strong need for what Robert Putnam (2000: 346) describes as 'connections, reciprocity, trust, networking, mutual benefit, bonding, bridging and engagement'. From a programme design perspective, a blended programme can lie anywhere along the continuum anchored at opposite ends by fully traditional and fully distance learning environments. The traditional component can be either on the main university campus, or faculty can travel to a remote site in order to meet with students, although the former approach is superior as it promotes stronger ties to the institution.

Residencies can create a bond between the distant student and the institution, which can result in other benefits, such as increased student satisfaction with the programme, increased student loyalty to the institution, increased student persistence and the formation of interpersonal connections with other students that facilitate online collaborative efforts. 'When people interact with one another, they have a model and foundation upon which to base further cooperative enterprises' (Putnam, 2000: 346). The result is an educational experience more robust than fully distance learning can offer. Moreover, the reduced seat time of blended learning versus traditional face-to-face courses is attractive as a cost savings approach for institutions coping with limited classroom space.

Annual residencies during the summer are a common programme requirement for both undergraduate and graduate programmes. Typically, the initial residency could constitute a cornerstone course and serve a purpose similar to that of the 'freshman experience' used in many undergraduate programmes. The purpose of this initial residency is to introduce students to the university, to each other, and to faculty and staff; to integrate students in university life; and to provide information and impart skills that promote and support academic success. Such a residency is consistent with various student development theory models (e.g. Tinto, 1987, 1993) that focus on academic involvement, student–faculty interaction, campus involvement and student–peer interaction. These elements can promote student persistence when included as part of an initial university experience.

Subsequent residencies build on the initial residency and can be used to provide opportunities for guest presentations and discussions by distinguished scholars on topics significant to the programme. Additionally, they can be used to conduct cooperative learning experiences that emphasise teamwork and promotion of leadership skills and involve small group face-to-face discussions and projects, nurture intra-cohort and inter-cohort community-building and conduct proctored, high-stakes testing.

Although the research evidence supports the inclusion of residencies in distance education programmes for the reasons outlined above, an alternative is to make attendance optional, that is, include a residency experience, but make it elective. This may be a practical solution for the global university that has achieved global reach where it is impractical for some students to travel great distances for the residency. When the residency is an optional part of the programme, students who do not opt for the face-to-face experience should be required to complete an alternative experience, perhaps in the form of a virtual residency described in the next section.

Single-mode online programmes

In addition to blended programmes, educational programmes can be either entirely face-to-face or entirely offered at a distance. Universities that offer only one type of programme are labelled single-mode universities, while universities that offer both traditional and distance education programmes are labelled dual-mode universities. In dual-mode universities, both the face-to-face and distance students may have the same teachers and textbooks and take the same or similar examinations. In such universities, one often encounters the concept of a 'university within a university' in order to differentiate the distance education school culture from the traditional school culture. However, despite distinct cultures, both types of programmes need to be equivalent in terms of infrastructure and support in order to ensure consistent quality across all university programmes.

Single-mode online programmes are designed without any on-campus components. That is, all the courses are single-mode online and the programme itself has no residencies. Although blended programmes are preferred for the reasons described above, single-mode online programmes may be better suited for the global university, where it is impractical for students to physically visit the campus because of their dispersion worldwide.

In the absence of any campus-based experience, the institution must seek alternative ways to satisfy the needs that residencies typically satisfy. As the major purpose of residencies deals with forming connections with the university and increasing sense of community, the university should plan on designing and developing an initial virtual residency for the distance education programme.

According to Michael Moore (Moore and Kearsley, 2005), the physical separation between members of a virtual learning community leads to special patterns of learner and teacher behaviours. This separation represents a psychological and communications space to be crossed, a space of potential misunderstanding between the inputs of the teacher and those of the learner. It is this psychological and communications space that Moore calls *transactional distance*.

To reduce transactional distance and concurrently build a sense of community and links to the institution, the virtual residency should include activities that orient new students to each other, the institution and their programme. These activities can include, but are not limited to the following high-context communication events (i.e. they include video with audio to the maximum extent possible):

- an inspiring keynote address on a topic relevant to programme content;
- a presentation, e.g. a video podcast, that provides a tour of the campus and includes short interviews with programme faculty members and selected students;
- a series of relatively short online learning objects (i.e. 5–20 minutes each) that orient students to the programme and to the distance education technologies used to deliver the programme, especially the learning management system;
- an orientation to student support services, including interviews with programme administrators and staff personnel with whom students will

interact during the programme, e.g. advisers, financial aid specialists, business office representatives, technology helpdesk personnel, etc.; and

- multiple opportunities for students and faculty participating in the virtual residency to become better acquainted with each other.

Support services

Much of student affairs' online presence in support of distance students involves essential support services, such as admission, registration, financial aid and help with technology (Rovai, Ponton and Baker, 2008). Student life, student activities and related services have yet to provide distance students with experiences equitable to those offered to traditional on-campus students.

The amount of student support services required will vary by student depending on his or her strengths and weaknesses. A student with low social resources will require more support from the institution. If these services do not satisfy student needs, the student is unlikely to persist in the programme and institution.

Student support systems for distance education programmes must be as complete and as customer-oriented as those provided for on-campus students. In most cases, these services may be the only link the student has with the institution apart from academic activities.

High-quality, comprehensive student support services are essential to student recruitment and retention. Students expect convenient access to the same types of support services as on-campus students to support their programme, such as bookstores, library, financial aid offices, academic advisers, and counselling and placement services. Moreover, the institution should provide an adequate means for students to resolve complaints. While many programmes may not require 24-hour services, seven days a week, evening and/or weekend support will be needed by many students as many engage the programme during these times. Accordingly, the institution should provide 'helpdesk' services that meet the needs of students in the programme. Consideration should be given to providing timely assistance for technical problems, academic questions, billing questions, library research and textbooks. International students who reside in different time zones will require access to support during times that are convenient to them.

Research evidence reveals a positive relationship between student satisfaction and success in college (e.g. Tinto, 1987). In order to promote student satisfaction, alternative student support methods must be employed to ensure that no distance student is significantly inconvenienced. As distance students have widely varying access methods available to them, redundant access points should be in place for many support functions, e.g. telephone and web-based access. Consequently, the online teacher's role extends to that of adviser and mentor. Faculty should become familiar with campus services in order to respond to student questions and to direct them to the appropriate campus office. In turn, involvement with students yields personal satisfaction for teachers as well as for students.

Workman and Stenard (1996) suggest that distance learners also value services such as tutoring, study skill training and, particularly, an orientation on the technology used for course delivery. The distractions created by technology must be minimised. Consequently, telephone service is more user-friendly and more effective than asynchronous communication for responding to online student problems and advising students. Additionally, student support services typically exist as separate units on campus, which can create problems for online students who do not have access to the campus. An integrated approach to student support services through a single web portal is more effective for online students.

In addition to providing support services to students, the institution should also provide support services to faculty, especially if the institution does not utilise the team approach to online course design. Olcott and Wright (1995) assert that many distance education faculty members lack adequate support for their efforts (faculty compensation and rewards, incentives and training).

Tracy Irani (2001) reports that the primary form of distance education faculty training in the USA is a formal, regularly scheduled, prescribed course or set of training materials provided to the teacher. Most programmes consist of two to four-hour workshops or personal sessions at the faculty member's discretion. Other forms of training are informal meetings or a combination of formal, informal and self-paced (e.g. CD-ROM or web-based) programmes.

Course design

Distance education programme design provides purpose, organisation and structure to the programme using programme courses, programme residencies and support services as the major building blocks. Course design serves a similar purpose at the course level. It uses technology tools, learning objects, readings, discussion topics and assessment tasks as the major building blocks. For blended courses, course design also incorporates a mix of online and face-to-face components.

The challenge in constructivist design of online courses is finding the balance between group and individual work, between asynchronous and synchronous tools, and between different teaching styles. Embracing constructivist views of learning does not suggest that there is no place for direct instruction. However, when instructivist-oriented strategies dominate, their pedagogical value diminishes.

Globalisation and global learning both have course design and pedagogical implications. Crozet, Liddicoat and LoBianco (1999) identify the various ways that teaching culture and language takes place in higher education:

- The traditional approach is through the teaching of literature. According this view, culture is limited to high culture only, with little emphasis on communication skills. Cultural competence is defined as 'control of an established canon of literature' (Crozet, Liddicoat and LoBianco: 1999: 8).

- The cultural studies approach uses the area studies method, which is learning about cultures through the history, geography and institutions of a country. Cultural competence is defined under this paradigm as a body of knowledge about a particular country as well as the ability to communicate with native speakers.

- The culture as practices approach portrays the culture in terms of its practices and values. Cultural competence is the ability to observe and interpret the words and actions of a person from another culture. This paradigm is limited in that the learner remains within his or her own cultural paradigm.

- The intercultural language teaching approach attempts to achieve a change in the learner's cultural or linguistic behaviour by portraying culture as embedded in language use (i.e. linguaculture) and also examines the learner's own linguaculture along with the linguacultures of others. According to Zeszotarski (2001), intercultural language teaching offers a new paradigm to allow learners to function better in foreign cultures and to respond critically to the notion of culture.

Analysing one's own culture is essential to intercultural competence. Additionally, intercultural language teaching allows students to understand how worldviews are shaped by language and culture. Zeszotarski (2001) suggests that it facilitates learners moving from being mere observers of another language and culture to allowing them to experience another culture by creating a 'third place' in which participants of different cultures can interact on equal terms.

Learning is unaffected by a particular medium, and effective learning can be achieved through a variety of paths (media) if the content is appropriate for the chosen media and the methods of providing information are well designed, have a theoretical basis and are well executed. A well-designed online course incorporates a user interface that is appealing and usable by all students. Usability is the measure of the quality of the user experience in interacting with the learning management system (Nielsen, 1997). Usability problems may arise due to variations in behaviours and cultural differences. These variations may be found in colour, graphics, phrases, icons, character sets, pictures, symbols, date and time format and so forth (Onibere, Morgan, Busang and Mpoeleng, 2000). Students from different cultures may understand the same user interface in different ways. Some metaphors, navigation, interaction or course appearance might be misunderstood and confuse, or even offend some users (Marcus and Gould, 2000).

Additionally, students choose what they need from a rich, networked database of information, examples and exercises as they engage online content. Many researchers argue that some learners can become disoriented and may miss information when they are overloaded by multiple-channel messages in nonlinear hypermedia environments (e.g. Ford and Chen, 2000). Disorientation leads to confusion, frustration and wasted time wandering around the online content, reducing the effectiveness of the learning process.

Such disorientation in learning tasks can be particularly relevant to a diverse, multicultural environment where some learners may not be as familiar with hypermedia as other learners. To minimise disorientation, educational hypermedia should enforce navigation restrictions on learners, especially when the order of the hypermedia content is essential. Navigation should also be as consistent as possible between courses. On entering an online programme, students who possess limited experience using information and computer technology should receive an orientation on using this technology so that no member of the learning community is placed at a disadvantage because of their limited knowledge and experience.

Course designers need to attend to the proper alignment of the following elements:

- programme goals;
- course goals;

- instructional objectives;
- learning objects and course materials;
- learner interactions and activities; and
- assessment tasks.

Course designers should be able to create a flowchart to demonstrate how these elements are interconnected.

There are two basic approaches to design an online course, with the more common being a single trained teacher responsible for the entire effort. However, the research literature suggests a project team approach that includes expertise in technology, instructional design, pedagogy and content will likely result in a superior course.

Faculty who design a single-mode online or dual-mode course should approach the course design task in terms of maximising the potential of the medium and e-learning system that is to be used for course delivery. It would be a serious mistake to take a course delivered in a traditional classroom setting and use it, without change, in an online programme. The designer should carefully consider the following course design elements in terms of the competencies that students are to master and their culturally-related learning and communication style preferences:

- presentation of content;
- student–teacher, student–student, student–content and student–technology interactions;
- individual and group activities; and
- assessment of student performance (Rovai, 2004).

The actual process of course design can be viewed from multiple perspectives, although it is often viewed from a classical systems perspective, with input, process, output and feedback components. However, there are numerous variations to this approach.

Arguably, the most popular instructional design model based on the systems approach is the ADDIE model. ADDIE is an acronym that represents five phases of instructional design: analyse, design, develop, implement and evaluate. However, some educators have criticised the ADDIE model as being too linear and inflexible. Reigeluth (1997) asserts that, as a result of the shift into the Information Age, instruction needs to be customised rather than standardised. He also suggests that as an alternative to the linear stages of most models, the entire process cannot be known in advance, so designers are required to analyse, synthesise, evaluate and change at every step in the instructional design process. To fit in with the demands of the Information Age, the designer also needs to become sensitive to the broader social context within which the instruction takes place. The major implication of this approach, according to Reigeluth, is that learners should become user-designers, with much of the design happening at the point of delivery. Consequently, as an alternative to the ADDIE model, there are a number of design models that emphasise a more holistic, iterative approach to the development of courses and provide students with a measure of choice regarding learning resources to access.

The course instructional design model presented in Figure 4.2 represents a synthesis of the classical systems model with the ADDIE model, while also attending to Reigeluth's concerns. It is an open model in the sense that it does not assume all is known or should be known about the environment. Consequently, the model allows for outside variables to affect the design process, as appropriate.

Figure 4.2   Course instructional design model

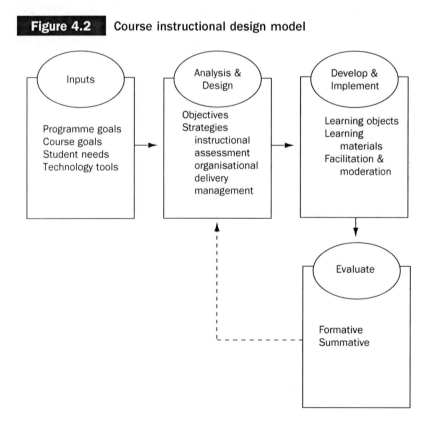

Reeves and Reeves (1997) emphasise that greater challenges may arise when the core pedagogical values in one culture are culturally inappropriate in another. Consequently, the model presented in Figure 4.2 permits a measure of flexibility in the design process as it provides the learner with the opportunity for flexible learning within a student-centred learning environment. Flexible design of an online course is required to address the cultural variables and specific learning needs of globally diverse students. Although online courses should be designed primarily based on the constructivist philosophy of learning, a broad range of teaching and learning theories, philosophies and methods should be used to provide students with increased choice, personalisation and control of their learning to suit their particular needs.

Input phase

The model starts with the input phase, during which the instructional designer collects relevant information regarding the course that is to be created. Much of this information is initially collected and/or developed during the programme design effort that precedes course design, such as identification of programme goals and outcomes. The basic input questions to be answered are:

- What modes will be used to deliver the programme and each course?
- What learning management system (LMS) and technology tools will be used?
- What types of technology and internet connectivity do students have access to, i.e. low bandwidth dial-up or broadband?
- What are the expected entering student competencies, e.g. standardised test scores?
- What are the characteristics of the students, e.g. culture and primary language?
- What is the scope and extent of international student enrolment in the programme and what cultural adaptations need to be included in the design of the course?
- What are the reasons for creating the course?
- What are the other courses in the programme and how does this course relate to the other courses?
- What support does the institution provide to help design and develop courses?

The course designer will consider the answers to these questions as well as the results of the programme design phase.

Normally, the institution offering the course will use an LMS consisting of an integrated set of technology tools as described in Chapter 3. Such a system is typically licensed and maintained by the institution, which makes use of this system mandatory. LMSs are very common, largely because they are template-driven and thus provide a common interface for all courses.

Analysis and design phase

Analysis and design are combined in this model to recognise that these functions are closely linked and iterative. During this phase, all inputs are analysed in order to inform course-level instructional objectives and determine the skills, knowledge and attitudes to be learned, the context in which students will learn, the conditions under which the new learning will take place, and the benchmarks or levels of mastery for successful performance.

Stephen Covey observes:

> To begin with the end in mind means to start with a clear understanding of your destination. It means to know where you're going so that you better understand where you are now so that the steps you take are always in the right direction. (Covey, 2004: 98)

Accordingly, a backward design process is a powerful way to approach the course design process. In other words, when a new programme is being designed, the intended programme impacts and outputs should be determined first. These outcomes are then translated into programme goals. Next, the intermediate steps or processes necessary to accomplish these goals are determined. Lastly, all the necessary ingredients to be used by the system are determined. After carefully analysing the results of the input phase, the course designer follows the following three steps (e.g. see Wiggins and McTighe, 2005):

- *Step 1*: The designer determines the enduring understandings and major student outcomes that are essential to the course. This stage concludes with identification of instructional objectives.

- *Step 2*: The designer determines the major topics to be covered in the course and identifies the learning activities that must be conducted for each topic. This stage concludes with identification of student assessments.

- *Step 3*: The designer identifies the sequence of learning activities required to promote understanding and permit students to do well on course assessments.

Quality instructional objectives require precise, observable and measurable student performance or behaviour. During Step 1, objectives are written in terms of levels of learning in the cognitive, affective and/or psychomotor domains. As described by Anderson and Krathwohl (2001), the cognitive domain consists of intellectual skills and includes the following levels of learning (from highest or most complex level to lowest or most simple level):

1. creation (reorganising knowledge into a new pattern);
2. evaluation (making judgments about information);
3. analysis (separating knowledge into its component parts);
4. application (applying knowledge in a new situation);
5. understanding (comprehending information); and
6. remembering (recalling information).

For example, an instructional objective from the cognitive domain for a research course could be written as follows: 'Given a research journal article [the condition], the student [the audience] will critique the research study and identify all major threats to validity [the behaviour] without error [the degree]'. This objective is written at the evaluation level of learning using the ABCD model (i.e. audience, behaviour, condition, degree).

The affective domain describes feelings and attitudes and includes the following levels of learning, again from highest to lowest levels (Krathwohl, Bloom and Masia, 1964):

1. characterising by value (behaviour is controlled by a value system);
2. organising and conceptualising (being able to form a hierarchy of values);
3. valuing (attaching a value);
4. responding (taking an active part); and
5. receiving (willingness to listen).

Finally, the psychomotor domain describes actions and consists of the following levels of learning rank ordered from most complex to simple (Dave, 1975):

1. naturalisation (automated mastery);

2. articulation (adapt and integrate actions);

3. precision (execute action reliably without help);

4. manipulation (reproduce action from instructions); and

5. imitation (copy action).

During Step 2 of the course design process, the designer takes each instructional objective identified during Step 1, determines the major topics and supporting learning activities, and identifies assessments to assess mastery of instructional objectives. Aligning all three components (i.e. instructional objectives, learning activities and assessments) is a dynamic process, as any change in one affects the other two.

Finally, during Step 3, the designer arranges the instructional activities in a hierarchy. The result is a diagram that depicts the hierarchical arrangement of all instructional activities necessary to achieve the instructional objective. Three major steps are required to produce this diagram (Seels and Glasgow, 1997):

- cluster instructional activities – once all instructional activities are identified, they are grouped based on the closeness of their relationship to each other;

- organise instructional activities – sequence instructional activities to ensure each activity reinforces the previously acquired knowledge or skills and introduces new concepts;

- confer with a subject matter expert to determine the validity of the organisational arrangement.

This hierarchical analysis is used to confirm learning outcomes and to sequence learning. If sequencing is poor, students will not learn as well. A popular sequencing model is based on elaboration theory (Reigeluth, 1987). This model starts the instruction with an overview that contains the simplest and most fundamental ideas, called the *epitome*. Subsequent modules add complexity or detail to one or more aspects of the epitome in layers called elaborations, while periodically reviewing and identifying relationships between the most recent ideas and those presented earlier.

This pattern of elaboration followed by summary and synthesis continues until the desired level of complexity is reached, i.e. mastery of the instructional objective.

Development and implementation phase

The creation and deployment of all learning objects, supporting learning materials and assessment tasks are completed in the development and implementation phase. The teacher will also draw on the analysis of student needs to estimate student learning preferences and to confirm the strategies best suited to meet instructional objectives based on student characteristics and needs as well as the capabilities of available technologies used to deliver instruction. These strategies include:

- instructional strategies (readings, collaborative group work and individual work, scaffolded instruction, case studies, online discussions, etc.);
- assessment strategies (e.g. performances, processes, products, portfolios and projects);
- organisational strategies (sequence of instructional events);
- delivery strategies (technology tools to be used); and
- management strategies (strategies that help the learner interact with the activities designed for learning).

During this process, the teacher draws on learning theory, systems theory, communication theory and instructional theory, as appropriate. Nothing should be left for development after the course commences. The use of learning objects helps organise content into small enough chunks for learners to engage successfully.

A learning object is a unit of instructionally-sound content centred on a learning objective or outcome intended to teach a focused concept (Gallenson, Heins and Heins, 2002). Learning objects include, but are not limited to, online lecture notes, podcasts, simulations, tutorials, glossaries, illustrations, etc. They are meant to be reusable and should be modularised into small units of instruction for assembly and reassembly into a variety of courses (Parrish, 2004). Van Someren (1998) suggests that technology allows integration of multiple representational formats or modalities, e.g. text, animations and diagrams, into a single learning object. Different modalities support different learning preferences and allow learners to select a suitable modality to help them construct understanding. This is especially important in a multicultural learning environment where students are likely to have different learning style preferences. Teachers and learners go about the process of creating linkages between learning objects in order to construct understanding (Polsani, 2003). Mayer (2003) asserts that multiple representations facilitate learning because different modalities are encoded and organised in different mind models, which lead to deeper understanding when mentally connected.

Learning objects are typically conceptualised for delivery over standard personal computers and often there are few attempts by designers to create learning objects for the mobile learning environment. The current practice is for students to transfer learning objects from their computers to mobile devices, such as an iPod, although the learning objects may not have been designed with mobile devices in mind. A learning object designed for a small mobile device display is likely to be effective when viewed on a larger computer display, but may not work in reverse. Consequently, designers of learning objects need to consider the need for students to use such objects with portable devices.

Cognitive load theory governs the design and development of instructional material. The major issue for the course designer is how to make efficient use of the limited capacity of each student's working memory when designing instructional material, both in the way it is presented and the way learners interact with the material (Sweller, 1988). Cognitive load theory posits that extraneous cognitive load should be minimised and germane cognitive load should be optimised. The level of extraneous cognitive load is determined by the format and manner in which the instructional material is presented and by the amount of working memory capacity that is available when students engage in instructional activities (Sha and Kaufman, 2005). Germane cognitive load, on the other hand, is determined by the effort that learners make in processing and comprehending the instructional material and is associated mainly with the process in which the construction and automation of schemas are required (Sha and Kaufman, 2005). Levin and Mayer (1993) suggest that concise material, such as figures that focus on essential elements of material, can significantly reduce cognitive load on working memory and enhance construction of schemas, thus improving understanding.

Additionally, the internet is changing the way individuals read and think. Consequently, Tom Kuhlman (2008) suggests that instructional designers incorporate this change into how they design e-learning materials. Thus they should design courses for learners who 'power-browse' because, as he notes:

> [they] are being conditioned to process online content a certain way. It impacts how they see, retrieve, and process information. If ... we're developing a new way of reading (or retrieving information), then this needs to be a consideration as we design our e-learning courses ... Design courses to accommodate these power browsing habits. If you don't, chances are you'll lose a connection with the learner which will make the course ineffectual. (Kuhlman, 2008: ¶ 6,7, 9)

The design of courses for a global or international university also requires the design to incorporate a global perspective and be sensitive to the ways in which culture influences learning. Culture shapes attitudes and behaviour, structures one's worldview, and is shared by most members of the same cultural group. It includes the values, customs, beliefs and communication patterns that are passed from one generation to the next. These factors serve as a cohesive cultural force, which, in turn, influences learning. Consequently, different cultural characteristics impact instructional design. Culturally-diverse students will likely have different preferences for the presentation and utilisation of learning objects and supporting materials and media elements.

Additionally, effective communication is essential to the reduction of potential problems associated with the clash of cultures in the classroom and to ensure the establishment of an appropriate environment for teaching and learning. Consequently, the course design needs to include a measure of student choice on how best to engage the content and to communicate.

Students from high-context cultures will prefer communication tools that facilitate the transmission of nonverbal cues, e.g. video teleconferencing and podcasting, whereas students from low-context cultures will be more satisfied with text-based communication. Field-dependent learners and learners from collectivist cultures will likely prefer collaborative work, whereas field-independent students and students from individualistic cultures will more likely prefer to work alone. Students from collectivist cultures will also avoid challenging or engaging in debates with other students, while students from individualistic cultures will freely challenge and debate other students. Male students from a masculine culture will be sensitive to losing face to a woman, whether it is another student or the teacher. Students from high uncertainty avoidance nations will require precise instructions and detailed guidance on assignment in addition to precise deadlines and timetables.

Careful consideration should be given to avoid the assignment of students from high power distance cultures to the same collaborative groups if their status is not equal in their heritage nation. However, the preference for individual students is not something designers can predict with certainty. National culture characteristics represent averages that can vary greatly between individuals who are members of a culture.

Instructional designers therefore need to incorporate multiple pedagogies and technology tools, such as providing graphics with accompanying text, videos with optional transcripts and audio to support graphic images. Each student should be permitted to select the best means to construct knowledge based on his or her cultural learning preferences and internet connectivity. Selected members of the cultures to whom the learning materials are intended should also comment on the design as part of the design's validation process.

In addition to developing learning objects and course materials, the course designer must also develop assessment tasks. The test designer must consider answers to the following questions when planning a summative (i.e. graded) assessment:

- What is the purpose of the test?
- What material and instructional objectives will the test cover?
- How much time should the test take to complete?
- How should the test be administered?
- What type of test should be developed, e.g. selected response or constructed response?
- Should alternative forms of the test be created to provide students a choice in how best to demonstrate competency, e.g. written presentation versus oral presentation?

Summative assessments are either selected response, e.g. multiple choice or true-false, or constructed response. Unlike selected response assessments, constructed response assessments are performance-oriented and require that students create an answer or product that demonstrates their knowledge and skills. Constructed response assessment tasks include, but are not limited to providing short answers to open-ended questions, writing an essay, assembling a portfolio, or completing a project either independently or as part of a collaborative group.

In constructivist learning environments where the emphasis is on collaboration, relationships, inquiry and invention in an authentic context, overreliance on selected response assessments that emphasise factual recall is not consistent with the nature of the learning that takes place in these learning environments. Constructivists view selected response assessments as shackling student responses to problems. Their view is that the more open-ended the assessment, the better (Rovai, 2000). Such assessments should reflect performance that is authentic in at least two respects. The tasks should be authentic in so far as feasible with respect to the content area; that is, the performance should demonstrate knowledge and skills that are consistent with the content area (e.g. repairing an automobile is an authentic task for an automobile repair course, whereas writing an essay about repairing an automobile is not). The performances should also be related to the actual demands of the real world, that is, they should not merely represent artificial indices meeting certain psychometric criteria (e.g. repairing an automobile in a garage is an important task that an automobile mechanic is expected to perform in the real world).

Students need to understand clearly what is expected of them in a summative assessment in order for the results to provide a valid indicator of content mastery. The following structure is suggested:

- *Introduction*: an introduction that sets the stage, provides some background information, identifies objectives that will be assessed, provides motivation and describes relevancy.

- *Task*: a short summary of the assessment task that is doable and interesting.

- *Resources*: a minimum set of information resources needed to complete the task, such as the course textbook and links to relevant lecture notes and other pertinent sources of information.

- *Process*: a description of the process the learners should go through in accomplishing the task. The process should be broken out into clearly described steps. The amount of detail should be tailored to the audience. Some students require substantial scaffolding to support their learning. For these students, the process section will be very detailed. However, for other audiences, e.g. advanced students, there may be a minimal amount of scaffolding necessary. It is reasonable to start students in a new content area with more scaffolding and then gradually reduce the scaffolding (referred to as 'fading') as they master the content.

- *Evaluation checklist or rubric*: the evaluation criteria used to grade students' work and perhaps a rubric or grading sheet that clarifies for students the expectations of the assessment and identification of 'look fors'.

- *Conclusion*: a conclusion that brings closure to the assessment task and allows learners to reflect about what they have learned. Students can share their reflections in a discussion forum.

Performance assessments do pose certain challenges. They require abandoning traditional notions about testing and evaluation, and they change teacher and student roles. Performance assessments are time-consuming for teachers to prepare and implement as they require clarity in goals, outcomes and criteria, and are more time-consuming to evaluate.

A portfolio is a form of student assessment that is especially relevant in a multicultural environment as it allows students a measure of choice in how to demonstrate mastery. A portfolio is an assortment of student products representing a variety of performances. It often is a folder or website (i.e. webfolio) containing a representative sampling of the student's performances and the student's assessment of the strengths and weaknesses of these performances. Some learning management systems contain tools for students to develop online portfolios. The requirement to develop a portfolio is often presented to students in the programme's cornerstone course. The student assembles the portfolio during regular coursework and completes and submits it for a summative evaluation during the programme's capstone course. Developing and maintaining a portfolio assists each student in taking charge of his or her own learning. Students learn to value their own work and, by extension, to value themselves as learners.

During the programme, evolving portfolios can be checked by faculty at set times for formative evaluation purposes and to provide feedback to students. A student portfolio often includes the following elements.

- *Introduction*: The introduction offers insight into students' thought processes, perspectives and process guiding portfolio construction. It also provides students with the opportunity to list their personal goals and aspirations, and describe how the programme assists them in achieving their goals. Although appearing first in the final portfolio, the introduction is usually written last.

- *Table of contents*: The table of contents helps the reader navigate through the portfolio. It references the appropriate programme goals, identifies each artefact by name and also the course names (where appropriate) and dates of each artefact.

- *Programme goals*: The student describes each programme goal and supporting instructional objective.

- *Artefact(s) of student work that respond to each goal*: This is the heart of the portfolio. Each student's artefacts are samples of actual work. Artefacts may include essays, reports, videotaped presentations, or models built by the student. The portfolio should include multiple artefacts that demonstrate fulfilment of each goal, and these artefacts should reflect a variety of media or tasks, or perhaps show growth over time.

- *Student reflection on the work and on themselves*: This narrative should not consist of a review or elaboration of the portfolio, but a thoughtful reflective analysis of the process of learning. Students include perceptions of their attitudes, motivations and self-assessments of their learning to include what they think and feel about their work, their learning environment and themselves. Students also reflect on and formulate statements about their personal beliefs and values.

Portfolios are organised and maintained by students based on teacher guidance that is characterised by a clear vision of the programme goals that are addressed and student involvement of what goes into the portfolio.

Faculty teams will evaluate portfolios by focusing on the following issues:

- *Change over time*: Do the artefacts demonstrate growth over time?

- *Diversity*: Does the portfolio include a variety of student products?

- *Programme goals*: To what degree does the portfolio provide evidence of student mastery of programme goals? Does the work provide evidence that the student has identified, analysed and solved problems associated with the goals?

- *Organisation, format and structure*: Has the student arranged the portfolio in a clear and inviting way? Are all the necessary elements included?

- *Self-reflection*: Are statements of self-reflection included that show thoughtful consideration of personal strengths and needs?

Rather than assessment 'of' learning, the focus of assessment in the multicultural classroom should be on assessment 'for' learning, in which both instructors and students seek to assess where students are in their learning so teaching and learning activities can be shaped by information gained from assessments. An online classroom assessment strategy characterised by the following principles will promote education equity in a multicultural learning environment:

- assessments should be based on clearly articulated instructional objectives;

- student progress should be monitored frequently;

- students should receive timely feedback;

- whenever possible, students should help determine how educational objectives will be assessed;

- a variety of assessment tasks are necessary to provide teachers with a well-rounded view of what students know and can do;

- to use assessments fairly, teachers must become knowledgeable about both the subject matter being assessed and about students' cultures and languages;

- teachers must pay particular attention to unequal participation of students in group work and employ strategies to address status problems;

- assessments should

  - resemble real life as closely as possible (i.e. be authentic);

  - recognise the vital importance of both the cultural characteristics and educational experiences of students;

  - be mostly performance-based, e.g. portfolio assessments;

  - consist of cooperative group work whenever possible;

  - focus on student growth, such as action-oriented projects, self-assessments and reflections on the course; and

  - include an evaluation checklist or grading rubric so that grading criteria are transparent, helping students to know what is expected and to promote fair grading by the teacher (Carter and Rovai, 2007: 157–8).

It is important that the teacher has a clear rationale for assessing students via certain products and performances and for the ways he or she interprets students' performances. The teacher must be vigilant at every step of the way for potential bias, looking at the student's behaviour and background as well as test performance to justify interpretations of scores and how they are used.

In addition, teachers must be extremely cautious in interpreting inadequate performances of students who are still developing proficiency in English (assuming English is the language used for instruction) or whose cultures do not match that of the school. A low performance cannot be assumed to mean that the student has not learned or is incapable of learning what is being assessed. A key element to meeting the assessment needs of a diverse student population is a flexible approach. It should be possible to design assessments that allow for a choice of tasks to demonstrate competency, while maintaining quality standards. The student should be able to select a task that reflects a context meaningful to the student.

Distance learning programmes assess learner progress by reference to expected learning outcomes. Summative assessments become even more important in online environments without the face-to-face interactions and observations that best enable teachers to assess student progress toward achieving instructional objectives. Courses offered at a distance often demand that instructors alter the manner in which they assess student performance. Student assessments in such environments become particularly challenging in courses where direct observation of the student by the teacher is the best approach. In each case, online instructors must devote additional preparation time to resolving issues related to assessment. Options include postponement of immediate assessment in favour of:

- a delayed telephone conversation, online chat, or e-mail;
- proctored testing at decentralised locations such as remote learning centres; and
- proctored testing at centralised on-campus residencies.

Proctored testing is particularly relevant when testing is for high-stakes, summative purposes. Proctored testing also enhances identity security and academic honesty, two related issues that frequently arise when discussing distance education. Instructors need to know that the individuals receiving course credit are, indeed, the individuals who do the work and that the work they do is their own. Depending on the risks associated with identity security and academic honesty in a specific course, some solutions in addition to proctored testing include:

- internet-based testing software that can be password protected;
- internet-based testing software that uses a different test form each time a different student logs in; and
- internet-based testing software that limits time on a test.

Evaluation phase

The evaluation phase focuses on evaluating the course and programme. Consequently, the focus of assessment of student work in this phase is to improve the course and programme, whereas the primary focus of student assessment in the previous phase is for summative purposes.

According to the principles of Total Quality Management, quality in manufacturing is the result of regular inspections or assessments along the production line, followed by needed adjustments. Quality is not achieved by end-of-line inspections alone – by then it is too late to make a difference. Similarly, assessments in education are used throughout the learning process, followed by needed adjustments, in order to achieve quality in education. Consequently, this formal evaluation phase runs concurrently with the development and implementation phase and is used to make adjustments to the course design throughout the duration of the course.

The instructional effectiveness of any course or programme design is judged based on students' satisfaction and success. The term 'formative evaluation' is used to help monitor the progress of learning and the acquisition of learning outcomes during instruction in order to provide periodic feedback to both students and teachers on learning successes and failures. Consequently, one purpose of formative assessments is to allow the teacher to evaluate course effectiveness. A 'summative evaluation', on the other hand, is used to assess student performance and the extent to which instructional objectives have been achieved. Performance indicators, outcome measurement and benchmarking are the major instruments of summative evaluation. As a result of both types of student assessments, the course is modified, as needed, to make it more effective.

Both summative and formative assessment data are collected throughout the duration of the course. Sources of assessment data include ungraded classroom assessments (i.e. formative assessments), graded assessments of student individual and group work (i.e. summative assessments), anonymous student evaluations of teaching, and peer evaluations of the course.

Angelo and Cross (1993) provide a useful list of discussion topics for teachers to include in their courses that can be used for formative classroom assessments. These topics include:

- *one-sentence summaries*: students select and articulate only the defining features of an idea;

- *most important point*: students describe the most important point of a reading assignment and why it is important to them;

- *muddiest point*: students identify the least understood point in a reading assignment;
- *test questions and model answers*: students write plausible test questions and model answers for specified topics;
- *self-confidence surveys*: students assess their self-confidence regarding specific skills; and
- *benefits analysis*: students describe how the skills learned relate to their goals and interests in life.

Using formative assessments can have the following beneficial effects (Angelo and Cross, 1993):

- more active involvement and participation;
- greater interest in learning;
- self-awareness as learners and greater metacognitive skills;
- higher levels of cooperation within the learning community; and
- greater satisfaction.

Conclusion

Although the same model is used to guide the design of face-to-face and distance education programmes and courses, there are differences regarding this process. For online courses, the teacher must plan all the components of the course prior to the course start date. There is also a greater need for the teacher to understand the impact that the technology has on the processes of learning and instruction, particularly in a multicultural virtual classroom.

A technology-led course design is common in distance education. Indeed, there is often a preoccupation with technology by some online course designers and a concurrent neglect of pedagogical theory. Instead of technology-led course design, teaching and learning is better served by a pedagogy-led course design philosophy. Ramsden (1992: 161) makes the point, 'No medium, however useful, can solve fundamental educational problems'. He also observes that although technology in itself is unlikely to solve fundamental educational problems, it might still allow us to see them in a new light.

Oscar Wilde, Irish playwright, novelist and poet, reportedly said, 'Consistency is the refuge of the unimaginative'. Applying this thought to distance education programme and course development leads one to question any design that does not permit flexibility, especially when considering the diverse learning needs and preferences of a globally-diverse student body. Bryant Griffith describes this situation thus:

> The point is we have constructed a theory of knowledge, an epistemology, about teaching and learning, which rejected randomness and deviations from the norm ... I believe that we need to focus more on the general in our teaching and learning and less on the precise. We also need to be open, attentive, and anticipatory to that which may surprise us, to that which we will not expect. (Griffith, 2008: 17)

Based on his review of the literature, Subramony (2004) points to a severe lack of attention regarding important issues of cultural diversity among online instructional designers as a whole. This situation must change if the global university is to design quality online courses for a culturally diverse student body. Designing courses for the international market requires awareness of the national culture, values and communication patterns of each nation represented. Some of the cross-cultural issues that have been reported in the distance education professional literature include:

- teaching style and learning style mismatches;
- problems relating to different educational values and cultures;
- problems of language and semantics, including linguistic sensitivities; and
- technical problems relating to platforms, operating systems and lack of standard interfaces. (Collis, Parisi and Ligorio, 1996)

The cultural values of individualism, secularism and feminism, which one finds in many Western nations, are not all recognised as desirable in other cultures, which may place higher values on religion, group efforts and well-defined gender roles (McIsaac, 1993). Consequently, Western distance education programme and course designers need to carefully consider the implicit cultural values inherent in the programmes and courses they design. They should carefully consider the national cultures of the international students who are likely to enrol in the programme and determine whether the instructional design contains cultural and social bias. The danger is that international students will be treated as inferior by the institution and host nation students. Because the appropriate design of online courses is an essential element in its effectiveness, the issue of 'who designs what and for whom' is central to any discussion of the economic, political and cultural dangers that face course designers using information and communication technologies to reach out to a global audience (McIsaac, 1993).

5

Global online teaching and learning

Introduction

Some students learn better when teaching emphasises concrete, social and holistic approaches. Conversely, such students often find it difficult to learn through abstract and analytical learning approaches – approaches that other students may well prefer. Other students learn better during activities involving a visual rather than a verbal approach. Some students, particularly from Asian cultures, are more accustomed to assuming a compliant role and prefer not to distinguish themselves from other students, whereas others may be more accustomed to exercising individual initiative and engaging in competition. Some students prefer independent work while others prefer collaborative group work. The challenge for the online teacher is to provide a student-centred learning environment that addresses the academic needs of all students. An equitable environment promotes high levels of learning for all students.

The philosophy that permeates online teaching and learning is constructivism. It is based on the premise that each individual constructs knowledge through his or her engagement with the environment, including learning resources and other learners. Thus, from a constructivist viewpoint, much of the knowledge one acquires is socially constructed, the learner is an active processor of information, and the teacher's major role is that of facilitator of learning. Depending on the circumstances, the online teacher also assumes the roles of content expert, collaborator, mediator, tutor, coach, encourager and community builder.

Online teachers should use constructivist principles to respond to the following issues (Huang, 2002) present in online learning environments:

- *humanity and the learner's isolation*: the use of online technologies often results in the loss of some aspects of humanity and can result in feelings of alienation and isolation;

- *quality and authenticity of learning*: interactions with fellow learners using computer-mediated communication can result in incomplete or erroneous understandings;
- *preauthentication*: the difficulties are in making learning materials and environments correspond to the real world prior to the learner's interaction with them;
- *evaluation of learner outcomes*: evaluation is time-consuming and relatively difficult in an online environment;
- *focus of teaching and learning*: teaching must focus on the individual learner – a one-size-fits-all approach is usually not effective;
- *collaborative learning is often in conflict with individual differences*: social constructivism contends that knowledge is constructed by social interaction and collaborative learning.

Manning and Baruth (1996) maintain that teachers in a multicultural learning environment require three types of competencies:

- knowledge and understanding of various cultures;
- skills in recognising learners' strengths and weaknesses and responding appropriately to their learning style preferences and cultural values and beliefs; and
- positive attitudes toward cultural diversity and creating a learning environment that provides respect and concern for people of all cultural, racial and religious backgrounds.

The basic premise for teaching and learning from a multicultural perspective is that this knowledge contributes to the development of cultural and global competence. Cultural competence includes the skill of interacting positively with all people – embracing their race, gender, class, religion, age, culture or abilities. Shealey and Callins (2007: 195) assert that 'culturally responsive teaching refers to the extent to which educators use students' cultural contributions in transforming their lives and the lives of their families and communities by making education relevant and meaningful'. Moreover, they observe that the demonstration of cultural sensitivity requires teachers to:

> learn about the cultures represented in their classrooms and translate this knowledge into instructional practice... [Culturally mediated instruction is] characterized by the use of culturally mediated cognition, culturally appropriate social situations for

learning, and culturally valued knowledge in curriculum content. (Shealey and Callins, 2007: 196)

Gordon Allport's contact theory of intergroup relations provides a basis for establishing a positive multicultural classroom climate. Allport (1954) theorises that when a member of one cultural group initially meets with member of a different cultural group and the experience is positive, an attitude change occurs on two levels. First, there is a target-specific attitude change. In other words, initial assumptions about the other person that arise from the (negative) stereotypes associated with his or her group are replaced by more positive attitudes regarding the individual. Second, these new positive perceptions will become extended to that individual's group as a whole, thus reducing negative attitudes toward the group. Allport (1954) identifies four key conditions for such a meeting: equal-group status within the situation, common goals, inter-group cooperation and institutional support. Additional conditions can be added to this, the most important of which are voluntary interaction and intimate (i.e. socio-emotional) contact. Moreover, research shows that, when effectively implemented, these conditions do lead to a positive attitude change that is target-specific (e.g. Hewstone and Brown, 1986), although evidence is weaker regarding an attitude change toward the individual's group. In particular, Hewstone and Brown (1986) argue that inter-personal contact is likely to have little impact at the inter-group level unless individual participants are seen as representatives of their group.

A major concern is how higher education develops the capacity to provide students with a global perspective, as well as the skills and frameworks for understanding different ways of thinking. Consequently, global learning is much more than extending the reach of schools across borders to embrace globally diverse students. It also includes pedagogical changes that promote respect for cultural and linguistic diversity and that integrate global content in academic programmes. Strategies that promote global learning include increasing faculty knowledge of various features of the world and how they work, educating students to compete and succeed in the new global economy, developing awareness of multicultural issues, and responding to cultural diversity.

Diverse learning communities require 'reciprocal mentoring' that nurtures students while increasing the cultural sensitivity of faculty to the needs of minority students. Under reciprocal mentoring, faculty members and students each assume the role of protégé and mentor at different times. The emphasis is on knowledge construction and collaborative group work. Content is reconceptualised through a shift in paradigm, as people no longer view content exclusively through the perspective of the dominant culture (Kitano, 1997).

However, taking on the role of learner during reciprocal mentoring in a multicultural group that includes Eastern culture students can create problems for the teacher. In Western cultures it is acceptable for students to question a teacher or for a teacher to respond to a question with 'I don't know'. However, in many Eastern cultures, the teacher loses respect by such a response. Indeed, in many Eastern cultures students are often reluctant to ask questions out of fear of insulting the teacher.

The teacher must guard against introducing cultural biases that may not be acceptable or viewed as positive by some cultures. In many settings in the Middle East, for example, students may view teachers who use a collaborative approach to teaching as being weak in their knowledge base (e.g. House, Hanges, Javidan, Dorfman and Gupta, 2004). While these culturally-based viewpoints may not alter the university's approach to an inclusive teaching model, they are aspects of a global awareness and perspective that instructors need in order to be effective in a global setting (where many more students may arrive with their cultural baggage) and to be effective in developing global competency. Learning to communicate is essential in a multicultural learning environment, for both teachers and students. Both groups need to develop intercultural skills, including learning to communicate across cultures and communicating for learning across cultures.

Effective online teaching

The seven principles for good practice in undergraduate education identified by Arthur Chickering and Zelda Gamson (1991) provide an excellent overview of effective teaching practices that can be applied to online courses. According to these principles, an effective teacher:

- encourages contact between students and faculty,
- develops reciprocity and cooperation among students,
- encourages active learning,
- gives prompt feedback,
- emphasises time on task,
- communicates high expectations, and
- respects diverse talents and ways of learning.

The first four principles have obvious linkages to constructivism, while the seventh principle is especially relevant to the multicultural classroom. Effective teaching affirms the presence of diverse ways of learning. The teacher should not attempt to match learning and teaching styles for each student. Instead, the teacher should broaden his or her repertoire of teaching methods and include instructional activities that touch all students in a special way while expanding the learning experiences for each student. In other words, the online teacher affirms the presence of diverse ways of learning by using diverse methods of teaching and by providing learners a measure of choice in engaging content and demonstrating their mastery of course competencies.

Ken Bain's (2004) description of what the best college teachers do is also very relevant to the online learning environment:

- *Teacher knowledge and understanding*: 'Without exception, outstanding teachers know their subjects extremely well. They are all active and accomplished scholars, artists, or scientists' (Bain, 2004: 15).

- *Preparation to teach*: 'Exceptional teachers treat their lectures, discussion sections, problem-based sessions and other elements of teaching as serious intellectual endeavors as intellectually demanding and as important as their research and scholarship' (Bain, 2004: 17).

- *Student expectations*: 'Simply put, the best teachers expect "more" … they avoid objectives that are arbitrarily tied to the course and favor those that embody the kind of thinking and acting expected for life' (Bain, 2004: 17–18).

- *Treatment of students*: 'Highly effective teachers tend to reflect a strong trust in students. They usually believe that students want to learn and they assume, until proven otherwise, that they can' (Bain, 2004: 18).

- *Continuous improvement*: 'All the teachers we studied have some systematic programme … to assess their own efforts and make appropriate changes. Furthermore, because they are checking their own efforts when they evaluate their students, they avoid judging them on arbitrary standards' (Bain, 2004: 19).

Finally, Kearsley and Blomeyer (2004) suggest that effective online teachers:

- provide timely and meaningful feedback;
- create learning activities that engage all students;
- keep students interested and motivated;

- ensure students interact with each other; and
- encourage students to be critical and reflective.

Providing feedback and guidance that will direct the learner towards mastery of course goals is especially important in the online classroom. Effective feedback provides the learner with two types of information: verification and elaboration (Kulhavy and Stock, 1989). Verification represents the judgment of whether a response is correct or incorrect, complete or incomplete. Elaboration provides relevant cues to guide the learner toward a correct or complete response. In the absence of timely feedback, there is a degree of uncertainty in online communication regarding how others perceive one's communication which does not typically exist in a face-to-face setting. This uncertainty can result in anxiety if left unattended.

The above descriptions of effective teachers suggest that the basic principles of effective teaching remain the same regardless of modality: face-to-face or online, live or asynchronous. Differences arise in how these principles are applied in different learning environments. Both online teachers and learners have access to more open and diverse forms of content than is typically available in the physical classroom and how they are best used can be a challenge. Additionally, students need to be guided toward greater levels of self-regulation and self-determination in the virtual classroom. The major differences for teachers are related to their interaction with learners in a computer-mediated communication environment, and how they manage and implement technology and nurture a sense of community that facilitates the social construction of knowledge.

Just as good teaching comes in many forms, so the ability to build community also comes in many forms, but most of all it comes from the heart and often takes the form of edifying conversation and honest encouragement. The question posed by Parker Palmer, addressing the spiritual dimension of teaching, provides online teachers with an opportunity for reflection:

> Does my pedagogy come from a place of connectedness in me so it can evoke in my students those connections that make learning possible? Or am I using my pedagogy in a way that distances me from my subject and sets me apart from my students, thus diminishing the chances that my classroom will become a place of live encounter? (Palmer, 1998: 187)

Mobile learning

Mobile learning is distance learning that is enhanced with mobile tools and mobile communication. Although the emphasis of this chapter is on online learning using personal computers, the principles addressed in this chapter also apply to mobile learning using portable devices and mobile web tools. Mobile learning devices offer a unique opportunity for teachers and students to capitalise on the flexibility and freedom afforded by these devices. Many individuals worldwide carry mobile phones, which are almost always switched on. Consequently, students with mobile phones are highly accessible. However, use of these devices requires modified pedagogies and approaches to delivering and facilitating instruction.

Naismith, Lonsdale, Vavoula and Sharples (2004) offer the following suggestions for adapting mobile learning to various types of learning:

- *behaviourism*: rapid feedback or reinforcement can be achieved using mobile devices;
- *constructivism*: mobile devices enable immersive experiences such as those provided by participatory simulations;
- *situated learning*: learners can take mobile devices into authentic learning environments, such as museums, and receive additional information about the exhibits as they move from exhibit to exhibit;
- *collaborative learning*: mobile devices provide portable means of communication for students to gather and share information as they work in collaborative groups.

The increasing range of Web 2.0 mobile technology tools facilitates the development of user-created content and provides greater opportunities for learners to collaborate. The ease of contacting students with mobile phones makes it a great tool for problem solving and exchanging information. Students can call or exchange short text messages and images with each other as well as opinions or advice. Indeed, some modern mobile phones now have the ability to record and transmit short video clips. Portable devices with cameras can also be used as tools for scientific data collection and documentation.

The easy access also makes portable devices a great tool for students to spend time learning while waiting or travelling. For example, students can listen to course-related podcasts, watch videos, or study online lecture notes. The teacher can also use short text messaging to provide students with learning reminders and encouragement, to poll students and to conduct quizzes. Internet browsers are also available in a growing number of portable devices, especially those with the third-generation (3G) wireless protocol. Moreover, websites designed for access by portable devices are growing in number.

Community of inquiry

Garrison, Cleveland-Innes and Fung (2004: 63) describe a 'Community of Inquiry' model that posits that learning is facilitated through the interaction of three important presences: social, cognitive and teacher. Social presence refers to the co-presence of students and teacher to create a climate that supports productive computer-mediated communication to accomplish shared learning objectives. It also refers to the ability of participants in an online course to project their personal characteristics into the online learning community and to reduce the social distance between members of the community. 'Social presence in cyberspace takes on more of a complexion of reciprocal awareness by others of an individual and the individual's awareness of others ... to create a mutual sense of interaction that is essential to the feeling that others are there' (Cutler, 1995: 18).

Cognitive presence is defined as the 'extent to which learners are able to construct and confirm meaning through sustained reflection and discourse in a critical community of inquiry' (Garrison, Anderson and Archer, 2001: 11). It refers to an individual student's constructivist learning via computer-mediated communication and, hence, level of engagement within the course. Garrison, Anderson and Archer (2001) divide the cognitive presence component into a four stage cognitive-processing model. This model classifies student responses into categories of triggering, exploration, integration and resolution.

Finally, Garrison, Cleveland-Innes and Fung (2004) hypothesise that teacher presence refers to the teacher's role in implementing an instructional design that promotes cognitive and social processes that catalyse individual cognitive activity and achievement. Teacher presence manifests itself in each of the roles that an online teacher assumes: instructional designer and activity organiser, discussion facilitator and subject matter expert.

Figure 5.1 depicts the hypothesised relationships between the processes of social, cognitive and teacher presence and the online course outcomes of learning and persistence. Increased presence results in stronger feelings of community, which, in turn, results in greater learning and persistence. Cognitive presence directly promotes sense of

Figure 5.1   Online learning and persistence model

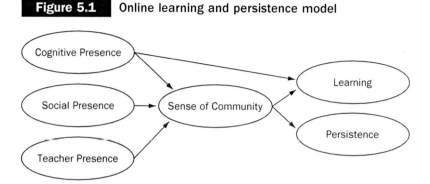

community and learning, whereas social presence and teaching presence influence learning and persistence by increasing sense of community.

What is not fully supported by research evidence is how sense of community is related to learning in online classroom environments, although empirical research evidence exists to support a relationship between these variables in traditional face-to-face classroom environments (Royal and Rossi, 1996). However, Rena Palloff and Keith Pratt (1999) warn that it is possible to develop a strong sense of community in an online classroom where very little learning occurs. They, therefore, suggest that it is important for online professors to be actively engaged in the learning process and to guide participants who stray from the learning goals, thus ensuring that a strong learning community emerges, not just a strong social community.

There are several issues that can hinder the natural progression of an inquiry. The teacher must be mindful of the issues associated with different culture-related communication patterns and cognitive preferences among members of the learning community. Because communication has both verbal and nonverbal components, some cultural groups show their feelings more readily than other groups, while some individuals rely more heavily on nonverbal messages to communicate. In the online environment, however, these nonverbal messages are reduced and subject to misinterpretation. Such cultural differences can have unintended negative consequences in cross-cultural interactions, leaving some students feeling isolated. Consequently, members of the learning community must learn to care for and value dialogue in order for it to achieve its full potential. According to Nel Noddings (2003), caring is the element that helps each participant to accept different points of view, a particularly important aspect of effective cross-cultural communication.

Students in an effective online community of inquiry must do more than watch, listen and read. They must actively engage themselves in the learning process. The focus is on student involvement in higher-order cognitive processing (i.e. analysing, judging and creating). Online students do not merely receive information; they also reflect on the information presented, think critically, participate in online discussions and do things, such as writing, role-playing and participating in collaborative group projects. Web technologies are especially suited to promote such active learning as they permit the creation of a rich nonlinear, multisensory environment that facilitates multiple forms of student–student, student–teacher and student–content engagement. In such an environment, students assume personal ownership of their learning because they are in control.

Contextual learning

An active, inquiry-based learning environment creates the means for deep learning to take place. To promote such learning, students also need to feel that learning focuses on issues that are meaningful to them as individuals. They need to reflect on what they are learning and why they are learning it. Motivation to learn comes from a sense of personal need:

> According to contextual learning theory, learning occurs only when students (learners) process new information or knowledge in such a way that it makes sense to them in their frame of reference (their own inner world of memory, experience, and response). This approach to learning and teaching assumes that the mind naturally seeks meaning in context – that is, in the environment where the person is located – and that it does so through searching for relationships that make sense and appear useful. (Hull, 1993: 41)

Contextual teaching and learning is an educational process that aims to help students see meaning in the academic material they are studying (Johnson, 2001). It requires the kinds of understanding, perspectives and skills that come from engagement with diverse communities and contexts. It also helps students understand the reciprocal ways that self and culture, social forces and institutions shape and give meaning to knowledge. Through such learning, students can:

- discover the lens through which they view the world and themselves,
- understand and appreciate diverse perspectives and how they differ from their own, and
- develop competencies for working in multicultural organisations and living in multicultural communities (Johnson, 2001).

Some educators argue that 'culture itself cannot be objectified as just another factor to be programmed into designing a distance learning course' (Chen and Mashhadi, 1998: 10). As a consequence, Rogers, Graham and Mayes (2007) suggest that online teachers must be culturally aware of the diverse backgrounds (e.g. norms, values, practices) of their students and make adjustments as situations dictate. They conclude that teachers need to situate themselves in the other culture and offer instructional activities that are meaningful to the learner. Additionally, the teacher must make the connection between theory and praxis by drawing on the diverse cultures represented within the community of learners. Assigning competence to all students means that the teacher publicly recognises the importance of the cultural perspectives each student brings to the classroom. Consequently, the teacher must make the case to students that everyone needs each other for successful cognitive engagement within a global learning environment.

Rod Sims and Elizabeth Stork (2007) suggest that classifying and predicting the particular characteristics learners bring to a course is presumptive, especially in a globally diverse learning environment. Instead, they suggest that such courses should focus on strategies and performance indicators while allowing learners, with their individual sets of characteristics, to manage their learning processes and engage with both teachers and other learners. As the student, rather than the teacher, takes up the creation of relevance, they suggest a more contextual and personal learning experience can be generated.

Additional research evidence is needed to determine the best way to implement a culturally diverse online course. Without such research, the teacher and the students should attend to the creation of relevance. The underlying premise is that all learners learn best in an environment reflecting three foundational principles: interdependence, differentiation and self-organisation (Johnson, 2001). These principles are reflected in the following components:

- active, self-regulated learning;
- making connections;

- significant work;
- critical and creative thinking;
- collaborating;
- nurturing the individual;
- recognising and reaching high standards; and
- using authentic assessment.

These principles and components suggest the online teacher, in recognising the cultural diversity present in the virtual classroom, should meet students at their frames of reference in so far as possible and teach using diverse methods and multiple contexts.

Teachers must strive to encourage all their students to be tolerant and respectful of differences. Stereotypical knowledge and beliefs about cultural groups limit the perspective students have available. Moreover, teachers must understand their own cultural self-awareness in order to recognise the cultural underpinnings of their teaching. Being culturally self-aware and providing an emphasis on the cultural predispositions of members of other cultures should create an attitude of cultural relativity and counteract attitudes of cultural superiority that might exist among any members of the learning community. As John Creswell writes:

> knowledge is within the meanings people make of it; knowledge is gained through people talking about their meanings; knowledge is laced with personal biases and values; knowledge is written in a personal, up-close way; and knowledge evolves, emerges, and is inextricably tied to the context in which it is studied. (Creswell, 1998: 19)

Teaching and learning strategies

Students filter instruction through their individual lenses, tend to manipulate perceived information in different ways, achieve understanding at different rates in various learning contexts (e.g. see Felder, 1993). It is not sufficient merely to provide information to students and to test them on their recall. Online teachers must foster in their students the ability to obtain and evaluate information, to think critically and creatively, to solve problems and to work skilfully both independently and collaboratively. They can best accomplish this goal if the teacher provides a mix of teaching and learning strategies. These strategies, rank-ordered in terms of amount of interactivity from least to most, fall into the general categories of independent study, direct instruction, experiential learning and interactive learning. The selection of specific teaching strategies by the teacher depends on such factors as the nature of the instructional objectives, the students' characteristics and the time available.

Independent study, the least interactive of the categories identified above, is planned independent activity under the general guidance or supervision of the teacher. It works best for students who possess the requisite maturity and the ability to work on a task with a minimum of supervision. Most independent studies are in-depth, personally shaped projects. Thus, independent studies provide students with a large measure of freedom to choose a type of study that best matches their independent learning style. Giving students options also provides them with a voice in how they satisfy their learning goals.

Independent learning requires that students take responsibility for their own learning. Such responsibility originates from the belief that learning can be achieved by personal effort. This belief is the critical factor that leads the student to persevere in the face of obstacles. Teachers can help students take responsibility for their learning by providing opportunities and strategies for learning independently and by encouraging them to initiate and actively participate in their own learning. Independent study reduces students' dependence on teachers for their learning and increases their ability to set and meet their own learning goals. Consequently, independent study helps promote lifelong learning skills.

Direct instruction is the next category. It is a set of highly structured teaching strategies that emphasise teacher direction and student–teacher interaction. It is most often used to provide new material and, in an online learning environment, often takes the form of advance organisers; online lectures in which the teacher explains, elaborates or summarises; demonstrations; and reading/study assignments. Direct instruction has an important role in a constructivist learning environment as it promotes teacher presence and incorporates interpersonal interactivity between students and the teacher.

Advance organisers contain information that is presented prior to learning, which students use to organise and interpret new incoming information. Research evidence (e.g. Mayer, 2003) suggests that advance organisers work best when students have little prior knowledge of the topic that is addressed. Online lectures can take many forms including webpages formatted with text and graphics, audio or video podcasts and other learning objects discussed in the previous chapter.

Experiential learning in an educational setting represents the type of learning undertaken by students who are given a chance to learn in an authentic setting. Consequently, experiential learning involves an encounter with the phenomenon being studied rather than reading or being told about the phenomenon. In the virtual classroom, experiential learning can occur using simulations and role-playing, in which students explore issues involved in complex social situations. By taking on a perspective other than their own, students can learn to appreciate the beliefs, attitudes and motivations of others. Role-playing activities using excursions into a virtual world or multiple user dimensions can provide students with authentic learning. Such role-playing can be particularly useful in a multicultural learning environment when students take on the roles of individuals from other cultures as they solve realistic problems.

Interactive learning is the final set of teaching and learning strategies described in this section and represents the strategy best aligned with social constructivism. It requires students to actively engage in discussions with each other, teachers and subject-matter experts, as appropriate, in order to construct knowledge. Web 2.0 technologies, such as blogs and wikis, as well as the more traditional discussion boards, are ideally suited to support these strategies. The use of these technology tools exposes students to divergent ideas in a collaborative learning environment and permits them to construct new knowledge.

Various interactive learning strategies are discussed below, starting with collaborative learning. These strategies are not comprehensive and there is a measure of overlap between them. Additionally, some forms of experiential learning, such as role-playing, can also be classified as interactive learning.

Collaborative learning

An effective online course promotes ongoing student interaction and collaboration in accordance with the principles of constructivism. The collaborative learning strategy begins with the observation that the traditional teacher-centred classroom can impede learning because teacher interference can reduce student–student interaction (Bruffee, 1995). Technology enables egalitarian participation in collaborative group work, but effective online collaboration is dependent on the participating individuals and structured tasks assigned by the teacher. A teacher who uses a collaborative learning strategy reduces or eliminates his or her involvement in collaborative group activities, thereby promoting free discussion and group member negotiation of understanding. Such a model:

> helps students become autonomous, articulate, and socially and intellectually mature ... and it helps them to learn the substance at issue not as conclusive 'facts' but as the constructed results of a disciplined social process of inquiry. (Bruffee, 1995: 17)

Numerous online activities fall under the umbrella of collaborative learning, including joint document creation, debates and group problem-oriented discussion topics. One popular collaborative activity is the creation and use of weekly discussion forums where, in each forum, the teacher posts the initial message, representing a problem or dilemma that the participating students must solve.

Regardless of the nature of the activity, collaborative group work involves the following three stages (Harasim, 1990):

- *idea generating*: indicators include verbalisation, brainstorming, information generating and democratic participation;
- *idea linking*: indicators include an increased number of replies, references to other messages, and a qualitative change in the nature of the discourse;
- *intellectual convergence*: indicators include an increased number of substantive contributions and more conclusive statements supported by the group.

When a group is tasked to prepare a single deliverable for a teacher's evaluation (i.e. a product), an equitable contribution by all group members may be impossible to assess unless additional information is available to the teacher. Disparate contributions suggest disparate student engagement, uneven individual learning and undeserved credit or blame for someone else's effort or lack of effort. Thus, teachers must use multiple methods to assess individual efforts; online discussion board participation and peer evaluation provide two good methods. Peer evaluation works best if the group agrees the focus of the evaluation beforehand.

Case-based learning

A teaching case is a story, usually based on real events and circumstances, which is told with a teaching purpose in mind. Ertmer and Russell (1995: 24) define case-based learning as 'a teaching method [that] requires students to actively participate in real or hypothetical problem situations, reflecting the kind of experiences naturally encountered in the discipline under study'.

Cases are best used to expose students to authentic decision-making situations. By using information and situations that experts in the field are likely to encounter, cases are used to teach students how to think like an expert. Consequently, they contextualise learning. Situated cognition theory encourages teachers to immerse learners in an environment that approximates as closely as possible the context in which their new ideas and behaviours will be applied (Schell and Black, 1997). Contextualised learning uses authentic materials and experiences to create opportunities for students to apply learning to their lives by drawing from their prior knowledge and experience as a starting place for instruction. Such learning can maximise student engagement, particularly in a multicultural setting with diverse student experiences.

Another popular form of case-based learning is the case study. According to Orngreen (2005), North American cases studies tend to take the student up to the point where an important decision is to be made and the student develops a recommendation. Frequently, the students are then given a description of the actual decision made, along with a description of the results. The European tradition of a case study, however, typically includes a description of the events leading to a decision in an organisation, the decision, and the first results of that decision. Consequently, this type of case study is more interpretative in nature and students focus on conducting a critique of the decision-making process.

Cases help train students preparing to enter a profession on how to respond to actual problems they will encounter in their field. They provide students with authentic situations to analyse, make judgments and create solutions. When students participate in analysis and discussion of alternative solutions they better understand difficult or complicated issues and analyse them more effectively (Lombardi, 2007).

Wasserman (1994) suggests that teachers should use the following guidelines to develop cases:

- draw the reader into the story during the opening;
- build the case around an important event;
- elevate the tension between conflicting points of view;
- write the story so that readers grow to care;

- be sure the case is believable; and
- end the case on the 'horns of the dilemma'.

Flynn and Klein (2001) report that the use of discussion groups in case-based learning activities can be an effective and motivating method of teaching if students are prepared and time is available for both individual preparation and group discussion.

Problem-based learning

Problem-based learning is a learning strategy closely aligned with constructivist principles that starts with a problem or puzzle that a group of learners must solve. It is closely related to case-based learning as cases can be framed in terms of a problem-based learning strategy. The teacher gives authentic, challenging, open-ended problems to small collaborative groups to solve with limited scaffolding (Rovai, Ponton and Baker, 2008). Students are provided the training to identify what they need to learn to solve the problem.

This strategy requires learners to acquire important knowledge during the process of solving the problem and demonstrate problem-solving proficiency, self-directed learning strategies and teamwork skills. Students assume responsibility for their learning, giving them more motivation and self-satisfaction, establishing the foundation for them to become successful lifelong learners. The teacher, in turn, becomes a resource, tutor, facilitator and evaluator. Problem-based learning approaches that combine small-group tutorials with case-based learning are now used worldwide (Salvatori, 2001).

Regardless of how it is implemented, all problem-based learning strategies adhere to the following principles (Savery and Duffy, 1995):

- learners construct knowledge through the process of solving problems;
- learning is situated in a context meaningful to the learner that leads to greater ability to transfer the learning to other settings;
- learning emphasises metacognitive skills as students generate their own strategies for defining the problem and working out a solution – the teacher's primary role is that of a facilitator who keeps the process moving;
- learning involves social construction of knowledge – students are able to challenge their thoughts, beliefs, perceptions and existing knowledge by interacting with others.

Problem-based learning requires careful planning and students must become familiar with the process before they can be expected to become proficient in its application. Additionally, as problem-based learning is often interdisciplinary in nature, it should be planned and monitored by an interdisciplinary team as required.

In a study of problem-based learning in an online learning environment, McConnell (2002) identifies the following three overlapping stages of group activity in such learning environments:

- negotiation of understandings and organisational decisions;
- research related to devising a solution; and
- development of the final product.

The process starts with students analysing the problem to understand it better, followed by assignment of roles, e.g. leader, recorder, technology specialist, planner and so forth. Using roles helps team members become interdependent and individually accountable for team success (Johnson, Johnson and Smith, 1991). Rotating roles discourages dominance by one student and provides all students with opportunities to practise social, communication and leadership skills (Millis and Cottell, 1998).

The next step involves students developing a problem statement that includes a listing of known and unknown facts regarding the problem. A research strategy is then developed to obtain the required knowledge to solve the problem, including identification of the resources and processes needed to solve the problem. Students then engage in independent study to acquire the needed information. Information sources include experts as well as web-based resources. Once all this information is acquired, the students share information with each other in a group setting and generate plausible solutions, choose the most viable solution, and answer the question that initiated the process.

Feedback is a critical aspect of this step. Student–student as well as teacher–student dialogue helps to monitor and promote progress. Possible feedback strategies include checklists, informal meetings, student self-assessment progress checks and journal entries using a wiki.

As a final step, each member of the group and the teacher evaluates the performance of each member as well as the group as a whole. This evaluation provides each student with positive reinforcement regarding his or her strengths, as well as constructive feedback for rectifying any identified areas for improvement (Barrows, 1994).

Using synchronous tools expedites the learning experience and also provides the advantages of co-presence. Use of asynchronous communication tools, on the other hand, brings the advantage of reflective thinking, but also involves delays in the exchange of ideas. Consequently, the online teacher needs to ensure adequate time is provided for the group to solve the problem and develop the final product. The best solution might be to offer the group both synchronous and asynchronous communication tools. Synchronous tools are particularly useful during the first stage of group activity (i.e. negotiation of understandings and organisational decisions).

It is essential for the teacher to emphasise the importance of student accountability during group work. Assessment of learning should be embedded in the learning experience itself, with assessment of both individual and group performances.

Inquiry-based learning

Problem-based learning becomes inquiry-based when students are active in creating the problem. Research suggests that inquiry-based learning can help students become more creative, more positive and more independent (Kuhne, 1995). Students drive inquiry-based learning projects. Teachers act as coaches, guides and facilitators who help learners arrive at their questions. The desired result of inquiry-based learning is that students learn to devise good questions, identify and collect appropriate evidence, present results methodically, analyse and interpret results, formulate conclusions and assess the value and significance of those conclusions (Prince and Felder, 2006).

Jakes, Pennington and Knodle (2002) suggest teachers facilitate learner development of questions to inform their inquiry-based project. They describe an 'essential question' as a question that requires students to make a decision or plan a course of action. Such essential questions go beyond the form of 'what is...' and take on the richer qualities of 'what decision should we take regarding...' or 'what plan can we develop to...' Once the essential question is developed and agreed, inquiry-based learning proceeds as problem-based learning.

Project-based learning

Project-based learning is another interactive strategy appropriate for the online constructivist learning environment. It is an approach to learning focusing on development of a product. The project may or may not be inquiry-based. Using this strategy, teachers and students attempt to

(a) identify a real-world problem, (b) develop a guiding question related to the problem, (c) explore the issues, (d) devise a solution, (e) create a product related to the solution and based upon investigative findings, (f) present the product to others, (g) assess students' work throughout the completion of the project, and (h) reflect (Brooks-Young, 2005).

Project-based learning is similar to problem-based learning in that both usually involve students working collaboratively in completing open-ended assignments that emulate real-world problems, and both require students to formulate solution strategies and to repeatedly re-evaluate their methodology in response to outcomes. However, there are several differences between project-based learning and problem-based learning.

A project normally has a broader range and can include several problems; it is focused on questions or problems that permit students to encounter the central concepts and principles of the content area or discipline under study. Furthermore, in project-based learning, the final product is the primary focus of the assignment, and the completion of the project involves the construction of new knowledge. The solution may be less important than the knowledge gained in arriving at the solution. Thus, the emphasis in project-based learning is on applying or integrating knowledge while that in problem-based learning is on obtaining knowledge (Prince and Felder, 2006). Consequently, a project often involves the application of interdisciplinary skills. The benefits to students include enhanced problem-solving skills, communication skills, teamwork skills and an understanding of the theoretical concepts behind the project (Allan, 2007).

Online discussions

Interaction is the interplay and exchange in which individuals and groups influence each other. Research evidence demonstrates that interaction is positively related to quality of learning processes and outcomes (e.g. Gao and Lehman, 2003). Interaction also plays a role in facilitating higher-order thinking skills such as critical thinking (Garrison, Anderson and Archer, 2001). Moreover, a multicultural discussion group can increase the level and value of interaction because learners take part in the interaction with different goals, values and characteristics.

However, productive interaction does not occur automatically because the available technology is capable of supporting discussion; online discussions must be planned, facilitated and moderated. The major purpose of facilitating and moderating online discussion is to promote and nurture online interactions, establish teacher presence in the virtual classroom, and, by doing so, promote both social presence and cognitive presence. In establishing teacher presence, the teacher must cultivate development of a community of inquiry in which he or she moves away from centre stage by promoting collaboration and cooperation among students.

Online discussions also provide the teacher with the opportunity to ask questions or pose problems that are to be solved by discursive (i.e. dynamic) interaction, which is, in principle, unbounded and open-ended. Different types of questions or questioning strategies can engage learners in deeper learning. Research suggests that questions help to activate prior knowledge and integrate it with new knowledge and the application of that knowledge (Osman and Hannafin, 1994). King (1992: 304) maintains that requiring students to ask and answer high-level questions facilitates their comprehension of textbook material by engaging them in tasks such as 'focusing attention, organizing the new material and integrating the new information with existing knowledge'.

By understanding the ways in which faculty members make direct contributions to students' learning, teachers can broaden their range of skills in the learning environment, especially regarding teacher immediacy, a concept first developed by Albert Mehrabian. Mehrabian (1969: 203) defines this concept as 'those communication behaviors that enhance closeness to and nonverbal interaction with another'. His concept suggests that nonverbal cues such as facial expressions, body movements and eye contact foster social presence and closeness. Additionally, Witt, Wheeless and Allen (2004: 199) report the results of a meta-analysis of teacher immediacy that includes 81 studies and 24,474 students. The results provide evidence that 'as verbal and nonverbal immediacy increase, students perceive that they are learning more ... [and] affective learning meaningfully increases'. However, they also caution, that 'even though students like more highly immediate teachers and think they learn more from their courses, actual cognitive learning is not affected as much as they think it is' (Witt, Wheeless and Allen, 2004: 201).

In a traditional classroom, eye contact, smiling, open body postures and moving around the classroom are all signals of social warming and regard for others. Online teachers are largely denied these behaviours and must find other ways of reflecting a positive classroom demeanour. For example, teachers can use personal examples, provide inviting feedback and address students by name. Many teachers find it useful to post autobiographical information or photos of their families, hobbies or pets as a means of keeping their personal information available to students in order to allow them to make connections and feel closer to their teacher.

Students can be made to feel comfortable in a traditional environment and there is little evidence to suggest that a teacher should sacrifice any of this comfort level in a distance environment. Teachers who are particularly effective at projecting their personalities using technology are at a distinct advantage. Brown (2001) argues that this form of communication and shared space for students involves a three-step process: (a) making friends, (b) gaining community conferment or acceptance, and (c) establishing camaraderie. By using this method of conceptualising teaching, online teachers are able to model behaviours that show sensitivity to diverse human needs and guide all students though increasing levels of interpersonal bonding and affiliation. Key to this kind of communication is a measure of authenticity that arises from genuine regard for other individuals, which is important within an online community of inquiry.

Active student participation in online discussions is viewed as the cornerstone of social constructivism. Consequently, online teachers often choose to grade learners according to the level of their participation in discussions. Rovai (2003c) reports research that reveals significantly more discussions per student per week and a greater sense of community in courses where discussions are a graded course component. In particular, he describes an ex post facto study in which 18 online courses were grouped based on the following three teacher-imposed grading strategies: (a) courses in which student discussions are not graded, (b) courses in which discussions represent 10–20 per cent of the course grade, and (c) courses in which discussions represent 25–35 per cent of the course grade. The study provides evidence that grading student discussions motivates students to increase the number and quality of weekly messages they post to group discussion boards.

The number of weekly messages posted by students was lowest for courses where discussions were not graded and significantly higher for courses where discussions were graded. Interestingly, there were no significant differences in the number or quality of weekly messages posted by teachers across the three grading strategies, suggesting that the messages posted by teachers each week had a negligible effect on the number and quality of student postings. Additionally, there were no additional benefits to increasing the weight of student participation (i.e. 10–20 per cent versus 25–35 per cent of the course grade) in terms of either increased number of student postings per week or increased sense of community.

Emphasis on asynchronous online discussions is justified in constructivist learning environments to facilitate knowledge construction. Awareness of teacher presence in online discussion boards is awareness that one is being watched (Gulati, 2008). The surveillance and power of the teacher may lead the naturally silent learner who prefers direct information acquisition over social constructivism to feel pressured and powerless to learn according to his or her preferred learning style. This pressure may force the naturally silent student to participate in online interactions and ultimately lead to student alienation as the student conforms to a teacher-imposed style of learning. The issue becomes whether or not mandatory participation in online discussions allows learners sufficient autonomy in the learning process to learn in the most productive manner. Gulati suggests:

> Online learning practices that aim for constructivist education need to recognize the impact of formal requirements that discourage different roles and learning processes. Course developers and facilitators, who may find themselves or their colleagues justifying compulsory participation in online learning discussions, could be persuaded towards greater reflexivity in their work. Compulsory participation in discussions may be a useful tool for engagement for some learning situations, but using it as a pedagogical strategy requires greater awareness of power differences due to monitoring and judging learners against a tutor-defined process. (Gulati, 2008: 188–9)

Facilitating discussions

Facilitating and moderating discussions are terms that are often used synonymously. When a distinction is made between moderating and facilitating discussions, the facilitator's role is to create a student-friendly online environment that promotes and provides structure to the discussion. The facilitator, typically the online teacher, participates in discussions as needed, in order to maintain teacher presence and serve as a content expert. The moderator, on the other hand, is the teacher or student who is in charge of leading the discussion. The facilitator:

- divides a large class into smaller groups (generally, it is best to limit the size of each discussion group to not more than 20 students each);

- creates separate forums for each discussion topic or project;
- establishes group goals;
- develops and posts each discussion topic or project requirement;
- assigns students on a rotating basis to moderate each conference for a grade (as deemed appropriate);
- provides learners with suitable scaffolding so they know what is expected of them, typically in the form of procedures and a grading rubric;
- establishes a date when discussions terminate for each topic;
- monitors all interactions;
- maintains a teacher presence in all active conferences by periodically providing words of encouragement and content-related critiques;
- points out themes that learners fail to identify in the course of their discussion;
- coordinates activities with the moderator;
- uses the discussions to assess class mastery of instructional objectives and to identify weak areas that require reinforcement;
- balances serving as the content expert and resource with allowing learners to construct deeper understanding through primarily learner–learner discourse; and
- trains moderators, as required (Rovai, Ponton and Baker, 2008).

Moderating discussions

Oftentimes, the teacher serves both roles of facilitator and moderator. However, the teacher may find it useful to assign the role of moderator to students on a rotating basis. Collison, Elbaum, Haavind and Tinker (2000), suggest three principles for moderating online discussions:

- moderating takes place in both professional and social contexts;
- the style of guide-on-the-side is more appropriate than sage-on-the-stage; and
- moderating online discussions is an art that has general guiding principles and strategies that can be learned by new online faculty members.

It is through active and appropriate intervention by a teacher that communication tools and strategies such as computer conferencing and cooperative learning become useful instructional and learning resources (Garrison, Anderson and Archer, 2001).

The moderator typically assumes the following responsibilities:

- introduces the topic;
- closely monitors the discussions by accessing the active conferences at least twice a day;
- sets a tone for an enthusiastic, smooth discussion;
- adopts an empathetic and nurturing approach for those learners who are struggling with course content or technology;
- elicits postings, as needed;
- responds to procedural and organisation issues as they arise;
- recognises high-quality contributions;
- maintains a social presence without becoming dominant or appearing authoritative;
- ensures all learners are encouraged to participate in the ongoing discussion;
- attends to issues of social equity based on different culture and gender-related communication patterns;
- allows learners time for reflection;
- identifies areas of agreement and disagreement;
- helps in the sorting of ideas and helps participants focus on key points;
- works toward reaching a consensus;
- gives timely and supportive feedback; and
- brings closure to the discussion topic by summarising discussions, and provides one last opportunity for learners to make final comments (Rovai, Ponton and Baker, 2008).

The moderator should not place himself or herself in the centre of all discussions. This is particularly true when the teacher serves as moderator. Higher education faculty already perceive teaching online as involving more work and time than teaching a traditional course (Hislop and Ellis, 2004). Thus, placing oneself in the centre of all discussions substantially increases workload and can become a major workplace stressor for the faculty member, resulting in teacher burnout, emotional exhaustion and feelings of low personal accomplishment. Moreover, numerous postings to read along with significant textbook readings and written assignments can result in student burnout as well, which results in reduced student engagement and hence attrition.

Neumann, Finaly-Neumann and Reichel (1990: 29–30) conclude that university students may experience burnout due to learning conditions that demand excessively high levels of effort and do not provide supportive mechanisms that facilitate effective coping. They suggest that 'development of learning environments that improve learning flexibility and students' involvement' can reduce this burnout phenomenon. They recommend strengthening the flexibility of academic programmes by emphasising electives, self-directed learning, independent study and courses concerned with critical questions. Within a course, flexibility can be achieved by allowing students a measure of choice regarding discussion topics, assessment tasks and course pacing.

Placing emphasis on student–student interactions and rotating students as moderators of small group online discussions can decrease teacher workload and increase student interest, motivation and learning. Humour can also moderate the effect of stressors on members of the learning community and help pre-empt teacher and student burnout. However, little research evidence exists regarding the use of humour in the virtual classroom, although much has been written on this topic in the traditional classroom. D. James (2004) summarises research findings that suggest humour can:

- create a more supportive learning environment;
- help students retain knowledge;
- create a sense of community; and
- reduce stress.

Teachers should exercise care regarding how they use humour in text-based computer-mediated communication as a comment intended to be amusing and positive can be difficult to decode in the absence of nonverbal cues and may be perceived as negative by some. Consequently, online teachers should focus on positive humour and avoid negative humour. Martin, Puhlik-Dorris, Larsen, Grey and Weir (2003) describe positive humour as consisting of affiliative humour (e.g. using humour to say funny things and using jokes to amuse others to facilitate relationships) and self-enhancing humour (e.g. reflective of a generally humorous outlook on life). Negative humour, on the other hand, consists of aggressive humour (e.g. using humour to hurt or tease other people, such as with sarcasm and ridicule), and self-deprecating humour (e.g. using humour to amuse others by disparaging about oneself).

Multicultural discussions

Biggs (1999) suggests that international students may experience three kinds of problems in an online course: sociocultural adjustment, language issues and teaching/learning issues relating to different expectations and perspectives on learning. International students in many Western cultures are often perceived to be too teacher-dependent, lacking in independent study skills and tending to adopt rote learning strategies. However, research suggests that international students often outperform their peers academically and that such conceptions may be misinterpreted (Kember, 2000).

As universities achieve global reach, so does the prospect that online courses will contain students from diverse cultures and nations. Consequently, in all likelihood there will be cultural barriers to cross when engaging in interpersonal communication. Educational efforts must take these barriers into account. There is therefore a need for the online teacher to facilitate and moderate discussions in ways that appeal to the preferences of learners from diverse cultures. To achieve true sensitivity to cultural differences, pedagogy should take on a multicultural approach and be sensitive to and respect the deep structures of different cultures (Roblyer, Dozier-Henry and Burnette, 1996).

Within a multicultural community of inquiry, cultural differences can affect how students share ideas, access course-related materials and construct knowledge. Effective instruction in international online classes requires teachers to address those cultural differences that could affect learning. In so doing, online teachers must assist students become acculturated to a multicultural learning environment.

Members of the learning community interact with each other based on shared values, which influence their norms and behaviour. In the global university, online classroom discussions can become more complex because of the presence of students who do not share the same values. Because the basic source of value differences is culture (Kitayama, Duffy, Kawamura and Larsen, 2003), culture becomes the basis for the perceptual filters on which people rely to guide their attention (Markus and Kitayama, 1991). In a multicultural learning environment, each constituency possesses strong arguments in defence of its own position. In such a situation, the foreign student may be pressured to choose pre-emptive self-criticism, carefully weighing the merits of the alternative perspectives and forming connections and reasonable trade-offs among them (Tetlock, 2002).

An international student who enrols in a global university where the dominant culture differs from his or her own culture, will encounter unfamiliar norms, values and beliefs. Because perceptual differences between cultures are rooted in difficult-to-detect values and normative prescriptions (Peng and Nisbett, 1999), a student who relies on more effort-demanding conscious processing will be better positioned to notice the discrepancies between the various cultures represented in the global classroom. These cultural differences are at the heart of the dissonance acculturating individuals will experience. Consequently, in a multicultural classroom, it is essential that members of the learning community come to understand the cultural differences present in the classroom at the start of the academic term so they can better understand and appreciate the cultural dynamics present in online discussions.

As students become increasingly acculturated in the multicultural classroom, different resolution styles are learned in situations that evoke cultural dissonance (Tadmor and Tetlock, 2006). For example, if a student from a collectivist culture solves a conflict between face-saving and honesty and this solution is positively reinforced, he or she is more likely to treat this conflict situation and mode of resolution as a relevant analogue when she or he is confronted with a conflict between expressing emotions and remaining professional with colleagues (Sanchez-Burks, 2002). As another example, students acculturated in high power distance cultures expect the teacher to exercise strong authority and to guide them. The teacher typically initiates communication and students do not speak unless invited to do so. However, if the teacher is acculturated in a low power distance culture, the teacher is more likely to treat students as equals and encourage student initiative, which makes students from higher power distance cultures uncomfortable. However, if these students understand such cultural differences and expectations early in the course, they are better able to cope as culturally uncomfortable situations occur. Additionally, the teacher will understand that lack of student initiative does not necessarily reflect poor learner behaviour.

Through successive dissonance-producing situations, repeated behaviour and positive reinforcement of the resolution style should produce an automatic response in the student's repertoire of coping mechanisms. As long as the student interprets situations similarly, they will activate similar appraisals, expectations, values and goals, and, consequently, will elicit similar solutions (Shoda, Tiernan and Mischel, 2002). However, the accountability pressures that students encounter during acculturation in the virtual classroom are likely to shift depending on both situational and dispositional factors. For example, in the virtual classroom, the student is accountable to a different audience than when at home and will be required to adjust behaviour accordingly. Additionally, a more extraverted and open-minded individual may be more susceptible to accountability pressures exerted by members of the new culture than individuals lower on these traits (e.g. see Hofstede and McCrae, 2004).

Hites (1996) makes the following recommendations for facilitating cross-cultural verbal communication:

- keep language simple and active;
- use consistent terminology;
- reduce or avoid the use of jargon, idioms and acronyms;
- define terms and provide glossaries;
- use relevant, specific examples familiar to the user;
- explain concepts using multiple examples;
- use multiple media to deliver the message through multiple senses; and
- develop and field-test the materials with representatives of the cultures for which the message has been written.

Conclusion

International students often experience the effects of culture shock arising from differences in social structure, customs, interpersonal relationships and communication between home and host nations. This same experience occurs when students in one nation are enrolled in a distance education programme offered by an institution located in another nation. Differences in the cultural norms and styles of interpersonal communication can lead to a range of individual uncertainties and anxieties associated with saving face and engaging in appropriate social interaction (Spencer-Oatey, 2000).

The natural inclination of teachers leads them to familiar ways of teaching, but most scholars now recognise that conventional methods may not work in a multicultural classroom. Providers of educational programmes across national boundaries have a responsibility to consider how their materials and practices can help promote effective cross-cultural interactions and learning.

Effective multicultural pedagogy creates knowledge and awareness of different cultures and the implications of these differences to the content area being taught. Such pedagogy does not teach individuals to become 'colour blind' or tolerant. Instead it teaches students to celebrate and respect differences. Teaching tolerance would be counter-productive, as it places one culture in a dominant position over others. The ultimate goal of multicultural pedagogy is to place all cultures on an equal footing. Consequently, multicultural pedagogy is much more than acquisition of knowledge about different cultures. It transcends the cognitive domain of learning and includes the affective domain as students learn to value and respect other cultures. In a pure sense, multicultural teaching is transformational teaching in which the teacher recognises how different forces affect and influence educational policies, curricula and practices. The multicultural teacher acknowledges that instructional decisions are often made based on ideologies not grounded in educational theory. Instead, they are often made based on beliefs influenced by history, politics, culture, language and power. Multicultural pedagogy also accommodates different learning styles, assists students to become acculturated to learning at a distance as well as learning using various technologies, and attends to different culturally-related communication patterns.

Online education tends to reflect the English-speaking world's perspective, with many of these values remaining implicit to users of online learning systems (Chase, Macfadyen, Reeder and Roche, 2002). Even the basic course design may be a new experience for some students. Many Western cultures emphasise learner-centred course designs, whereas teacher-centred course designs are more common in many Eastern cultures.

'The preconditions of cyber culture usually involve the linguistic and communication norms of Anglo-American societies in which the aggressive, competitive individual is enshrined' (Jordan, 2001: 13). Aggressiveness and competition on the part of some students may silence other students who are not accustomed to such behaviour. Such silence can adversely influence the grades of silenced students when discussions are a graded component of the course. As learning is largely a social undertaking, silenced students do not have the same opportunity to learn as students who freely participate in discussions.

Additionally, culturally diverse students may hold widely different expectations of how to exchange information, give and receive feedback, or evaluate information. Unfortunately, cultural and linguistic differences and sensitivities present in diverse students are not always incorporated into the design and delivery of distance education courses, even when the institution is attempting to reach a global audience.

Global universities that expect students to adapt to the institution's academic values and forms of communicating are practising a form of intellectual imperialism (Pincas, 2001).

Online teachers can facilitate powerful, effective courses geared to achieve specific learning outcomes using the vast resources and capacities of the internet. A key element in effective cross-cultural communication is being aware of the influence of culture on communication and understanding. Different worldviews and cultural characteristics colour perceptions, values and communication patterns. Without an awareness of these differences, communication in the virtual classroom can result in misunderstandings, prejudice, stereotypes and discrimination. Ineffective communication prevents the exchange and exploration of diverse perspectives that can enrich lives and promote a strong sense of community.

6

Quality assurance and institutional effectiveness

Introduction

Numerous international initiatives, such as the Declaration from the UNESCO Conference on Higher Education in 1998, aim to guarantee the quality of higher education in an international setting. These agreements, together with several national and international trends, have resulted in heightened interest in higher education quality and the policies of quality assurance and institutional effectiveness. These trends include the transition from elite to mass participation in higher education since the 1980s and the increased burden of higher education on national budgets (Santiago, Tremblay, Basri and Arnal, 2008). Given the high level of public investment in higher education (an average of 1 per cent of GDP among Organisation for Economic Cooperation and Development nations, according to the OECD, 2007), there is also increased interest in the sector's cost-effectiveness.

Additionally, the recent growth in international student mobility and the increase in various forms of cross-border provision of distance education, increasing demands for accountability in higher education, rising expectations of employers and students, growing financial pressures, expansion of consumerism and academic capitalism, growing importance of globalisation, emergence of lifelong learning, efforts to make instruction more learner-centred, and the explosive growth of distance education, are forcing institutions to take a closer look at quality (Rovai, Ponton and Baker, 2008).

The US Department of Education (2006) lists several red flags associated with the quality of distance education programmes that point to quality assurance problems. These red flags are:

- new programmes are launched on the basis of perceived need, but without any research indicating there is a market for them;
- faculty members engage in distance education course development, while carrying a full-time teaching load;
- large numbers of students in online courses with insufficient faculty for effective student–teacher interaction;
- little discussion board activity in online courses;
- the majority of student postings lack substance and show little evidence of reflection or critical thinking;
- poor student evaluation of teaching;
- rapid adjunct faculty turnover;
- outdated course materials;
- faculty members are given primary responsibility for solving students' technical problems;
- students do not know who to contact if they have questions or problems; and
- low student persistence.

The quality of higher education must be assured to justify the allocation of public resources and ensure effective use of these resources. UNESCO describes quality in education as follows:

> Two principles characterize most attempts to define quality in education: the first identifies learners' cognitive development as the major explicit objective of all education systems. Accordingly, the success with which systems achieve this is one indicator of their quality. The second emphasizes education's role in promoting values and attitudes of responsible citizenship and in nurturing creative and emotional development. The achievement of these objectives is more difficult to assess and compare across countries. (UNESCO, 2005a: 2)

The *Guidelines for Quality Provision in Cross-Border Higher Education* (UNESCO, 2005b: 15–17) include the following guidelines for institutions/providers:

- Ensure that programmes delivered across borders and in the home nation are of comparable quality and that they also take into account the cultural and linguistic sensitivities of the receiving nation. It is desirable that a commitment to this effect should be made public.

- Recognise that quality teaching and research is made possible by the quality of faculty and the quality of their working conditions that foster independent and critical inquiry.

- Develop, maintain or review current internal quality management systems so that they make full use of the competencies of stakeholders such as academic staff, administrators, students and graduates, and take full responsibility for delivering higher education qualifications comparable in standard in their home nation and across borders.

- Consult competent quality assurance and accreditation bodies and respect the quality assurance and accreditation systems of the receiving nation when delivering higher education across borders, including distance education.

- Share good practices by participating in sector organisations and inter-institutional networks at national and international levels.

- Develop and maintain networks and partnerships to facilitate the process of recognition by acknowledging each other's qualifications as equivalent or comparable.

- Where relevant, use codes of good practice such as the UNESCO/ Council of Europe *Code of Good Practice in the Provision of Transnational Education* and other relevant codes such as the Council of Europe/UNESCO *Recommendation on Criteria and Procedures for the Assessment of Foreign Qualifications*.

- Provide accurate, reliable and easily accessible information on the criteria and procedures of external and internal quality assurance, and the academic and professional recognition of qualifications they deliver, and provide complete descriptions of programmes and qualifications, preferably with descriptions of the knowledge, understanding and skills that a successful student should acquire.

- Ensure the transparency of the financial status of the institution and/or educational programme offered.

Consequently, the quality of cross-border higher education is a shared responsibility between importing and exporting nations and should be of the same quality as home nation delivery.

The 11 principles of the UNESCO/Council of Europe *Code of Good Practice in the Provision of Transnational Education* (2001) are consistent with this view. Summaries of each of these principles are provided below:

1. Transnational arrangements should be elaborated, enforced and monitored so as to widen the access to higher education studies, fully respond to the learners' educational demands, contribute to their cognitive, cultural, social, personal and professional development, and comply with the higher education standards in both receiving and sending countries.

2. Academic quality and standards should be comparable to those of the awarding institution as well as to those of the receiving country.

3. The policies and the mission statements of institutions, their management structures and educational facilities, as well as the goals, objectives and contents of specific programmes, courses of study and other educational services, should be made available upon request.

4. Information given to prospective students should be appropriate, accurate, consistent and reliable, and include directions regarding concerns, complaints and appeals.

5. Staff and faculty members should be proficient in terms of qualifications, teaching, research and other professional experience.

6. Transnational education arrangements should encourage the awareness and knowledge of the culture and customs of both the awarding institutions and receiving country among the students and staff.

7. The awarding institution should be responsible for the agents it, or its partner institutions, appoint to act on its behalf.

8. Awarding institutions should provide clear and transparent information on the qualifications, in particular through the use of the Diploma Supplement. This information should include the nature, duration, workload, location and language(s) of the study programme leading to the qualifications.

9. The admission of students for a course of study, the teaching/learning activities, and the examination and assessment requirements should be equivalent to those of the same or comparable programmes delivered by the awarding institution.

10. The academic workload in transnational study programmes should match comparable programmes in the awarding institution.

11. Qualifications (i.e. whether for access to higher education, for periods of study, or for higher education degrees) should be assessed

in accordance with the stipulations of the Lisbon Recognition Convention.

Both the *Guidelines for Quality Provision in Cross-Border Higher Education* (UNESCO, 2005b) and the *Code of Good Practice in the Provision of Transnational Education* (UNESCO, 2001) emphasise openness and quality assurance. Moreover, these documents make clear that no discrimination shall be made based on the applicant's gender, race, colour, disability, language, religion, political opinion or national, ethnic or social origin.

Quality assurance

Evidence-based practice, such as distance education, requires quality assurance in order to achieve and improve quality. The definition of quality assurance differs slightly from nation to nation although the basic concept is the same. Quality assurance assumes that quality for a product or service is first defined in order to establish a standard so that it can be evaluated. It also requires the development of quality improvement goals to meet institutional goals and objectives, and the identification of performance metrics (i.e. measures or key performance indicators) to assess quality. Metrics have the potential to serve as barometers of programme quality, efficiency and adequacy. Once metrics are identified, they become the operational definitions of quality, so care is necessary in developing a sound, valid and adequate set of metrics.

Quality assurance activities are carried out by the distance education service provider and are customer-oriented. Most importantly, quality assurance requires an institutional culture that promotes and enforces quality and continuous improvement. Quality assurance applies both to the institution itself as an organisational entity and to the academic programmes it offers.

Judith Eaton (2001: 13), President of the US Council for Higher Education Accreditation, writes that 'whatever our opinions may be about distance learning and its future, there is no disputing the evidence that some elements of the distance learning experience are significantly different from a site-based educational experience'. She goes on to note that some of the more significant differences include curricula development, computer-mediated classrooms, separation in time of communication between teachers and students, and online support services. Quality assurance must consider these differences, and quality standards for distance education programmes must differ from those of traditional face-to-face programmes along these lines of difference.

Phipps, Wellman and Merisotis (1998), in reviewing US distance education programmes versus traditional programmes, note that there is a greater tendency for the assessment process of distance education programmes to be led by the administration instead of by the faculty, with greater use of outside consultants and assessment by experts in lieu of internally-generated peer reviews. The quality assurance process for these programmes tends to be less process-driven, where there is a high value placed on consultation, consensus building and dialogue, and a greater orientation toward bottom-line or market-oriented results. Moreover, Phipps, Wellman and Merisotis (1998) describe other differences between distance education and traditional programmes as including:

- *difference in focus*: distance learning has a sharper focus on the teaching/learning process;
- *focus on student*: the educational activities that the student desires predominate in the design and implementation of programmes;
- *less control by faculty over curriculum*: the tendency to develop or use pre-packaged courses and learning objects as well as the preponderance of adjunct faculty are characteristics of many distance learning programmes;
- *less emphasis on process*: the traditional academic culture relies heavily on process, is substantially consultative, and is consensus-driven, while the delivery of distance education programmes tends to abandon, at least partially, these traditional quality assurance activities, and appears to be more assessment-driven;
- *contracting for services*: many distance learning programmes contract with other entities to provide many administrative and student services not directly related to the teaching/learning process.

Institutions establish quality assurance structures to manage institutional effectiveness. Insung Jung (2005) describes the different quality assurance structures used by mega-universities worldwide. Each structure falls into one of the following three categories:

- *Centralised quality assurance structure*: One approach is to establish a centralised office to provide university-wide oversight. For example, the British Open University uses such an approach with a quality assurance team and a pro-vice-chancellor for learning and teaching.

- *Collective quality assurance structure*: Another approach is to utilise the boards, the councils, and/or the committees rather than an independent quality assurance unit in administration. Each organisational element has distinctive roles at different stages of quality assurance or in different areas of quality assurance activities. For example, at Anadolu University in Turkey, the university senate, university executive board, academic advisory board, course accreditation and review committee and instructional design committee exercise significant roles in quality assurance.

- *Dispersed quality assurance structure*: Using this approach, quality assurance is dispersed throughout several university administrative offices. For example, the Korean National Open University has a decentralised quality assurance system where quality is a responsibility of all relevant offices and academic divisions.

Regardless of the organisational approach to manage quality assurance, all nationally accredited universities must comply with their national standards. For example, the quality assurance policies and regulations at the Indira Gandhi National Open University are in conformity with the quality assurance guidelines established by the Distance Education Council of India. For most institutions, the predominant objectives of internal quality assurance activities are self-improvement and accountability to the public and to the national quality assurance authority (Jung, 2005). Thus, internal quality assurance results are used for self-improvement and to support external accreditation and institutional effectiveness.

Quality assurance standards

Quality assurance standards vary from nation to nation. Jung (2005) identifies several key quality assurance areas. For example, the key areas reported by the Alama Iqbal Open University in Pakistan are:

- courses and their effectiveness;
- tutorial support system;
- assessment system;
- student problems;
- methods of course production;
- cost-effectiveness of courses;

- outcomes of courses and programmes;
- servicing/operational departments; and
- administration.

In the USA, the Council for Higher Education Accreditation (CHEA) is the primary national voice for voluntary accreditation and quality assurance, and is answerable to Congress and the Department of Education. According to the CHEA Institute for Research and Study of Accreditation and Quality Assurance, many recognised US accrediting organisations routinely review the following seven key areas of institutional activity when examining the quality of distance learning programmes:

1. *Institutional mission*: Does offering distance learning make sense in this institution? Distance education programme content, purposes, organisation and enrolment history should be consistent with the institution's role and mission.

2. *Institutional organisational structure*: Is the institution suitably structured to offer quality distance learning? Distance learning programmes offered by an institution should be integrated into the institution's administrative structures, as well as its planning and assessment systems. Moreover, institutional evaluation of distance education programmes should take place in the context of the institution's regular evaluation of all academic programmes and adhere to similar levels of quality.

3. *Institutional resources*: Does the institution sustain adequate financing to offer quality distance learning? The institution's budgets and policy statements should reflect its commitment to distance education students.

4. *Curriculum and instruction*: Does the institution have appropriate curricula and design of instruction to offer quality distance learning? The institution should research the industry, review curricula of programmes offered by mainstream schools and adopt mainstream texts. Additionally, academically qualified persons should participate fully in the decisions concerning programme curricula and programme coordination.

5. *Faculty support*: Are faculty members competent to engage in offering distance learning and do they have adequate resources, facilities and equipment? Faculty members should receive appropriate training that goes beyond software training and includes distance education

pedagogy, with specific emphasis on instructional strategies to foster interaction, to convey concepts and to assess student learning.

6. *Student support*: Do students have the necessary counselling, advising, equipment, facilities and instructional materials to pursue distance learning? Students should have easy and timely access to the range of services appropriate to support online programmes.

7. *Student learning outcomes*: Does the institution routinely evaluate the quality of distance learning based on evidence of student achievement? When examinations are employed, they should take place in circumstances that include firm student identification. Additionally, sufficient opportunities should be present for students to acquire comparable levels of knowledge and competencies as in similar programmes or courses offered in more traditional ways (CHEA, 2002).

These seven areas are consistent with the Alfred P. Sloan Consortium's five pillars of a quality online course (J. C. Moore, 2002). These pillars are:

- *learning effectiveness*: learners who complete an online programme receive education that represents the distinctive quality of the institution;

- *cost-effectiveness*: institutions should offer their best educational value to learners and control costs so that tuition is affordable yet sufficient to meet development and maintenance costs, and provide a return on investment;

- *access*: institutions should provide students with the means to complete courses and programmes in their disciplines of choice in terms of three areas of support: academic (e.g. tutoring, advising and library), administrative (e.g. financial aid and disability support), and technical (e.g. hardware reliability, uptime and helpdesk);

- *faculty satisfaction*: online teachers should find the online teaching experience personally rewarding and professionally beneficial; and

- *student satisfaction*: online students should express satisfaction with course/programme rigour and fairness, with professor and peer interaction, and with student support services.

ISO 9000/9001 quality standards

The International Organization for Standardization (ISO) 9000 family of international quality assurance standards establishes international quality assurance schemes for distance education programmes. Although the standards originated in manufacturing, they are now employed across a wide range of other types of organisations to encompass the services sector, including distance education.

The ISO 9000 Quality Standard is a model that provides a framework for any organisation to establish a customer satisfaction oriented quality assurance system that is internationally recognised and can be independently assessed and certified. The original ISO 9000:1994 Standard emphasised quality assurance via preventive actions. The newer ISO 9001:2000 Standard combines previous standards with a focus on monitoring and optimising an institution's activities and consists of a generic set of requirements for implementing a quality management system. The goal is to improve institutional effectiveness via process performance metrics with expectations of continual process improvement and tracking customer satisfaction. Implementation involves deliberate efforts to document, implement and improve the institution's processes, programmes and methods.

Sections 4 through 8 of the ISO 9001:2000 Standard identify the following requirements:

- *Systemic requirements (section 4)*
  - establish a quality management system;
  - document the quality management system, e.g. develop, approve and control quality management documents and maintain suitable records.
- *Management requirements (section 5)*
  - support quality;
  - satisfy customers;
  - establish a policy on quality;
  - carry out quality planning;
  - control the quality management system and perform periodic management reviews.
- *Resource requirements (section 6)*
  - provide quality resources;
  - provide quality personnel;
  - provide quality infrastructure;
  - provide a quality environment.

- *Realisation requirements (section 7)*
  - control realisation planning, e.g. define product quality objectives and requirements;
  - control customer processes, e.g. identify and review customer needs;
  - control product development, e.g. define product design and development;
  - control the purchasing function, e.g. ensure purchased products meet standards;
  - control operational activities, e.g. control production and service provision;
  - control monitoring devices, e.g. identify the monitoring and measuring that should be accomplished.
- *Remedial requirements (section 8)*
  - perform remedial processes;
  - monitor and measure quality, e.g. regular internal audits and customer satisfaction surveys;
  - control nonconforming products;
  - analyse quality information;
  - make quality improvements.

As ISO does not certify institutions, many nations have formed accreditation bodies to authorise certification. These bodies audit institutions applying for ISO 9001 compliance certification. Once an institution's quality system is documented and implemented, the institution can invite an accredited external auditor to evaluate the effectiveness of the system. The auditor will certify the quality system once it determines that the system meets all relevant ISO requirements.

Institutional effectiveness

The effectiveness of an institution rests upon the contribution that each of the institution's programmes and services makes toward achieving its mission. Accordingly, institutional effectiveness is the system designed to improve an institution and demonstrate the extent to which it has been effective in fulfilling its mission. Institutional effectiveness is therefore a management system used to assure quality and is thus closely related to quality assurance. It is oriented towards measuring inputs, processes and outcomes, and using those results to support decision-making and continuous improvement. Because student learning is a fundamental component of the mission of higher education institutions, the assessment of student learning is an essential component of the assessment of institutional effectiveness. Institutional effectiveness consists of three interrelated components that are each related to the budgeting process:

- planning;
- assessment and evaluation; and
- institutional and programme improvement.

Strengthening institutional strategic planning, assessment and evaluation capacity is a fundamental focus for improving institutional effectiveness. Among the obstacles to successful institutional effectiveness efforts are lack of sustained attention by institutional leadership, limitations of assessment tools, poorly designed systems to use assessment results and the lack of faculty commitment (Ewell, 2005; Palomba and Banta, 1999).

Robert Birnbaum (2001) argues that one of the most significant reasons that managerial strategies fail is that they do not succeed in attracting the allegiance or support of large numbers of institutional administrators or faculty. Institutional effectiveness activities are often presented to faculty by administrators in terms of common sense appeals for improvement and accountability, yet faculty often see them as (a) attacks on tenure and academic freedom, (b) attempts to reduce faculty lines, (c) selling out to business ideologies, and/or (d) caving-in to governmental bureaucracies (Ryan, 1993). Therefore, the design and implementation of institutional effectiveness processes must encourage active faculty and staff participation beyond passive acceptance of institutional mandates (Ewell, 2005).

The appendix to this book includes examples of both unit and academic programme effectiveness report templates that institutions can tailor to help satisfy their internal institutional effectiveness reporting requirements. Naturally, institutions should use their own sets of key performance indicators for their reports. The example templates, when completed by the institution in the form of an actual report, allow administrators to track the alignment of university mission and goals with unit and programme inputs and outcomes. Additionally, the academic programme effectiveness report format facilitates checking the alignment of each academic programme's purpose statement with programme and course learning goals and outcomes. It also facilitates a systems analysis approach to programme evaluation by examining programme inputs, processes, and outcomes. Finally, and most importantly, the report provides a description of how assessment results are used to improve programme effectiveness. This last part satisfies the institutional effectiveness requirement of measuring inputs, processes and outcomes, and using those results to support decision-making and continuous improvement. Although this systems analysis approach emphasises research-based techniques in the evaluation of academic programmes, it is also important for professional knowledge obtained from experience, teaching and the study of educational purpose to influence evaluation results.

Planning

Strategic planning is a process in which an organisation envisions its future and develops the necessary strategies, programmes and activities to create that future. In so doing it seeks to better align itself with its environment. Rowley, Lujan and Dolence describe strategic planning in higher education as:

> [a] formal process designed to help a university identify and maintain an optimal alignment with the most important elements [of] the environment ... within which the university resides. [This environment consists of] the political, social, economic, technological, and educational ecosystem, both internal and external to the university. (Rowley, Lujan and Dolence, 1997: 14–15)

For educational institutions, distance education can mean movement toward new directions, particularly in the growing area of lifelong learning, and outreach to a wider and more diverse student population. Strategic planning assists the institution in realising these outcomes efficiently and can help provide a solution to the adult educational needs of educationally isolated communities, physically handicapped persons who cannot attend on-campus classes, individuals who move frequently and persons whose work and family schedules make it difficult or impossible to attend scheduled classes or commute to campus.

Typically, distance education planning is fully integrated in the school's overall planning process. Strategic planning activities can be viewed as involving three sequential phases that comprise a cyclical planning model: the startup phase, the scanning and diagnosis phase and the strategy formulation and implementation phase (Rovai, Ponton and Baker, 2008). Each phase addresses an increased level of strategic focus on the information and issues defined and analysed in the preceding phase. The process ends with the implementation and monitoring of the strategic plan as a new strategic planning cycle begins.

Startup

The startup phase consists of the formation of the strategic planning committee (SPC). The SPC performs the following tasks:

- identifies the institution's key services, products and markets, including distance education, as appropriate;
- reviews strategic plans and reports from the previous strategic planning cycle;
- identifies the broad information needs for the second phase;
- identifies organisational constraints to conducting the strategic planning process.

The output of this phase is a detailed work plan with timeline.

Scanning and diagnosis

During the scanning and diagnosis phase, the SPC performs a situational analysis by accomplishing two major tasks. First, it conducts an analysis of strengths, weaknesses, opportunities and threats (SWOT) by diagnosing the internal strengths and weaknesses and external opportunities and threats facing the overall organisation and each of its key services, products and markets (Bryson, 2004). Second, it identifies the core values that form the heart of the institution's approach to intellectual, moral, social and cultural development.

Bryson (2004) describes SWOT analysis as a tool for auditing an organisation and its environment. It helps planners focus on the strategic issues, that is, the issues that are the fundamental challenges the organisation must address to achieve its mission and move towards its desired future. This focus helps the organisation relate to what it should be doing to meet the needs of its clients or potential clients. The SWOT analysis is carried out by identifying and assigning each significant factor, positive and negative, to one of the four SWOT categories, allowing one to take an objective look at the environment. This analysis is a useful tool in developing and confirming a strategic vision and supporting goals and strategies.

The rise of consumerism and academic capitalism in higher education, the growing cross-border activity among faculty and students, and the increasing importance of a more knowledgeable workforce and of lifelong learning, all represent opportunities for the well-situated university that point to extending its global reach. The university can forge a powerful niche for itself within the emerging twenty-first century global education environment by seizing the opportunity for innovation and international responsibility. Maximising this opportunity will require a university initiative to strategically apply its expertise in information and communication technologies for the purpose of delivering quality educational services to a rapidly growing international market. Doing so has the potential to benefit the university economically and to promote the global good by promoting international social and cultural harmony.

The SPC also identifies or revises the institution's core values, which largely define organisational culture. For example, shared governance, faculty control of the curriculum, and non-proprietary basic research and scholarship detached from revenue considerations are likely to be important values for not-for-profit institutions. In contrast, strong hierarchical organisational structure with centralised power and realisation of a profit from operations are valued by for-profit institutions. For the global university, core values could include pursuit of global social and cultural harmony.

One possible method of identifying organisational values is to first examine the values that faculty, staff and students bring to the school before examining the institution's values. By identifying and publicising core values, the school makes clear what is expected and provides the basis for individual accountability. Moreover, the core values become a recruitment tool and allow hiring to address the congruence of the applicant's values to those of the school.

Strategy formulation and implementation

In the final phase, strategy formulation and implementation, the SPC develops a strategic vision and the strategies, programmes and activities that will achieve this vision. The SPC performs the following tasks in this final phase:

- Recommends refinement of the school mission statement, if needed. The mission statement outlines what the school does now. A well-articulated mission statement identifies (a) the needs the organisation fulfils, (b) the products and markets required to fulfil the organisation's purpose, and (c) unique competencies that distinguish the organisation from competitors (Hax and Majluf, 1996).

- Refines the school's vision statement, if needed. It focuses on tomorrow and provides a clear decision-making standard. A school's vision does not determine how the school will work, but rather how it will look and act if the strategic plan is implemented successfully.

- Sets strategic direction by identifying strategic university goals that lead the school from where it is at present, as defined by its mission, to where it wants to go, as defined by its vision. In so doing, the SPC should reflect on the needs of a globalised world as well as on the challenges associated with an increasingly competitive distance education marketplace.

- Develops strategic objectives, metrics and targets that reflect statements of attainable and quantifiable achievements that move the school toward its strategic goals.

- Develops appropriate strategies, activities and programmes to enable key services, products and markets to best respond to the issues and challenges flowing from the previous phase.

- Develops resource and budgetary requirements. Budgetary decisions are made based on the requirements of processes related to educating students.

- Directs the preparation of unit strategic plans that address implementation of strategic objectives at the departmental level. These plans identify the specific steps that will be taken to achieve the initiatives and strategic objectives, and focus on operations, procedures and processes.

- Implements and monitors the institution's strategic plan and supporting unit plans through institutional research and programme evaluations that focus on key metrics.

- Directs the refinement of unit plans, as needed, as the result of monitoring activities.

- The most important issue to be addressed is development of the institution's vision statement. A good vision statement is specific, attainable and measurable. Higher education administrators and educators should heed what the Cheshire cat said to Alice in Lewis Carroll's *Alice in Wonderland*, 'if you don't know where you are going, any road will take you there'. A vision statement outlines what a school wants to become and identifies where the institution is going. Opportunities that can inform a vision statement include extending global reach in order to meet growing demands for higher education worldwide. Strategies to respond to this opportunity include building universities capable of competing at world-class level, forging meaningful alliances and partnerships with higher education institutions around the world, and using the internet to deliver courses.

Programme evaluation

Institutions often have a variety of plans, such as a strategic plan, academic plan, budget, facilities master plan and technology plan. Just as these plans are interrelated and aligned to provide mutual support to advance the institution's mission, assessments should also be interrelated and aligned with the institution's strategic goals and objectives.

Quality assurance in business and industrial environments is usually based on an assessment and evaluation of customer satisfaction. Assessment refers to measurement, while evaluation refers to forming a value judgment based on assessments. The purpose of higher education evaluation varies somewhat from nation to nation, but generally tends to address one or more of the following factors: (a) mission achievement, (b) product/service delivery, (c) accreditation, (d) improvement by providing feedback, and (e) accountability to stakeholders. The outcomes of evaluation are specific decisions regarding educational programmes and supporting services in order to improve quality. Consequently, the evaluator must examine effectiveness, appropriateness of processes, adequacy and value.

Lee Harvey and Diana Green (1993) draw from the business literature and analyse higher education in terms of the following overlapping views of quality and how quality can be assessed:

- *Quality as being exceptional*: This traditional view of quality is that universities embody quality and thus do not need to demonstrate it. This view of quality is of little value when it comes to assessing quality because it provides no standards.

- *Quality as perfection (i.e. consistency and zero defects)*: This view focuses on process and sets targets that institutions aim to meet.

- *Quality as fitness for purpose*: This view judges quality in terms of the extent to which the product or service fits its purpose. As the primary purpose of higher education is to provide an educated workforce, this view of quality suggests that quality is assessed in terms of student outcomes and impacts.

- *Quality as value for money*: This view places emphasis on institutional accountability, particularly in terms of public institutions and efficiencies. It judges the quality of processes and outcomes in terms of the monetary cost of undertaking the processes or achieving the outcomes.

- *Quality as being transformative*: This view of quality focuses on the extent to which the educational experience enhances the skills, knowledge and attitudes of students by enhancing or empowering each student. The emphasis is on value added.

These varied views of quality suggest a comprehensive model of quality in higher education can be based on systems theory by examining quality in terms of inputs, processes, outputs and impacts. Outputs and impacts are especially important when one views quality as 'fitness for purpose' and where public accountability is a driving force. Such a model includes both formative and summative components and incorporates both professional and managerial considerations.

Refining and specifying a distance education programme into an evaluable programme model involves making explicit the various components of the programme, and demonstrating how the various activities link to one another and progress from immediate programme effects, through intermediate effects, to ultimate programme effects (i.e. programme impacts). Consequently, the activities that link programme components with immediate and ultimate effects will be explicitly defined. It is however important to acknowledge that programme theory is more than a flowchart of programme activities, as flowcharts do not necessarily explain 'how programme activities are understood to lead to intended outcomes', and do not 'convey what it is about the programme activities that seems to help bring about the goal' (Rogers, 2000: 227).

A key consideration in using the systems model is the acknowledgment that a distance education programme is an open system, and, consequently, feedback from a variety of internal and external stakeholders is essential for system adjustment and improvement. Stakeholders include students and teachers, staff, administrators, policymakers, the board of trustee members, vendors, consultants, community groups, accrediting agencies, government organisations, businesses and employers.

Input evaluation

The purpose of an input evaluation is to provide information on the quality of resources used by the programme and to determine how best to use these resources to achieve programme goals. It identifies and judges programme resources and capabilities, including equipment and technical expertise, faculty and student abilities, and the designs used to satisfy student educational needs.

An input evaluation can also help forecast future costs and the sustainability of the programme being evaluated, validate programme and course objectives, and provide information for refining and positioning the programme in competitive distance education markets. Metrics that can be used to assess programme inputs focus on student and faculty profiles and programme opportunities and include:

- quality of students entering the programme, e.g. standardised test scores and previous grade point averages;
- student characteristics, e.g. age, gender, nationality and primary language;
- student access, e.g. faculty and student diversity, number of international students, etc.;
- number of study abroad programmes;
- number of students studying foreign languages;
- relevance (i.e. the extent to which the programme corresponds to student perception of needs);
- teacher credentials, e.g. experience teaching online and expertise in the content area taught;
- faculty satisfaction, e.g. with compensation, workload, training and teaching;
- faculty salaries;
- faculty participation rate in professional development opportunities, e.g. regarding strategies to foster interaction, to convey concepts, and to assess online student learning;

- incentives to faculty members for innovative practices to encourage development of distance learning courses;
- amount of institutional rewards for the effective teaching of distance learning courses;
- currency of course materials;
- student to faculty ratio;
- staff to faculty ratio;
- availability and nature of student support services for online students;
- capabilities and limitations of the learning management system; and
- programme demand:
  - number of telephone enquiries per academic cycle;
  - number of applications requested per academic cycle;
  - number of completed applications received per academic cycle;
  - number of students admitted per academic cycle; and
  - number of new students enrolling in courses per academic cycle.

Academic audit

Given a set of programme inputs, programme processes determine the extent to which programme outcomes are achieved. Processes are evaluated using an academic audit, often referred to as a process evaluation. The prototype academic audit systems were developed in the early 1990s in the UK, New Zealand and Hong Kong (Ewell, 2001). The academic audit's main focus is on the adequacy of the processes that the institution employs. The audit is used to determine the overall quality of the processes in place compared with a standard 'ideal type' for such processes and the extent to which the institution actually follows its own processes.

The evaluator must examine not only what is happening within the programme as it is being implemented but also what should be happening and is not. In other words, the evaluator monitors programme implementation and identifies any changes from the documented programme model that may have occurred, any defects in the procedural design or its implementation, and documents process activities and events. Its purpose is to facilitate better learning while that learning is ongoing. Consequently, an academic audit determines how well a programme is working and identifies, early on, any problems or inefficiencies that occur in order to make adjustments before weaknesses become permanent. It provides information about the state of all programme components for formative purposes.

The evaluator must also analyse and evaluate the e-learning system as a whole, as well as by subsystems, including teacher effectiveness. After all, technology is not self-implementing. In large measure, the teacher influences the effectiveness of any learning environment. For example, a great e-learning system may be resulting in poor learning because of teacher ineffectiveness (a process problem). Similarly, an exceptional teacher may be able to achieve a superior learning experience despite a marginal e-learning system (an input problem).

As part of the academic audit, the evaluator should also address the ongoing instructional efficiency of the teaching/learning process. As learning is inherently a social process, measurement of variables, such as sense of community and weekly rates and quality of student–student and student–teacher interactions, can be useful as proxy measures of learning. In particular, online students are more motivated when contacts with teachers are frequent, especially regarding feedback pertaining to how well they are performing on their assignments. They also value participation in small groups, particularly discussion groups. Metrics that can be used for a programme audit focus on programme processes and include:

- gratification (i.e. the extent to which the programme enhances the students' self-esteem and sense of integrity);
- student satisfaction, as measured by regular surveys;
- number and nature of student complaints;
- number and nature of student technical difficulties, e.g. summary of helpdesk logs;
- timeliness of faculty and staff feedback;
- quality of teaching;
- group learning experiences;
- peer evaluation of teaching;
- number of students dropping from the programme per academic cycle;
- student reasons for refunds and enrolment termination;
- student achievement on major assignments;
- quality of student effort, e.g. grade trends;

- affordability, e.g. total cost of attendance, tuition assistance, etc.;
- faculty and staff turnover ratios;
- faculty use of support services;
- student participation rates in support services;
- quality of vendor support;
- reliability of the technology delivery system; and
- focus group results.

Output evaluation

An output evaluation seeks to determine the immediate or direct effects of the programme, that is, the changes that occur in terms of the institution, the programme and the student. It makes little sense to conduct an output evaluation in the absence of input and process evaluations. If a programme is not implemented as intended or not well implemented, the outputs of the programme will not reflect its true potential.

The emphasis during the output evaluation is on the student and determining the extent to which instructional objectives have been achieved as students complete the programme. An output evaluation also examines institutional and programme outputs, mostly in terms of productivity, cost-effectiveness and cost-efficiency. Cost-effectiveness entails accomplishing the intended programme goals by providing maximum values for limited expenditures. Programme elements to be measured are applied against the cost, and the comparison of cost and effectiveness form the basis of this analysis. Metrics that can be used to assess programme outputs focus on student academic success and include:

- numbers of credits produced through instruction;
- extent to which student learning matches intended outcomes;
- changes in student skills, knowledge, and/or attitudes as a result of the programme (i.e. value added);
- percentage of graduates believing the programme has met their educational goals and expectations (i.e. satisfied their educational needs);
- graduation rates, including variations over time;

- degrees awarded by discipline;
- job placements after graduation;
- attitudes of graduating students concerning the programme;
- end-of-course student evaluation of teaching;
- types of service or research products generated;
- research and development expenditures;
- research grants;
- student enrolment and academic fee growth;
- revenue by source;
- programme revenue per academic cycle;
- private support;
- average credit hours per student;
- expenditures by function;
- programme costs per academic cycle;
- non-instructional costs as a share of all costs;
- average cost per student by dividing the total annual cost of the institution by the number of registered students in a particular academic cycle (this assumes that the teaching/learning experience of all students is similar);
- average cost per graduate by multiplying the average cost per student by the average number of years that it takes to graduate, adjusting for dropouts; and
- each programme's bottom line contribution to the institution as a percentage of the programme's gross revenues.

Impact evaluation

For programme evaluations, the ultimate issue is whether or not the observed results of the programme are judged to be of value. This issue involves programme effectiveness and typically addresses such areas as career success and personal development. To evaluate effectiveness, the evaluator focuses on impacts – the longer-term results that are expected to satisfy the programme's goals. While output evaluations focus on determining the extent to which specified instructional objectives are met, impact evaluations go well beyond this focus by examining the worth or value of these outputs. Such evaluations focus on what graduates should be able to do when they leave an educational programme and the degree to which the programme has met its ultimate goals.

Impact evaluations typically involve tracking the performance of programme graduates in their programme-related job and often include the use of graduate and employer surveys. Such evaluations seek evidence of the degree to which the programme has reduced/eliminated student educational needs, longer-term as well as unintended programme effects, and evidence of programme effectiveness (value) at the societal level (Fitzpatrick, Sanders and Worthen, 2003). Impact evaluation also seeks to determine how staff and faculty attitudes, behaviours and goals have changed because of the programme. Often, the focus of impact evaluation is on determining longer-term value-added by the programme, such as determining the economic dividend of the programme in terms of the increased individual earnings by graduates that can be attributed to the programme. Metrics that can be used to assess programme impacts include:

- performance on external or professional licensure examinations;
- success of graduates in their profession;
- employment and career mobility;
- benefits of the learning to an employer;
- changes in graduates' job performance;
- percentage of graduates seeking further education (i.e. commitment to lifelong learning);
- changes in staff and faculty perceptions regarding the programme;
- enhanced incomes and lifestyles;
- economic dividend to society; and
- return on investment by measuring the monetary benefits of the programme versus programme costs.

Administrators and educations must be cautious of how they apply and interpret value-added metrics. For example, value-added measurements for incoming students with strong academic preparation will likely be modest compared with those who enter the institution with poor preparation. Additionally, some institutions may experience perverse incentives to have their entering students score poorly on pre-tests or entrance tests to make the performance of their graduates look especially good (Lederman, 2008).

Assessment of programme utility is a critical element of a summative programme evaluation. The evaluator assesses programme utility by combining the results of programme impact (i.e. value added in terms of outcomes) and programme efficiency (i.e. benefits in terms of costs). The ultimate purpose of such evaluations is to help determine whether continuing the programme in its current form is worth the cost. Unless one assesses programme costs and balances these costs against programme outcomes, one cannot determine whether the impact was worth the cost. For example, some programmes may not be worth their high cost when compared with their impact. However, improving efficiencies as the result of process evaluations can possibly reduce high costs and improve programme utility.

Course evaluation

Course evaluation is an important aspect of distance education programme evaluation, programme accreditation and programme improvement. Course evaluations should be based on information collected from multiple sources, such as student evaluation of teaching, peer review of teaching, teaching portfolios, virtual classroom observations and self-evaluation (Seldin, 2007). These evaluations typically include four steps: selection of the standards or objectives and related performance indicators; setting the level of planned performance (i.e. the target); collecting data and comparing actual performance versus the target; and making a value judgment regarding the course (Reiser and Dempsey, 2007). Course evaluations are most often used to obtain evidence to support merit pay, promotion and tenure decisions, as well as inputs to programme evaluations. When used for high-stakes decisions regarding faculty members, the focus of the evaluation is on summative evaluation of teaching effectiveness. However, formative purposes are also essential to maintaining and improving the quality of teaching and learning.

The danger is that course evaluation as implemented at specific institutions may place too much emphasis on supporting summative purposes and too little emphasis on formative purposes. A comprehensive course evaluation system should embrace both high-stakes decision-making regarding the course and the teacher as well as developing faculty, improving the course and nurturing the scholarship of teaching.

Parker Palmer (1998) criticises institutional culture that keeps teaching privatised. He notes the tendency of many teachers to teach solo and out of collegial sight. As a result, the teacher has little or no shared experience related to teaching and therefore does not tend to speak to colleagues about what has happened or what needs to happen next. He claims that one price we pay for such privatisation is evaluation practices that are distanced, demoralising and even disreputable.

Four pillars of valid course evaluation and quality assurance are student evaluation of teaching, peer review of teaching, supervisor evaluation and self-evaluation. Most researchers and educational administrators believe that student evaluation of teaching results are the single most reliable indicator of teaching effectiveness, assuming the underlying construct or model of teaching effectiveness is an accurate reflection of local values and orientations (e.g. see Rovai, Ponton, Derrick and Davis, 2006). Notwithstanding these positive views, there are weaknesses.

Student evaluation of teaching

Simplistic questionnaires used in student evaluations or questionnaires that ask the wrong questions 'are not simply the result of administrative malfeasance, as faculty sometimes complain. They are the outcome of a faculty culture that offers no alternative' (Palmer, 1998: 143). Consequently, 'good talk about good teaching is unlikely to happen if presidents ... deans and department chairs and others who have influence without position, do not expect it and invite it into being' (Palmer, 1998: 156).

Although administrators view teacher evaluations based on student ratings as valid, faculty members often tend to question this source of assessment data. Nonetheless, student evaluations are used more than any other method to evaluate teaching performance (Seldin, 2007). However, there are risks in placing too much emphasis on such evaluations. As James asserts:

> Students are well-equipped to judge the quality of certain aspects of higher education and we should trust their intuitions on these matters. Generally speaking, students are in a reasonable position to judge the more tangible, short-term components of the experience and to judge aspects of the process of higher education ... But the student expectation-quality relationship is not altogether this straightforward ... There are deeper dimensions to quality in

higher education ... [that] are usually less tangible, less intuitive and require a longer term view. Students are not necessarily in the best position to judge these aspects... (R. James, 2001: 8)

Evidence of faculty concerns and unintended negative consequences of using student evaluation of teaching scores for high-stakes decisions are evident in Michael Birnbaum's (1998) survey of 208 college faculty members at a large California public university. He reports that 65.4 per cent of surveyed faculty members believe that stricter grading standards would have a negative effect on students' evaluations, while 72.1 per cent of the respondents admitted to watering down their courses in an attempt to increase evaluation scores. Ironically, this outcome conflicts with the formative purpose of student evaluations, namely to improve the quality of instruction.

In a review of the professional literature, Rovai, Ponton, Derrick and Davis (2006) report that while research results tend to be mixed on this topic, student evaluation of teaching may include the following response biases:

- *Course characteristics*
  - smaller on-campus courses are evaluated more favourably than larger courses;
  - elective courses are rated higher than required courses;
  - courses in the humanities and arts are evaluated the highest, social science courses come next, followed by mathematics and science courses.
- *Student characteristics*
  - low positive relationships exist between student evaluations and the student's expected or actual course grade;
  - little to no bias based on student gender, age, or personality.
- *Teacher characteristics*
  - teacher's rank, experience, autonomy and research productivity influence evaluations only slightly in a positive direction;
  - gender has a negligible effect;
  - teachers with positive self-regard, self-esteem, energy, enthusiasm and a positive view of others have a positive influence on student evaluations, but a very small effect on student achievement, suggesting student ratings may be unduly influenced by teacher personality and form of presentation.

The response rate issue is also a serious threat to the validity of student evaluations. If non-responding students differ from respondents in their evaluation of the course, then the conclusion one draws from responding students is questionable. Generally, response rates need to be 70 per cent or higher for the assessment data to be credible.

Ponzurick, France and Logar (2000) have found evidence to suggest that many online students enrol in online courses primarily because of convenience but also feel that the online learning format is less satisfying than the traditional classroom. One would expect that students possessing such feelings could introduce bias in the student evaluation process by evaluating online courses lower than on-campus courses because of the delivery medium rather than teacher effectiveness. The issues then become: (a) how professors can become more effective in online learning environments, and (b) whether professors should be held accountable for lower course evaluations introduced as the result of the course delivery medium.

Peer review of teaching

While students are best qualified to evaluate the teaching process from the perspective of learners, supervisors and peers are in a much better position to provide judgments on course goals and objectives, course organisation and content, assessment of disciplinary competence, currency of course materials, course design, and the teacher's subject matter expertise (Chism, 1999). Consequently, supervisor and peer reviews are important components of a complete, balanced and fair evaluation of teaching effectiveness. Moreover, while student evaluations are valuable for course improvement, they should not be used for summative decision-making because of their potential for bias, unless confirmed by other sources of information.

Research evidence (e.g. Brinko and Menges, 1997) shows that the simple provision of student evaluation data has little or no improvement effect on teaching, whereas data accompanied by support from knowledgeable peers, supervisors and faculty development staff can enhance teaching success. However, the validity and reliability of peer ratings of teaching are not as well established as they are for student evaluations.

Institutions using peer review to evaluate teaching effectiveness should follow sound procedures in selecting and training reviewers; establish guidelines, criteria and standards for the reviews; and collect data to assess the validity and reliability of the reviews (Chism, 1999). The risk in using peer reviews without careful planning is the possibility of a clash between the institutional culture of collegiality and accountability on the one hand, and valid peer evaluations on the other, particularly if such evaluations are to be used for summative purposes. Parker Palmer (1998: 103) recommends the adoption of a holistic approach to peer review based on multiple observations and collegial conversations, as well as self-reflections that result in 'a communal effort to stretch each other and make better sense of the world'.

Peer reviews of online courses should be based on best practices confirmed by research as well as institutional and accreditation standards. The review should address course design, the specific teaching methods used by the online teacher, course content and delivery. The review should be team-based and consist of a course designer and two or three faculty peer reviewers, if possible. All peer reviewers should be experienced in online teaching and have completed institutional training in the purpose and conduct of peer reviews, focusing on the quality and alignment of the following course components:

- *course introduction*: the course provides students with an overview that clearly identifies all course requirements and expectations, identifies how students can obtain help or get their questions answered and provides an opportunity for the teacher and students to become acquainted;
- *instructional objectives*: objectives are SMART (i.e. they are specific, measurable, achievable, realistic and time-bound);
- *instruction*: instruction and content are appropriate for the audience and aligned with both the instructional objectives and assessments, active learning is fostered, multiple teaching methods are evident, and both independent and collaborative learning techniques are used;
- *student interactions*: requirements are clearly articulated, both socio-emotional and task-oriented interactions are valued, teacher presence and student presence are evident, and constructivist discourse is promoted and maintained;
- *use of resources and technology*: appropriate technology tools and media are used to facilitate learning, and navigation throughout the course is consistent and clear;
- *assessment of student learning*: assessments are properly aligned with instructional objectives and instruction, moreover, they are mostly performance-oriented, possess a meaningful and authentic context,

are linked to pedagogy, and tap higher-level thinking and problem-solving skills. Feedback is comprehensive and timely.

Conclusion

Planning, assessment, evaluation and continuous improvement represent the cornerstone of institutional effectiveness. Evaluation in higher education is an instrument of public policy associated with efficiency, performance measurement, quality assurance and accountability. On the basis of evaluation, programmes are improved and quality is assured. The design of the institution's or programme's assessment system is an important element in monitoring institutional effectiveness. Credible assessment systems (Ewell, 2001):

- provide evidence about the full range of student learning outcomes established by the institution or programme;
- utilise multiple sources of evidence in a mutually reinforcing way to examine outcomes;
- examine different facets of student performance with respect to established learning outcomes so that patterns of strength and weakness can be identified; and
- emphasise direct measures of student attainment instead of self-reports about learning or proxy indicators of attainment like graduation rates or graduate placement.

However, there remains the question of whose vision of quality is being assured? Is quality defined by outside sources, such as government, accrediting agencies or school administrators, or do academicians who were presumably hired because of their expertise in the field determine quality? Clearly there must be a balance between increased public scrutiny and accountability of the quality of academic processes and outcomes in the form of externally-imposed standards, and the need for self-management of the university and academicians setting their own agendas and standards. Moreover, the increased emphasis on conformity versus non-conformity has unknown implications for the academy over the longer term.

Each nation possesses its own system for quality assurance in higher education and each system continues to evolve. As a result, what constitutes a quality programme will vary from nation to nation as there are many variations of evaluation and institutional accreditation. Guy Neave (2004) notes that one dimension of this transition is a move away from viewing higher education as a subset of the political system (i.e. the selection, formation and enculturation of elites) to its redefinition as a subset of the economic system (i.e. the training of the masses for the private sector). Moreover, the globalisation of higher education and the use of distance education in the cross-border reach of institutions have led and will continue to lead to additional pressures for change, such as represented by the Bologna Process.

The quality of distance education programmes influences both the accreditation status of the institution as whole as well as individual programmes for which accreditation is sought. Additionally:

> the high probability that cross-border and for-profit provision is not covered by national systems for quality assurance, accreditation and recognition of qualifications may increase the risk that students/learners are victim of rogue providers ('degree mills'), offering low quality educational experiences and qualifications of limited validity. (OECD, 2004: 23)

Higher education is traditionally viewed as an investment in human capital. The benefits of higher education cannot be fully known or realised during the short term. Consequently, what Robert Birnbaum (2001: 216) refers to as 'a trust market, in which people do not know exactly what they are buying [in higher education] and may not discover its [true] value for years', will likely become increasingly irrelevant as colleges move toward the corporate economic model and accrediting agencies insist on evaluating programmes based on measurable shorter-term outcomes. Bok (2003) cautions:

> No university can measure the value of its research output or determine reliably how much its students are learning ... For this reason, efforts to adapt the corporate model by trying to measure performance ... are much more difficult and dangerous for universities than they are for commercial enterprises. (Bok, 2003: 30)

Consequently, there is a risk that the needs of institutions to expand enrolments and meet financial goals by adopting the business model will take precedence over serving the public good. Consumerism and the utilitarian value of higher education, e.g. increased prestige and opportunities for better employment, should not trump educating students, especially they do not foster an environment conducive to nurturing intellectual inquiry and development, providing a liberal education and infusing civic engagement in academic life (Rovai, Ponton and Baker, 2008).

7

Summary and conclusion

Introduction

The purpose of this book is to make accessible, in a clear and concise form, a body of current evidence-based knowledge regarding online distance learning in higher education to increase understanding of the major theories, issues, challenges and possible solutions. The focus is on global learning and cross-border provision as this book explores the implications of a culturally and nationally diverse student base and issues related to quality assurance and accreditation of domestic and cross-border programmes. The following six sections summarise the first six chapters of this volume.

Key concepts of global online higher education

The key concepts described in the first chapter include copyright and intellectual property rights, globalisation and internationalisation, multicultural online learning, constructivism, adult learning, sense of community, presence and self-direction. These concepts are briefly summarised below.

The internet facilitates information access as well as the unauthorised copying of information. The central feature of the Berne Convention for the Protection of Literary and Artistic Works is automatic copyright protection. No copyright notice is required. Most nations follow this convention. Individuals should assume other people's works are copyrighted and may not be copied unless one knows otherwise. Individuals charged with the development and delivery of distance education programmes need to become aware of the scope of copyright protection as well as the exceptions to the provisions of copyright laws regarding fair use and dealing. As many of the provisions of copyright law focus on the behaviour of institutions, online teachers and students must become familiar with their institution's copyright policy and procedures.

The next concept, globalisation, is the process of increasing international interdependence. As applied to higher education, it refers to extending global reach and integrating global learning in university programmes. The major goal of global reach is to increase student diversity in order to provide the diverse human resources needed for meaningful and authentic communication about real-world issues from multiple perspectives. The major goals of global learning consist of acquiring knowledge about global cultures and issues, gaining skills related to cooperative problem solving, viewing issues from multiple perspectives and attaining attitudes related to global awareness and respect for diversity.

One theoretical approach to achieving global competence is posited by M. J. Bennett (1993). This model incorporates concepts from constructivism and cognitive psychology to describe six stages of sensitivity to cultural differences. Bennett describes three ethnocentric stages of development (denial, defence and minimisation) and three ethnorelative stages (acceptance, adaptation and integration). This model assumes that intercultural competence increases as people progress through these increasingly complex reactions to different cultures. A global learning experience is more effective for the learners when a high degree of cultural contrast is provided.

Multicultural education combines global competence education with domestic education in a culturally diverse learning community to meet the educational needs of the twenty-first century. It is a field of study and an emerging discipline where the major aim is to create equal educational opportunities for students from diverse racial, ethnic and cultural groups (Banks and Banks, 1995). It interrogates, challenges and reinterprets content, concepts and paradigms, as appropriate, from various fields and uses the results to modify pedagogy and curricula. Multicultural education provides inclusive, interactive and collaborative teaching and learning. Applied to an international environment, an important goal of multicultural education is to prepare students to become global citizens by becoming globally competent. Without global competence, students lack the skills to address national security needs and are unlikely to compete successfully in the global marketplace.

Social constructivism and adult learning theory support multicultural education and form the basis for much of the learning that takes place in distance education programmes. Constructivism emphasises the importance of culture, context and social interaction in constructing knowledge, while adult learning emphasises experiential, self-directed and applied learning. Instruction based on these perspectives stresses the need for collaboration among learners and practitioners, and to use the life experiences of students. These principles are important aspects of multicultural education.

Because of the emphasis by social constructivism on interaction, effective communication is an important prerequisite to effective learning, and effective online communication requires the elimination of technical, psychological and semantic barriers. Elimination of these barriers is especially important in a global learning environment where multiple cultures are likely to be represented with their culturally-related communication patterns and ways of communicating.

Successful distance education students tend to be self-motivated, independent and self-directed. Self-directed learners autonomously control their own learning and manifest such characteristics as independence, self-management and motivation to learn, and make use of learning resources and personally-developed learning strategies to overcome the difficulties that occur in the learning process. Such characteristics are especially valuable in a multicultural virtual classroom.

A strong sense of community has an important role in supporting self-direction. It does so by building trust among learning community members, encouraging teacher and student presence in the virtual classroom, facilitating social construction of knowledge, and providing students social support as they progress through their own self-directed activities. Ultimately, a strong sense of community can facilitate learning.

Global distance education issues

The major global distance education issues discussed in the second chapter deal with student outcomes, student access to technology and higher education, student global diversity, racial and cultural discrimination, and academic capitalism and consumerism. The quality of student outcomes is especially important, as the student is the major focus of distance education programmes.

Physical separation of students from each other and the teacher can lead to a weak sense of community, disconnectedness, isolation, distraction and reduced personal attention, which, in turn, can contribute to lower student persistence, reduced student success and lower student satisfaction when compared with traditional classroom programmes. Developing a strong sense of community can improve student outcomes by promoting cohesiveness, consistency, affiliation and satisfaction with group efforts.

The exclusion of some people from higher education and from the technology to participate in distance education is another important issue. A major reason for the exclusion of some people from distance education is inequitable access to information and communication technologies, both within and between nations. This is often referred to as the first-level digital divide. The second-level digital divide is a result of the poor technology knowledge and skills of some individuals. While economic, cultural and social factors have a greater role to play in narrowing the gap in the first-level of the digital divide, educational factors are more important in closing the gap in online skills. Rapid changes in technology and the proliferation of information sources require individuals to possess the knowledge and skills that enable them to identify information needs, locate relevant information sources, and synthesise information from a variety of sources for productive uses, as well as being able to participate effectively in online distance education.

The next issue is student global diversity. Respect and trust are fundamental to learning. The integration of multiple cultural perspectives in the content and structures of distance learning programmes and the use of a multicultural approach to teaching and learning require the establishment of a climate of respect and trust with minimal miscommunication. It is therefore important that teachers understand how culture influences teaching and learning along multiple dimensions. The major dimensions described in this book include high and low power distances, individualism and collectivism, masculinity and femininity, high and low uncertainty avoidances, long and short-term orientations, high and low-context communications and field dependent and independent orientations.

Cultural diversity is often accompanied by racial and cultural discrimination, which represents another major global distance education issue. Freedom, without distinction to race, colour or national origin, is recognised by the United Nations as a basic human right. Nonetheless, discrimination is often a feature of cross-cultural social interaction.

In a classroom setting, discrimination can manifest itself with an 'us' versus 'them' orientation. Such an attitude can lead to the ability of the dominant group to control the flow of communication and to influence the behaviour and thought processes of others. Such a climate can hinder minority student contribution to classroom discussions and other activities fostered by intellectual engagement. The resulting sense of alienation can create an unfriendly classroom climate for minorities where social connections are limited or do not exist. In a global distance education programme, in-class validation is the most practical approach, and the most important validating agent in this environment is the online teacher.

Academic capitalism and consumerism is the final major issue discussed in the second chapter. The new and growing international competition in higher education is increasingly based on economics rather than the political, cultural and academic rationales that were historically the main driving forces in higher education. Academic capitalism is not simply a matter of entrepreneurial universities seeking to generate more revenues. It is also a matter of these institutions behaving more like private enterprises (Rhoades, 2006). Consequently, more market-susceptible universities are taking such actions as eliminating non-self-supporting departments, increasing activities that generate revenues, outsourcing services that can be provided by others at less cost, and adjusting or creating programmes that respond to student interests and desires, rather than to societal needs, in order to attract more student customers.

Consumerism assumes the consumer student knows best what must be learned and how best it should be taught, notwithstanding the fact that the student, by definition, is not the expert in either area, although one can argue that students do know some of the things they need to learn to be successful in their chosen field (Rovai, Ponton and Baker, 2008). Additionally, the economic model that is typically aligned with consumerism values market-oriented decision-making, efficiency, product standardisation and tight control of the workforce in order to achieve cost-effectiveness and productivity gains. These values differ from the more traditional higher education values of shared governance, academic freedom, public service and pursuit of scholarship. The risk is that higher education institutions will become retailers of instructional commodities and will take care of some of their customers by tailoring academic rigour and standards to their customers' demands.

Technology and the internet

Advances in information and communication technology have had a significant impact on the way teachers teach and the way students learn. Old pedagogy delivered with new technology does not work.

Additionally, a major challenge for distance education is keeping up with the rapid advances in educational technology, especially Web 2.0 technologies and the advent of the social web to further empower discourse and allow members of the learning community to extend their social reach using a variety of technological tools. These technologies provide additional communication tools that foster a social constructivist learning environment.

The effects of computer-mediated communication (CMC) depend upon the type of CMC as well as on the communicators and their culturally-related communication-style preferences. The biggest appeal of CMC is its ability to eliminate the physical distance between individuals and thus provide the means to facilitate online distance education at a relatively low cost. However, CMC can also reduce the social boundaries imposed by traditional norms and social rules because of the relative increase in anonymity it has over face-to-face communication. Because of the global reach of distance education, different cultures within the same nation as well as cross-border cultural differences must be considered.

The emergence of new social web tools, such as video podcasts that provide a richer form of communication, can help level the communication playing field in a multicultural online learning environment, especially for students who are acculturated in high context cultures. The social web helps expand online learning from mostly instrumental learning using one-way transfer of information, to expressive learning, which supports self-fulfilment during the learning process and nurtures critical thinking skills. Moreover, richer forms of communication have the ability to assist all members of the learning community to improve social information processing, which is essential in a multicultural environment. The major challenge facing the global university is to determine how these cultural considerations influence the design and delivery of cross-border online distance education and the use of new Web 2.0 tools.

Designing global online programmes and courses

A new or revised distance education programme must fit within the mission of the university and support a defined need. Such programmes can be either blended or single-mode. There is a growing consensus in the literature that blended programmes are preferred over single-mode programmes. Consequently, there is a growing interest in combining distance education and face-to-face instruction into a blended learning model. Designers create a blended programme by adding face-to-face residencies to a distance education programme and/or including any mix of single-mode face-to-face and blended courses. Such blended designs help create a bond between the distant student and the institution, its faculty and other students, which can result in other benefits, such as increased student satisfaction with the programme, increased student loyalty to the institution, increased student persistence, and the formation of interpersonal connections with other students that facilitate online collaborative efforts.

In addition to blended programmes, distance education programmes can also be offered entirely at a distance. Such single-mode online programmes are designed without any on-campus components. In the absence of a campus-based experience, the institution must seek alternative ways to satisfy the needs that these experiences typically satisfy.

Student support services for both blended and single-mode distance education programmes must be as complete and as customer-oriented as those provided for on-campus students. In the case of the single-mode online programme, these services are likely to be the only link students have with the institution, apart from academic activities.

Distance education programme design provides purpose, organisation and structure to the programme using courses, residencies, as appropriate, and support services as the major building blocks. Course design serves a similar function at the course level. However, it uses technology tools, learning objects, readings, discussion topics and assessment tasks as the major building blocks. For blended courses, course design also incorporates a mix of online and face-to-face components. The challenge in constructivist design of online courses is finding the balance between group and individual work, between various asynchronous and synchronous tools, and between different teaching styles.

Instead of a technology-led course design, teaching and learning is better served by a pedagogy-led course design philosophy. Cultural values such as individualism, secularism and feminism, which one finds in many Western nations, are not all recognised as desirable in other cultures. Consequently, Western distance education programme and course designers need to carefully consider the implicit cultural values inherent in the programmes and courses they design. They should carefully consider the national cultures of the international students who are likely to enrol in the programme and determine whether the instructional design contains cultural and social bias. The danger is that international students will be treated as inferior by the institution and host nation students. Alternatively, there is the danger that the institution will be viewed as practising intellectual or academic imperialism. In other words, the institution may be viewed as an instrument of the host nation as it attempts to dominate the thinking of international students and change their culturally-related values and beliefs.

Global online teaching and learning

Some students learn better when teaching emphasises concrete, social and holistic approaches. Conversely, such students often find it difficult to learn through abstract and analytical learning approaches – approaches that other students may well prefer. Other students learn better during activities involving a visual rather than a verbal approach. Some students, particularly from Asian cultures, are more accustomed to assuming a compliant role and prefer not to distinguish themselves from other students, whereas others may be more accustomed to exercising individual initiative and engaging in competition. Some students prefer independent work while others prefer collaborative group work. The challenge for the online teacher is to provide a student-centred learning environment that addresses the academic needs of all students in an equitable manner.

An equitable environment promotes high levels of learning for all students. Interactive learning requires students to actively engage in discussions with each other, teachers and subject-matter experts, as appropriate, in order to construct knowledge. Web 2.0 technologies, such as blogs and wikis, as well as the more traditional discussion boards, are ideally suited to support these strategies. Online teachers must carefully select appropriate media based on student characteristics and the curriculum and offer balance in their use.

As universities achieve global reach, online courses will contain an increasing number of students from diverse cultures and nations. In all likelihood there will be cultural barriers to cross when engaging in interpersonal communication. Educational efforts must take these barriers into account. There is therefore a need for the online teacher to facilitate and moderate discussions in ways that appeal to the preferences of learners from diverse cultures. To achieve true sensitivity to cultural differences, pedagogy should be sensitive to and respect the deep structures of different cultures.

The natural inclination of teachers leads them to familiar ways of teaching, but most scholars now recognise that conventional methods may not work in a multicultural classroom. Providers of educational programmes across national boundaries have a responsibility to consider how their materials and practices can help promote effective cross-cultural interactions and learning.

Effective multicultural pedagogy creates knowledge and awareness of different cultures, and the implications of these differences to the content area being taught. Such pedagogy does not teach individuals to become 'colour blind' or tolerant. Instead it teaches students to celebrate and respect differences. Teaching tolerance would be counter-productive, as it places one culture in a dominant position over others. The ultimate goal of multicultural pedagogy is to place all cultures on an equal footing. Consequently, multicultural pedagogy is much more than acquisition of knowledge about different cultures. It transcends the cognitive domain of learning and includes the affective domain as students learn to value and respect other cultures.

In a pure sense, multicultural teaching is transformational teaching in which the teacher recognises how different forces affect and influence educational policies, curricula and practices. The multicultural teacher acknowledges that instructional decisions are often made based on ideologies not grounded in educational theory. Instead, they are often made based on beliefs influenced by history, politics, culture, language and power. Multicultural pedagogy also accommodates different learning styles, assists students to become acculturated in learning at a distance as well as learning using various technologies, and attends to different culturally-related communication patterns.

Quality assurance and institutional effectiveness

Numerous factors are forcing institutions to take a closer look at quality assurance and institutional effectiveness. These factors include the recent growth in international student mobility and the increase in various forms of cross-border provision of distance education, increasing demands for accountability in higher education, rising expectations of employers and students, growing financial pressures, expansion of consumerism and academic capitalism, growing importance of globalisation, emergence of lifelong learning, efforts to make instruction more learner-centred and the explosive growth of distance education (Rovai, Ponton and Baker, 2008).

Quality assurance assumes that quality is first defined in order to establish a standard so that it can be evaluated. It also requires the development of quality improvement goals to meet institutional goals and objectives, and the identification of performance metrics to assess quality. Quality assurance issues for the global university include whether or not curricula should be standardised or tailored for targeted markets and how to handle the cultural issues described above.

Institutional effectiveness is a closely related construct. It is a system designed to improve an institution and demonstrate the extent to which it has been effective in fulfilling its mission. Planning, assessment and evaluation, combined with continuous improvement represent the basic tenets of institutional effectiveness. Because student learning is a fundamental component of the mission of higher education institutions, the assessment of student learning is a key element of institutional effectiveness.

Each nation possesses its own system for quality assurance in higher education and each system continues to evolve. As a result, what constitutes a quality programme will vary from nation to nation, as there are many variations of quality assurance and institutional accreditation. Additionally, national efforts focus on domestic delivery by domestic institutions. International distance education students must be protected from low-quality provision and disreputable distance education providers. Consequently, there is a need for additional national and international initiatives regarding cross-border accreditation and the recognition of qualifications.

Conclusion

The six major themes or strands of this book are:

- the emergence of a global learning society and the role of online distance education to satisfy the higher educational needs of this society;

- transformational changes in higher education on a global scale as the result of advances in information and communication technology, the expansion of distance education using the internet, and the resurgence of interest in diversifying methods of educational delivery;

- the changing patterns of learning required to respond to evolving individual and societal needs as learning becomes more open and accessible, largely as the result of a growing need for lifelong learning as the knowledge and skills needed by the workforce require periodic renewal;

- the impact of online delivery on course and programme design and delivery, especially regarding media selected to provide course content and computer-mediated communication using Web 2.0 technologies;

- the importance of a multicultural approach to higher education as the result of the presence of globally diverse students; and

- the incorporation of global learning themes across the curriculum, such as peace and conflict, human rights and social justice, cultural diversity, global awareness, interdependence, environmental education and sustainable futures, development education, the role of religion, and global problem solving.

A major advantage the virtual classroom holds over the face-to-face classroom is the ease of its ability to bring together a culturally and physically diverse learning community. However, this ability is not without its own set of challenges. These challenges, discussed below, consist of:

- assuring the quality of distance education;

- improving access to distance education;

- implementing fair and equitable teaching methods;

- globalising the curriculum; and

- determining the institution's multiculturalist-assimilationist orientation.

The first challenge is assuring the quality of distance education. Some critics of distance education suggest that its expansion is being driven by demand rather than sound pedagogy. Improving quality in a rapidly-changing technological environment with diverse student needs requires sustained research to identify best practices.

Instructional methods used in traditional face-to-face classrooms remain relatively constant over time, resulting in a fairly stable course design. However, this is not necessarily the case with online distance education courses. One impact of the rapid pace of technological advances is the need to continuously assess how these advances can improve online course delivery and to redesign online courses as needed.

Such efforts are based on pedagogy-led use of technology, where technological enhancements clearly advance learning outcomes.

The focus of distance education quality assurance is on the student, however, which can promote consumerism. Consumerism and the utilitarian value of higher education, e.g. increased prestige and opportunities for better employment, should not trump educating students, especially if it does not foster an environment conducive to nurturing intellectual inquiry and development, providing a liberal education, and infusing civic engagement in academic life (Rovai, Ponton and Baker, 2008). Attempting to satisfy some students may become synonymous with lowering the degree of challenge, refraining from intellectually stretching students beyond their comfort zones during the educational process, awarding higher grades, and placing more emphasis on entertaining rather than educating students. Consequently, there is a risk that the needs of institutions to expand enrolments and meet financial goals by fully embracing the business model will take precedence over serving the public good.

To assure quality in a global learning environment, it is vital that distance education programmes use student data to make programme improvements. Student data should include information on student exposure to global content, but more importantly, data must also address how the programme impacts student understanding, attitudes and behaviour, and the extent to which it meets programme quality standards.

The second challenge is improving access to distance education. Internet technology, which is the backbone of online distance education, has challenges regarding access and equity for disadvantaged groups. Equity is achieved by providing equal opportunity for everyone to achieve his or her potential. Individuals who would benefit the most from online distance education do not all have personal computers and internet connectivity, or possess the knowledge and skills to use computers. Although internet access worldwide is growing, many nations still possess a poor telecommunications infrastructure. Given the ongoing global expansion of the internet and online distance education, there is an urgent need for national and international bodies to adopt effective measures to bring affordable internet access to personal users.

Additionally, institutions seeking to extend their global reach through online distance education must make their programmes affordable to individuals in less-developed nations, perhaps based on a strategy of economy of scale and the judicious use of partnerships. However, the institution is likely to incur substantial start-up expenses in establishing programmes for a global audience, particularly in the development of programme content and the design of courses.

The third challenge is implementing fair and equitable teaching methods. A culturally diverse learning community presents a challenge on how best to integrate students with different culturally-related values, beliefs, worldviews, learning styles and communication patterns. Cultural differences can result in unequal treatment of students and differential impact on learning. Consequently, institutional quality assurance efforts should collect and disaggregate data on student retention, participation and learning outcomes based on culture, gender and ethnicity in order to judge whether or not students are treated fairly.

The professional literature highlights the importance of using a variety of learning and teaching styles in a multicultural learning environment. Typically, higher education faculty members focus on using teaching styles that are compatible with the nation's dominant culture. For example, North American and Eurocentric education tends to focus on teaching to students who are competitive, inquiry-driven and prefer independent work. However, multicultural education is grounded in the democratic values of equality and justice. It is about equalising opportunities to learn, and it involves designing and presenting instruction that attends to individuals with diverse learning needs and learning style preferences.

The fourth challenge is globalising the curriculum. Figure 7.1 provides an example of a global learning programme that includes two programme components, implementation strategies for each component, desired student learning outcomes, and direct programme effect for students and ultimate goal effect for graduates. Globalising the curriculum not only benefits international students, but also benefits domestic students and the institution itself. Educators must rethink traditional approaches to higher education, both in and outside of the classroom and develop new methods and content that nurture global competence among students.

Globalising the curriculum is not limited to adding international issues to the curriculum, learning about other cultures and increasing proficiency in cross-cultural communication. Each profession must carefully consider what globalising the curriculum means, as it can mean different things for different professions. One purpose for globalising the curriculum is to improve the understanding and global application of each profession, e.g. by addressing how world societies face common problems and examining the multiple ways in which the profession can address these problems. Another purpose is to prepare students for

Figure 7.1 Example of a global learning programme

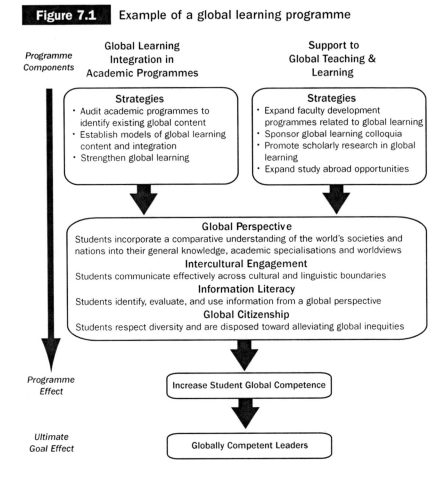

global citizenship in an era of globalisation by making their outlook less insular regarding global issues.

The final challenge is determining the institution's multiculturalist-assimilationist orientation. As education touches everyone, its impact can change society. Consequently, global universities must carefully consider how their programmes are changing diverse global societies. Institutions seeking a globally diverse student body need to identify and publicise where they situate themselves on the multiculturalist-assimilationist continuum. The major issue to address is how to overcome the weaknesses of multiculturalism and assimilation while reinforcing their strengths. Global universities must find their own level of comfort along the multiculturalist-assimilationist continuum.

Assimilation can injure minority cultures by removing their distinctive features. Moreover, global universities should not automatically assume the role of delivering programmes to assimilate or integrate their international students in the domestic culture. They should also avoid practices that promote the maintenance of one group's cultural values while merely tolerating the values of others. On the other hand, universities should guard against relativism and the concept that all beliefs and values are equal. The imperative is to create a proper balance between the need to treat all cultures as equal and the need to recognise universal truths that everyone must follow, regardless of cultural heritage. Global universities must focus on dealing with diverse cultures without creating new boundaries or reinforcing old ones between cultural groups. In so doing they must first look introspectively at who they are and what and how they teach, in order to align teaching with their guiding values and beliefs.

Appendix

Example of a unit effectiveness report template

Academic unit name	Academic year

Unit mission

Unit conceptual framework

Unit inputs

Proportion of full-time faculty by academic rank, gender, and race
Full-time female faculty salaries as a proportion of male salaries by rank
Full-time minority faculty salaries as a proportion of Caucasian salaries by rank
Domestic and international student aid as a ratio of tuition fees
Part-time/full-time faculty ratio
Percentage of courses that are single-mode online

University goals/objectives	Measures	Unit statistics
University goals/objectives	Unit goals	Unit accomplishments

Faculty scholarship

Bibliography of faculty publications, performances, shows, etc. by faculty member
(a) Books (exclude self-published books)
(b) Book chapters
(c) Volume editing
(d) Journal publications (peer-reviewed journals only)
(e) Exhibitions and performances
(f) Proceedings, manuals, supplementary materials, and book reviews

Faculty service and ongoing activity

Internal unit and university service
External service

Unit outcomes

Gross profit (income less expenses), shown over last five years
Percentage of expenses for personnel (faculty and staff), shown over last five years
Percentage operating expense by expense category, shown over last five years
Other relevant outcomes (if any)

Use of assessment results to improve unit effectiveness

Findings
How has the unit been affected?
What specific actions remain to be taken? By what date?
What changes, if any, were made to the unit strategic plan as a result of these findings?

Example of an academic programme effectiveness report template

Academic programme name	Academic year

Programme purpose

Brief programme description

Type of programme (single-mode online, blended, single-mode face-to-face)
Programme accreditation status
Description of the criteria for admission, retention, and exit from the programme
Description of the relationship of the programme to the unit's conceptual framework

Programme inputs (current year)

Mean score on entrance examination
Entering student previous grade point average
No. applicants
   No. applicants accepted
   No. applicants enrolled
Percentage male
Percentage female
Percentage international
Percentage national minority
Ratio of full-time international students versus domestic students
Student/faculty ratio
Part-time/full-time student ratio
Part-time/full-time faculty ratio
Percentage of faculty with terminal degree
Percentage of courses taught by full-time faculty
Other relevant inputs (if any)

Programme learning goals

Describe the relevant learning goals from the programme

Course learning goals

List supporting courses and identify relevant learning goals from each course

Course learning outcomes

Describe desired course learning outcomes

Programme processes (current year)

Gratification (i.e. the extent to which the programme enhances the students'
    self-esteem and sense of integrity)
Peer evaluation of teaching
Student satisfaction, as measured by regular surveys
Number and nature of student complaints
Timeliness of faculty and staff feedback
Quality of faculty
Student reasons for refunds and enrolment termination
Quality of student effort
Faculty satisfaction
Adequacy of support services
Student participation rates in support services
Quality of vendor support
Achievement on major assignments
Other relevant inputs (if any)

Programme outcomes (current year)

Student satisfaction
Faculty satisfaction
Staff satisfaction
Learning proficiencies (% not meeting, % meeting, % exceeding standards)
First attempt comprehensive exam pass rate (if appropriate)
Graduation rates by entering cohort after seven years at the university
Graduation rates (by male, female, international, national minority)
First attempt licensing examination pass rate (if appropriate)
Ratio of net tuition revenue over gross tuition revenue
Other relevant outcomes (if any)

Use of assessment results to improve programme effectiveness

Findings
How have results been used to improve the instructional process?
How have programme and academic courses been affected?
What specific actions remain to be taken? By what date?
What changes, if any, were made to the unit strategic plan as a result of these findings?

Bibliography

Abrami, P. C. and Bures, E. M. (1996) 'Computer-supported collaborative learning and distance education', *The American Journal of Distance Education* 10(2): 37–42.

Agar, M. (2002) *Understanding the Culture of Conversation*, New York: Perennial.

Allan, J. (2007) 'Snapshot of a generation: bridging the theory–practice divide with project-based learning', *Australian Journal of Adult Learning* 47(1): 78–93.

Allen, E. and Seaman, J. (2004) *Entering the Mainstream: The Quality and Extent of Online Education in the United States, 2003 and 2004.* Needham and Wellesley, MA: Sloan Consortium.

Allport, G. W. (1954) *The Nature of Prejudice*, Cambridge, MA: Addison-Wesley.

American Council on Education (2006) 'Global learning for all', available at: *http://www.acenet.edu/AM/Template.cfm?Section=IntCurrent&Template=/CM/HTMLDisplay.cfm&ContentID=9391* (accessed 1 March 2008).

American Council on International Intercultural Education (1996) *Educating for the Global Community: A Framework for Community Colleges*, Washington, DC: American Council on International Intercultural Education.

Anderson, J. R., Greeno, J. G., Reder, L. M. and Simon, H. A. (2000) 'Perspectives on learning, thinking, and activity', *Educational Researcher* 29(4): 11–13.

Anderson, L. W. and Krathwohl, D. R. (eds) (2001) *A Taxonomy for Learning, Teaching, and Assessing: A Revision of Bloom's Taxonomy of Educational Objectives*, New York: Longman.

Angelo, T. A. and Cross, P. K. (1993) *Classroom Assessment Techniques* (2nd edn), San Francisco, CA: Jossey-Bass.

Anzai, Y. (2007) 'Empowering English learning utilizing podcasts', in G. Richards (ed.) *Proceedings of World Conference on E-Learning in Corporate, Government, Healthcare, and Higher Education, Quebec, 15–19 October 2007*, Chesapeake, VA: AACE, pp. 10–15.

Ashby, C. M. (2002) *Distance Education: Growth in Distance Education Programs and Implications for Federal Education Policy*, United States General Accounting Office Report GAO-02-1125T, Washington, DC: Government Printing Office.

Bain, K. (2004) *What the Best College Teachers Do*, Cambridge, MA: Harvard University Press.

Bal, J. and Teo, P. K. (2001) 'Implementing virtual team working: Part 2: A literature review', *Logistics Information Management* 14(3): 208–22.

Banks, J. A. (1988) *Multiethnic Education: Theory and Practice* (2nd edn), Boston, MA: Allyn and Bacon.

Banks, J. A. and Banks, C. A. M. (eds) (1995) *Handbook of Research on Multicultural Education*, New York: Macmillan.

Barker, B. O., Frisbie, A. G. and Patrick, K. R. (1989) 'Broadening the definition of distance education in light of the new telecommunications technologies', *The American Journal of Distance Education* 3(1): 20–9.

Barrows, H. S. (1994) *Practice-Based Learning: Problem-Based Learning Applied to Medical Education*, Springfield, IL: Southern Illinois University School of Medicine.

Bates, A. W. (1995) *Technology, Open Learning and Distance Education*, London and New York: Routledge.

Belenky, M., Clinchy, B., Goldberger, N. and Tarule, J. (1997) *Women's Ways of Knowing: The Development of Self, Voice, and Mind (10th Anniversary Edition)*, New York: Basic Books.

Bell, J. E. and Watkins, R. A. (2006) 'Strategies in dealing with the Bologna process', *International Educator* 15(5): 70–3.

Bennett, C. I. (2006) *Comprehensive Multicultural Education: Theory and Practice* (6th edn), Needham Heights, MA: Allyn and Bacon.

Bennett, M. J. (1993) 'Towards ethnorelativism: a developmental model of intercultural sensitivity', in R. M. Paige (ed.) *Education for the intercultural experience*, Yarmouth, ME: Intercultural Press, pp. 21–71.

Berger, J. B., Cohen, B. P. and Zelditch, M., Jr. (1966) 'Status characteristics and expectation states', in J. Berger and M. Zelditch, Jr. (eds) *Sociological Theories in Progress, Vol. I*, Boston, MA: Houghton-Mifflin, pp. 26–46.

Bernard, R. M., Abrami, P. C., Lou, Y., Borokhovski, E., Wade, A., Wozney, L., Wallet, P. A., Fiset, M. and Huang, B. (2004) 'How does distance education compare with classroom instruction? A meta-analysis of the empirical literature', *Review of Educational Research* 74(3): 379–439.

Berne Convention (Paris Act) (1886/1979) *Berne Convention for the Protection of Literary and Artistic Works*, available at: *http://www.wipo.int/clea/docs_new/pdf/en/wo/wo001en.pdf* (accessed 24 June 2008).

Bhawuk, D. P. S. and Brislin, R. (1992) 'The measurement of intercultural sensitivity using the concepts of individualism and collectivism', *International Journal of Intercultural Relations* 16(4): 413–36.

Biggs, J. (1999) *Teaching for Quality Learning at University*, Oxford: Society for Research into Higher Education and Open University Press.

Birnbaum, M. H. (1998) 'A survey of faculty opinions concerning student evaluations of teaching', available at: *http://faculty.fullerton.edu/senatenews/page2.html* (accessed 18 September 2008).

Birnbaum, R. (2001) *Management Fads in Higher Education: Where They Come From, What They Do, Why They Fail*, San Francisco, CA: Jossey-Bass.

Bok, D. (2003) *Universities in the Marketplace*, Princeton, NJ: Princeton University Press.

Bonfadelli, H. (2002) 'The internet and knowledge gaps: a theoretical and empirical investigation', *European Journal of Communication* 17(1): 65–84.

Bordia, P. (1992) 'Face-to-face versus computer-mediated communication: a synthesis of the experimental literature', *The Journal of Business Communication* 34(1): 99–120.

Breneman, D. (2005) 'Entrepreneurship in higher education', in B. Pusser (ed.) *Arenas of entrepreneurship: Where nonprofit and for-profit institutions compete*, San Francisco, CA: Jossey-Bass, pp. 3–10.

Brinko, K. T. and Menges, R. J. (1997) *Practically Speaking: A Source Book for Instructional Consultants in Higher Education*, Stillwater, OK: New Forums Press.

Brooks-Young, S. (2005) 'Project-based learning: technology makes it realistic!', *Today's Catholic Teacher* 38(6): 35–9.

Brown, R. (2001) 'The process of community-building in distance learning classes', *Journal of Asynchronous Learning Networks* 5(2): 18–35.

Bruffee, K. A. (1995) 'Sharing our toys: cooperative learning versus collaborative learning', *Change* 27(1): 12–18.

Bryson, J. M. (2004) *Strategic Planning for Public and Nonprofit Organizations* (3rd edn), San Francisco, CA: Jossey-Bass.

Bull, P., Tyler, D. and Eaton, D. (2007) 'A neo-constructivist teaching tool: perceptions of HBCU faculty to podcasting as a teaching and learning tool', in C. Crawford, D. A. Willis, R. Carlsen, I. Gibson, K. McFerrin, J. Price and R. Weber (eds) *Proceedings of Society for Information Technology and Teacher Education International Conference, Antonio, TX, 26–30 March 2007*, Chesapeake, VA: AACE, pp. 1404–9.

Caffarella, R. S. (1993) 'Self-directed learning', in S. B. Merriam (ed.) *An Update on Adult Learning Theory. New Directions for Adult and Continuing Education, Vol. 57*, San Francisco, CA: Jossey-Bass, pp. 25–35.

Carr, S. (2000) 'As distance education comes of age, the challenge is keeping the students', *The Chronicle of Higher Education* 46(23): A39–A41.

Carter, J. A. and Rovai, A. P. (2007) 'Assessment for learning', in A. P. Rovai, L. B. Gallien, Jr. and H. R. Stiff-Williams (eds) *Closing the African American Achievement Gap in Higher Education*, New York: Teachers College Press, pp. 143–64.

Carter, R. T. (ed.) (2005) *Handbook of Racial-Cultural Psychology and Counseling: Theory and Research*, New York: John Wiley and Sons.

Case, R. (1993) 'Key elements of a global perspective', *Social Education* 57(6): 318–25.

Cayton, M. K. (2007) 'The commodification of wisdom', *The Chronicle of Higher Education* 53(45): B16.

Cerych, L. and Sabatier, P. (1986) *Great Expectations and Mixed Performances: The Implementation of European higher education reforms*, Stoke-on-Trent: Trentham Books.

Chambers, E. (2003) 'Cultural imperialism or pluralism? Cross-cultural electronic teaching in the humanities', *Arts and Humanities in Higher Education* 2(3): 249–64.

Chan, A. and Lee, M. J. W. (2005) 'An MP3 a day keeps the worries away: exploring the use of podcasting to address preconceptions and alleviate pre-class anxiety amongst undergraduate information technology students', in D. H. R. Spennemann and L. Burr (eds) *Good Practice in Practice. Proceedings of the Student Experience Conference, 5–7 September 2005*, Wagga Wagga, NSW: Charles Sturt University, pp. 58–70.

Chase, M., Macfadyen, L., Reeder, K. and Roche, J. (2002) 'Intercultural challenges in networked learning: hard technologies meet soft skills', *First Monday* 7(8), available at: *http://firstmonday.org/issues/issue7_8/chase/index.html* (accessed 3 August 2008).

Chen, A. and Mashhadi, A. (1998) 'Challenges and problems in designing and researching distance learning environments and communities', paper presented at the 1st Malaysian Educational Research Association Conference, Penang, 28–30 April.

Chickering, A. and Gamson, Z. (1991) 'Applying the seven principles for good practice in undergraduate education', *New Directions for Teaching and Learning, Vol. 47*, San Francisco, CA: Jossey-Bass.

Chism, N. V. (1999) *Peer Review of Teaching*, Bolton, MA: Anker.

Cohen, E. G. (1994) *Designing Groupwork Strategies for the Heterogeneous Classroom* (2nd edn), New York: Teachers College Press.

Cohen, E. G. (1997) 'Understanding status problems: sources and consequences', in E. G. Cohen and R. A. Lotan (eds) *Working for Equity in Heterogeneous Classrooms: Sociological Theory in Practice*, New York: Teachers College Press, pp. 61–76.

Collis, B. (1998) 'New didactics for university instruction: why and how?' *Computers and Education* 31(4): 373–93.

Collis, B. and Moonen, J. (2001) *Flexible Learning in a Digital World: Experiences and Expectations*, London: Kogan Page.

Collis, B., Parisi, D. and Ligorio, M. B. (1996) 'Adaptation of courses for trans-European tele-learning', *Journal of Computer Assisted Learning* 12(1): 47–62.

Collison, G., Elbaum, B., Haavind, S. and Tinker, R. (2000) *Facilitating Online Learning: Effective Strategies for Moderators*, Madison, WI: Atwood Publishing.

Conceição, S. (2002) 'The sociocultural implications of learning and teaching in cyberspace', in M. V. Alfred (ed) *New Directions for Adult and Continuing Education* No. 96, New York: Jossey-Bass, pp. 37–46.

Council for Higher Education Accreditation (CHEA), Institute for Research and Study of Accreditation and Quality Assurance (2002) *Accreditation and Assuring Quality in Distance Learning*, CHEA Monograph Series 2002, No. 1, Washington, DC: CHEA.

Covey, S. R. (2004) *The 7 Habits of Highly Effective People*, Glencoe, IL: Free Press.

Creswell, J. W. (1998) *Qualitative Inquiry and Research Design: Choosing among Five Traditions*, Thousand Oaks, CA: Sage.

Crozet, C., Liddicoat, A. J. and Lo Bianco, J. (1999) 'Intercultural competence: from language policy to language education', in J. Lo Bianco, A. J. Liddicoat and C. Crozet (eds) *Striving for the Third Place: Intercultural Competence through Language Education*, Geelong: Australian National Languages and Literacy Institute, Deakin University, pp. 1–20.

Cutler, R. H. (1995) 'Distributed presence and community in cyberspace', *Interpersonal Communication and Technology: A Journal for the 21st Century* 3(2): 12–32.

Cyr, D. (2002). *The Art of Global Thinking: Integrating Organizational Philosophies of East and West*, West Lafayette, IN: Purdue University Press.

Daft, R. L. and Lengel, R. H. (1986) 'Organizational information requirements, media richness and structural design', *Management Science* 32(5): 554–71.

Daniel, J. S. (2004) *Equity of Access to Quality Education: The Road to Poverty Alleviation*. Paris: UNESCO, available at: *http://portal.unesco .org/education/en/ev.php-URL_ID=31440&URL_DO=DO_TOPIC&URL_ SECTION=201.html* (accessed 31 August 2008).

Daniel, J. S., Kanwar, A. and Uvaliæ-Trumbiæ, S. (2005) 'Who's afraid of cross-border higher education? A developing world perspective', *Higher Education Digest* 52(Supplement): 1–8.

Daniel, J. S., Kanwar, A. and Uvaliæ-Trumbiæ, S. (2006) 'A tectonic shift in global higher education', *Change* 38(4): 16–23.

Darkwa, O. and Mazibuko, F. (2000) 'Creating virtual learning communities in Africa: challenges and prospects', *First Monday* 5(5), available at: *http://firstmonday.org/issues/issue5_5/darkwa/* (accessed 15 June 2008).

Dave, R. H. (1975) 'Psychomotor levels', in R. J. Armstrong (ed.) *Developing and Writing Behavioral Objectives*, Tucson, AZ: Educational Innovators Press, pp. 33–4.

Davison, C. and Williams, A. (2001) 'Integrating language and content: Unresolved issues', in B. Mohan, C. Leung and C. Davison (eds) *English as a Second Language in the Mainstream*, New York: Longman/Pearson, pp. 51–70.

Deardorff, D. (2006) 'Identification and assessment of intercultural competence as a student outcome of internationalization', *Journal of Studies in International Education* 10(3): 241–66.

Dennis, A. R. and Kinney, S. T. (1998) 'Testing media richness theory in the new media: the effects of cues, feedback, and task equivocality', *Information Systems Research* 9(3): 256–74.

Dick, W., Carey, L. and Carey, J. O. (2005) *The Systematic Design of Instruction* (6th edn), New York: Pearson.

DiMaggio, P., Celeste, C., Hargittai, E. and Shafer, S. (2004) 'Second-level digital divide: from unequal access to differential use', in K. Neckerman (ed.) *Social Inequality*, New York: Sage, pp. 355–400.

Dirkx, J. M. (1997) 'Nurturing soul in adult learning', in P. Cranton (ed.) *Transformative Learning in Action. New Directions for Adult and Continuing Education, No. 74*, San Francisco, CA: Jossey-Bass, pp. 79–88.

Dixon, C. and Greeson, M. (2006) 'Recasting the concept of podcasting (Part I)', available at: *http://news.digitaltrends.com/talkback109.html* (accessed 16 July 2008).

Du Bois, W. E. B. (1989) *The Souls of Black Folk*, New York: Penguin.

Eaton, J. S. (2001) *Distance Learning: Academic and Political Challenges for Higher Education Accreditation*, CHEA Monograph Series 2001, No. 1, Washington, DC: Council for Higher Education Accreditation.

Eduventures (2008) *Global Competency: Competitive Scan and Analysis of Bachelor Program Viability*, Boston, MA: Eduventures, Online Higher Education Learning Collaborative.

Edwards, R. and Usher, R. (2008) *Globalisation and Pedagogy: Space, Place and Identity* (2nd edn), New York: Routledge.

Ellsworth, P. (1994) 'Sense, culture, and sensibility', in S. Kitayama and H. Markus (eds) *Emotion and Culture: Empirical Studies of Cultural Influence*, Washington, DC: American Psychological Association, pp. 23–50.

Ertmer, P. A. and Russell, J. D. (1995) 'Using case studies to enhance instructional design education', *Educational Technology* 55(4): 23–31.

Ess, C. M. (2001) 'We are the Borg: the web as agent of assimilation or cultural renaissance?', available at: *http://sammelpunkt.philo.at:8080/1156/1/We_are_the_Borg_Charles_Ess.pdf* (accessed 10 July 2008).

Ewalt, P., Freeman, E. M., Kirk, S. A. and Poole, D. L. (eds) (1996) *Multicultural Issues in Social Work*, Washington, DC: NASW Press.

Ewell, P. T. (2001) *Accreditation and Student Learning Outcomes: A Proposed Point of Departure*, Washington, DC: Council for Higher Education Accreditation, National Center for Higher Education Management Systems.

Ewell, P. T. (2005) 'Can assessment serve accountability? It depends on the question', in J. C. Burke and Associates (eds) *Achieving Accountability in Higher Education: Balancing Public, Academic, and Market Demands*, San Francisco, CA: Jossey-Bass, pp. 104–24.

Fabos, B. and Young, M. D. (1999) 'Telecommunication in the classroom: rhetoric versus reality', *Review of Educational Research* 69(3): 217–59.

Falicov, C. J. (1996) 'Mexican families', in M. McGoldrick, J. Giordano and J. K. Pearce (eds) *Ethnicity and Family Therapy*, New York: Guilford Press, pp. 169–82.

Felder, R. (1993) 'Reaching the second tier: learning and teaching styles in college of science education', *Journal of College Science Teaching* 23(5): 286–90.

Fitzpatrick, J. L., Sanders, J. R. and Worthen, B. R. (2003) *Program Evaluation: Alternative Approaches and Practical Guidelines* (3rd edn), New York: Longman.

Flynn, A. and Klein, J. (2001) 'The influence of discussion groups in a case-based learning environment', *Educational Technology Research and Development* 49(3): 71–86.

Ford, N. and Chen, Y. (2000) 'Individual differences, hypermedia navigation and learning: An empirical study', *Journal of Educational Multimedia and Hypermedia* 9(4): 281–311.

Forrest, S. (2008) 'Staying competitive with Europe', *International Educator* 17(3): 88–91.

Francesco, A. M. and Gold, B. A. (2004) *International Organizational Behavior* (2nd edn), Upper Saddle River, NJ: Prentice-Hall.

Frankola, K. (2001) 'Why online learners drop out', *Workforce* 80(10): 53–9.

Friedman, T. L. (2005) *The World is Flat: A Brief History of the Twenty-First Century*, New York: Farrar, Straus and Giroux.

Friedman, T. L. and Ramonet, I. (1999) 'Dueling globalizations: A debate', *Foreign Policy* 116(Fall): 110–27.

Fulk, J. and Collins-Jarvis, L. (2001) 'Wired meetings: technological mediation of organizational gatherings', in L. L. Putnam and F. M. Jablins (eds) *New Handbook of Organizational Communication* (2nd edn), Newbury Park, CA: Sage, pp. 624–703.

Gaede, S. D. (1993) *When Tolerance is no Virtue: Political Correctness, Multiculturalism, and the Future of Truth and Justice*, Downers Grove, IL: Intervarsity Press.

Gallenson, A., Heins, J. and Heins, T. (2002) 'Macromedia MX: creating learning objects', available at: *http://download.macromedia.com/pub/elearning/objects/mx_creating_lo.pdf* (accessed on 17 July 2008).

Gandhe, S. K. (1998) 'Access and equity: the needs of the disadvantaged', paper presented at The Asian Distance Learner, the 12th Annual Conference of the Asian Association of Open Universities, Hong Kong, 4–6 November.

Gao, T. and Lehman, J. (2003) 'The effects of different levels of interaction on the achievement and motivational perceptions of college learners in a web-based learning environment', *Journal of Interactive Learning Research* 14(4): 367–86.

Gardner, H. (1999) *Intelligence Reframed*, New York: Basic Books.

Garrison, R. (2000) 'Theoretical challenges for distance education in the 21st century: A shift from structural to transactional issues', *International Review of Research in Open and Distance Learning* 1(1): 1–17.

Garrison, D. R., Anderson, T. and Archer, W. (2001) 'Critical thinking, cognitive presence, and computer conferencing in distance education', *The American Journal of Distance Education* 15(1): 7–23.

Garrison, D. R., Cleveland-Innes, M. and Fung, T. (2004) 'Student role adjustment in online communities of inquiry: model and instrument validation', *Journal of Asynchronous Learning Networks* 8(2): 61–74.

Gay, G. (2000) *Culturally Responsive Teaching: Theory, Research and Practice*, New York: Teachers College Press.

Gladieux, L. E. and Swail, W. S. (1999) *The Virtual University and Educational Opportunity: Issues of Equity and Access for the Next Generation, Washington*, DC: The College Board.

Glasersfeld, E. von (1987) 'An introduction to radical constructivism', in E. von Glasersfeld (ed.) *The Construction of Knowledge*, Seaside, CA: Intersystems Publications, pp. 193–217.

Glasser, W. (1986) *Control Theory in the Classroom*, New York: Harper and Row.

Glenn, D. (2003) 'Scholars who blog: the soapbox of the digital age draws a crowd of academics', *The Chronicle of Higher Education* 49(39): A14.

Goldsmith, E. (1993) *The Way: An Ecological World View*, Boston, MA: Shambala.

Green, M. F., Luu, D. T., Calderon, L. and Eckel, P. D. (2007) *Venturing abroad: Delivering US Degrees through Overseas Branch Campuses and Programs*, Washington, DC: American Council on Education.

Griffin, E. (2008) *A First Look at Communication Theory* (7th revised edn), Boston, MA: Irwin/McGraw-Hill.

Griffith, B. (2008) *Cultural Narration*, Rotterdam: Sense Publishers.

Groen, J., Tworek, J. and Soos-Gonczol, M. (2008) 'The effective use of synchronous classes within an online graduate program: building upon an interdependent system', *International Journal on E-Learning* 7(2): 245–63.

Grow, G. O. (1996) 'Teaching learners to be self-directed', *Adult Education Quarterly* 41(3): 125–49.

Gudykunst, W. B. (1995) 'Anxiety/uncertainty management (AUM) theory: current status', in R. L. Wiseman (ed.) *Intercultural Communication Theory*, Thousand Oaks, CA: Sage, pp. 8–58.

Gudykunst, W. B. and Matsumoto, Y. (1996) 'The influence of cultural individualism-collectivism, self construals, and individual values on communication styles across cultures', *Human Communication Research* 22(4): 510–43.

Gulati, S. (2008) 'Compulsory participation in online discussions: is this constructivism or normalisation of learning?' *Innovations in Education and Teaching International* 45(2): 183–92.

Guy, R. (1990) 'Research and distance education in the third world cultural context', in T. Evans (ed.) *Research in Distance Education I*, Geelong, Victoria: Deakin University.

Haag, S. (2006) *Management Information Systems for the Information Age*, New York: McGraw-Hill.

Habermas, J. (1987) *The Theory of Communication* (Vol. 2) Oxford: Basil Blackwell.

Hall, E. T. and Hall, M. R. (1990) *Understanding Cultural Differences*, New York: Intercultural Press.

Hall, P. (1996) 'Distance education and electronic networking', *Information Technology for Development* 7(2): 75–89.

Hammer, M. R., Bennett, M. J. and Wiseman, R. (2003) Measuring intercultural sensitivity: The Intercultural Development Inventory. *International Journal of Intercultural Relations* 27: 421–43.

Hanna, D. E. (ed.) (2000) *Higher Education in an Era of Digital Competition: Choices and Challenges*, Madison, WI: Attwood.

Harasim, L. (1990) 'Online education: An environment for collaboration and intellectual amplification', in L. Harasim (ed.) *Online Education: Perspectives on a New Environment*, New York: Praeger, pp. 39–64.

Hartsell, T. and Yuen, S. (2006) 'Video streaming in online learning', *AACE Journal* 14(1): 31–43.

Harvey, L. and Green, D. (1993) 'Defining quality', *Assessment and Evaluation in Higher Education* 18(1): 9–34.

Hax, A. C. and Majluf, N. S. (1996) *The Strategy Concept and Process: A Pragmatic Approach*, Upper Saddle River, NJ: Prentice-Hall.

Heaton, L. (1999) 'Preserving communication context: Virtual workspace and interpersonal space in Japanese CSCW', *AI and Society* 13(4): 357–76.

Hernandez, H. (1989) *Multicultural Education. A Teacher's Guide to Content and Process*, Columbus, OH: Merrill Publishing.

Herring, S. C. (1996) 'Bringing familiar baggage to the new frontier: gender differences in computer-mediated communication', in V. J. Vitanza (ed.) *CyberReader*, Needham Heights, MA: Allyn and Bacon, pp. 144–54.

Hewstone, M. and Brown, R. J. (1986) 'Contact is not enough: An intergroup perspective on the Contact Hypothesis', in M. Hewstone and R. J. Brown (eds) *Contact and Conflict in Intergroup Encounters*, Oxford: Blackwell, pp. 1–44.

Heyneman, S. P. (2006) 'Global issues in higher education', *eJournal USA* 11(1): 52–5.

Hislop, G. and Ellis, H. (2004) 'A study of faculty effort in online teaching', *Internet and Higher Education* 7(1): 15–32.

Hites, J. M. (1996) 'Design and delivery of training for international trainees: A case study', *Performance Improvement Quarterly* 9(2): 57–74.

Hofstede, G. (1984) *Culture's Consequences: International Differences in Work-Related Values*, Newbury Park, CA: Sage.

Hofstede, G. (1991) *Culture and Organizations: Software of the Mind*, London: McGraw-Hill.

Hofstede, G. (2004) *Cultures and Organizations: Software of the Mind* (2nd edn), New York: McGraw-Hill.

Hofstede, G. and McCrae, R. R. (2004) 'Personality and culture revisited: linking traits and dimensions of culture', *Cross-Cultural Research* 38(1): 52–88.

Hong,Y., Morris, M. W., Chiu, C. and Benet-Martinez, V. (2000) 'Multicultural minds – a dynamic constructivist approach to culture and cognition', *American Psychologist* 55(7): 709–20.

House, R. J., Hanges, P. J., Javidan, M., Dorfman, P. W. and Gupta, V. (eds) (2004) *Culture, Leadership, and Organizations: The GLOBE Study of 62 Cultures*, Thousand Oaks, CA: Sage.

Huang, H-M. (2002) 'Toward constructivism for adult learners in online learning environments', *British Journal of Educational Technology* 33(1): 27–37.

Hull, D. (1993) *Opening Minds, Opening Doors: The Rebirth of American Education*, Waco, TX: Center for Occupational Research and Development.

Hurtado, S., Milem, J., Clayton-Pedersen, A. and Allen, W. (1999) *Enacting Diverse Learning Environments: Improving the Climate for Racial/Ethnic Diversity in Higher Education*, ASHE-ERIC Higher Education Report, Vol. 26, No. 8, Washington, DC: George Washington University, Graduate School of Education and Human Development.

Hwang, A., Franscesco, A. M. and Kessler, E. (2003) 'The relationship between individualism-collectivism, face, and feedback and learning processes in Hong Kong, Singapore, and the United States', *Journal of Cross-Cultural Psychology* 34(1): 72–91.

Ibarra, R. A. (2001) *Beyond Affirmative Action: Reframing the Context of Higher Education*, Madison, WI: University of Wisconsin Press.

Ibarra, R. A. (2006) 'Context diversity: reframing higher education in the 21st Century', available at: *http://www.compact.org/20th/read/context_diversity* (accessed 25 June 2008).

Ibrahim, M., Rwegasira, K. S. P. and Taher, A. (2007) 'Institutional factors affecting students' intentions to withdraw from distance learning programs in the Kingdom of Saudi Arabia: the case of the Arab Open University (AOU)', *Online Journal of Distance Learning Administration* 10(1), available at: *http://www.westga.edu/~distance/ojdla/spring101/ibrahim101.htm* (accessed 30 August 2008).

International Telecommunication Union (ITU) (2007) *ICT Indicators Database 2007*, Geneva: ITU.

Irani, T. (2001) 'Going the distance: developing a model distance education faculty training program', available at: *http://campustechnology .com/articles/38638/* (accessed 19 July 2008).

Jakes, D. S., Pennington, M. E. and Knodle, H. A. (2002) 'Using the internet to promote inquiry-based learning', available at: *http://www .biopoint.com/inquiry/ibr.html* (accessed 1 August 2008).

James, D. (2004) 'A need for humor in online courses', *College Teaching* 52(3): 93–4.

James, R. (2001) 'Students' changing expectations of higher education and the consequences of mismatches with the reality', paper presented at the OECD-IMHE Conference: Management Responses to Changing Student Expectations, Brisbane, 24 September, available at: *http:// www.cshe.unimelb.edu.au/people/staff_pages/James/James-OECD_ IMHE.pdf* (accessed 24 August 2008).

James, W. B. and Gardner, D. L. (1995) 'Learning styles: implications for distance learning', *New Directions for Adult and Continuing Education* 67(1): 19–32.

Johnson, E. B. (2001) *Contextual Teaching and Learning: What it is and Why it's Here to Stay*, Thousand Oaks, CA: Corwin Press.

Johnson, D. W., Johnson, R. T. and Smith, K. A. (1991) *Active Learning: Cooperation in the College Classroom*, Edina, MN: Interaction.

Joinson, A. (2006) 'Causes and implications of disinhibited behavior on the internet', in J. Gackenbach (ed.) *Psychology and the Internet: Intrapersonal, interpersonal, and transpersonal Implications* (2nd edn), New York: Academic Press, pp. 43–60.

Jonassen, D. H. (1995) 'Operationalizing mental models: strategies for assessing mental models to support meaningful learning and design-supportive learning environments', *Proceedings of the Computer Support for Collaborative Learning Conference, Bloomington, IA, 17–20 October 1995*, Mahwah, NJ: Lawrence Erlbaum Associates.

Jonassen, D. H. (2000) 'Transforming learning with technology: beyond modernism and postmodernism or whoever controls the technology creates the reality', *Educational Technology* 40(2): 21–5.

Jordan, T. (2001) 'Language and libertarianism: the politics of cyberculture and the culture of cyberpolitics', *The Sociological Review* 49(1): 1–17.

Jung, I. (2005) 'Quality assurance survey of mega universities', in C. McIntosh (ed.) *Perspectives on Distance Education: Lifelong Learning and Distance Higher Education*, Vancouver and Paris: Commonwealth of Learning and UNESCO, pp. 79–95.

Kälvermark, T. and van der Wende, M. C. (eds) (1997) *National Policies for Internationalisation of Higher Education in Europe*, Stockholm: National Agency for Higher Education.

Katz, J. and Aspden, P. (1997) 'Motivations for and barriers to internet usage: results of a national public opinion survey', *Internet Research: Electronic Networking Applications and Policy* 7(3): 170–88.

Katz, R. N. and Oblinger, D. G. (eds) (2000) *The 'e' is for Everything: E-Commerce, E-Business and E-Learning in the Future of Higher Education*, San Francisco, CA: Jossey-Bass.

Kearsley, G. and Blomeyer, R. (2004) 'Preparing K-12 teachers to teach online', *Educational Technology* 44(1): 49–52.

Kember, D. (2000) 'Misconceptions about the learning approaches motivation and study practices of Asian students', *Higher Education* 40(2): 99–121.

Kim, Y. Y. (1988) *Communication and Cross Cultural Adaptation: An Integrative Theory*, Clevedon, PA: Multilingual Matters.

King, A. (1992) 'Comparison of self-questioning, summarizing, and notetaking – review as strategies for learning from lectures', *American Educational Research Journal* 29(2): 303–23.

King, J. E. (1991) 'Dysconscious racism: ideology, identity, and the mis-education of teachers', *Journal of Negro Education* 60(2): 133–66.

Kitano, M. K. (1997) 'What a course will look like after multicultural change', in A. Morey and M. K. Kitano (eds) *Multicultural Course Transformation in Higher Education: A Broader Truth*, Needham Heights, MA: Allyn and Bacon, pp. 18–34.

Kitayama, S., Duffy, S., Kawamura, T. and Larsen, J. T. (2003) 'Perceiving an object and its context in different cultures: a cultural look at new look', *Psychological Science* 14(3): 201–6.

Knowles, M. S. (1989) *The Making of an Adult Educator: An Autobiographical Journey*, San Francisco, CA: Jossey-Bass.

Knowles, M. S., Holton, E. F., III and Swanson, R. A. (2005) *The Adult Learner: The Definitive Classic in Adult Education and Human Resource Development* (6th edn), Woburn, MA: Butterworth-Heinemann.

Kosecoff, J. and Fink, A. (1982) *Evaluation Basics: A Practitioner's Manual*, Newbury Park, CA: Sage.

Kotler, P. and Fox, K. A. (1995) *Strategic Marketing for Educational Institutions*, New York: Prentice-Hall.

Krathwohl, D. R., Bloom, B. S. and Masia, B. B. (1964) *Taxonomy of Educational Objectives, The Classification of Educational Goals – Handbook II: Affective Domain*, New York: McKay.

Kuhlman, T. (2008) 'Is Google making our e-learning stupid?', available at: *http://www.articulate.com/rapid-elearning/is-google-making-our-e-learning-stupid/* (accessed 31 August 2008).

Kuhne, B. (1995) 'The Barkestorp project: investigating school library use', *School Libraries Worldwide* 1(1): 13–27.

Kulhavy, R. W. and Stock, W. A. (1989) 'Feedback in written instruction: the place of response certitude', *Educational Psychology Review* 1(4): 279–308.

Kumar, K. L. and Bhattacharya, M. (2007) 'Designing for learning effectiveness across borders in a multicultural context', *Journal of Interactive Learning Research* 18(1): 111–21.

Labi, A. (2005, December 16) 'Two agencies announce quality controls', *The Chronicle of Higher Education* 52(17): A41.

LaFromboise, T., Coleman, H. and Gerton, J. (1993) 'Psychological impact of biculturalism: evidence and theory', *Psychological Bulletin* 114(3): 295–412.

Lagorio, C. (2007) 'The ultimate distance learning', available at: *http://www.nytimes.com/2007/01/07/education/edlife/07innovation.html?_r=1&ex=1175572800&en=9ca2aab9111bf8d8&ei=5070&oref=slogin* (accessed 7 September 2008).

Larreamendy-Joerns, J. and Leinhardt, G. (2006) 'Going the distance with online education', *Review of Educational Research* 76(4): 567–605.

Larsen, K., Martin, J. P. and Morris, R. (2002) 'Trade in educational services: trends and emerging issues', working paper, available at: *http://www.oecd.org/dataoecd/54/44/2538356.pdf* (accessed 8 July 2008).

Lea, M. and Blake, N. (2004) *H805: Understanding Distributed and Flexible Learning, Block 3, Globalisation, Knowledge, Learning and Identity*, Milton Keynes: The Open University.

Lederman, D. (2008) 'Let the assessment PR wars begin', available at: *http://www.insidehighered.com/news/2008/08/18/cla* (accessed 18 August 2008).

Lenzer, R. and Johnson, S. S. (1997) 'Seeing things as they really are', available at: *http://www.forbes.com/forbes/1997/0310/5905122a.html* (accessed 25 June 2008).

Lerner, M. (2000) *Spirit Matters*, Charlottesville, VA: Hampton Roads Publishing Company.

Levin, J. R. and Mayer, R. (1993) 'Understanding illustrations in text', in B. Britten, A. Woodward and M. Binkley (eds) *Learning from Textbooks: Theory and Practice*, Hillsdale, NJ: Erlbaum, pp. 95–113.

Librero, F., Ramos, A. J., Ranga, A. I., Triñona, J. and Lambert, D. (2007) 'Uses of the cell phone for education in the Philippines and Mongolia', *Distance Education* 28(2): 231–44.

Lockee, B., Moore, M. and Burton, J. (2001) 'Old concerns with new distance education research', *Educause Quarterly* 2: 60–2.

Lombardi, M. M. (2007) 'Authentic learning for the 21st century: an overview', available at: *http://www.educause.edu/ir/library/pdf/ELI3009.pdf* (accessed 31 July 2008).

Lovett, M., Meyer, O. and Thille, C. (2008) 'The open learning initiative: measuring the effectiveness of the OLI statistics course in accelerating student learning', available at: *http://www.cmu.edu/oli/publications/LovettMeyerThille-OpenLearn.pdf* (accessed 10 July 2008).

Macfarlane, B. and Ottewill, R. (eds) (2001) *Effective Learning and Teaching in Business and Management*, London: Kogan Page.

Mancy, R. and Reid, N. (2004) 'Aspects of cognitive style and programming', paper presented at the 16th Workshop of the Psychology of Programming Interest Group, Carlow, 5–7 April.

Maness, J. M. (2006) 'Library 2.0 theory: Web 2.0 and its implications for libraries', *Webology* 3(2), available at: *http://www.webology.ir/2006/v3n2/a25.html* (accessed 5 July 2008).

Manning, L. and Mayor, B. (1999) 'Open and distance learning in a cross-cultural Context.' Paper presented to the International Conference on Distance Education, Vienna, June 1999.

Manning, M. L. and Baruth, L. G. (1996) *Multicultural Education of Children and Adolescents*, Boston, MA: Allyn and Bacon.

Marcus, A. and Gould, E. (2000) 'Cultural dimensions and global web user-interface design: What? So what? Now what?' *Proceedings of the 6th Conference on Human Factors and the Web, Austin, TX, 19 June 2000*, pp. 1–15.

Markus, H. R. and Kitayama, S. (1991) 'Culture and the self-implications for cognition, emotion, and motivation', *Psychological Review* 98(2): 224–53.

Marshall, P. L. (2002) *Cultural Diversity in our Schools*, Belmont, CA: Wadsworth/Thomson.

Martin, R. A., Puhlik-Dorris, P., Larsen, G., Gray, J. and Weir, K. (2003) 'Individual differences in uses of humor and their relation to psychological well-being: development of the humor styles questionnaire', *Journal of Research in Personality* 37(1): 48–75.

Mason, R. (1998) *Globalizing Education: Trends and Applications*, London: Routledge.

Matsumoto, D. (2007) 'Individual and cultural differences in status differentiation: the status differentiation scale', *Journal of Cross-Cultural Psychology* 38(4): 413–31.

Matthews, D. (1999) 'The origins of distance education and its use in the United States', *THE Journal*, September, available at: *http://www .thejournal.com/articles/14278* (accessed 15 June 2008).

Mayer, R. E. (2003) 'The promise of multimedia learning: using the same instructional design methods across different media', *Learning and Instruction* 73(1): 125–39.

Mayfield, R. (2006) 'There is no Web 3.0, part, uh 2', available at: *http://ross.typepad.com/blog/2006/11/there_is_no_web.html* (accessed 5 July 2008).

McConnell, D. (2002) 'Action research and distributed problem-based learning in continuing professional education', *Distance Education* 23(1): 59–83.

McGivney, V. (1993) 'Participation and non-participation. A review of the literature', in R. Edwards, S. Sieminski and D. Zeldin (eds) *Adult Learners, Education and Training*, London: Routledge, pp. 11–30.

McIsaac, M. S. (1993) 'Economic, political and social considerations in the use of global computer-based distance education', in R. Muffoletto and N. Knupfer (eds) *Computers in Education: Social, Political, and Historical Perspectives*, Cresskill, NJ: Hampton Press, pp. 219–32.

McMillan, D. W. (1996) 'Sense of community', *Journal of Community Psychology* 24(4): 315–25.

McMillan, D. W. and Chavis, D. M. (1986) 'Sense of community: a definition and theory', *Journal of Community Psychology* 4(1): 6–23.

Mehrabian, A. (1969) 'Some referents and measures of nonverbal behavior', *Behavior Research Methods and Instrumentation* 1(6): 205–7.

Merisotis, J. P. and Phipps, R. A. (1999) *What's the difference? A Review of Contemporary Research on the Effectiveness of Distance Learning in Higher Education*, Washington, DC: Institute for Higher Education Policy.

Merriam, S. B. and Caffarella, R. S. (1999) *Learning in Adulthood* (2nd edn), San Francisco, CA: Jossey-Bass.

Miller, G. E. (2008) 'Global trends in distance education', *Sloan-C View* 7(6), available at: *http://www.sloan-c.org/publications/view/v7n6/viewv7n6.htm* (accessed 16 June 2008).

Mills, J. (1999) 'Improving the 1957 version of dissonance theory', in E. Harmon-Jones and J. Mills (eds) *Cognitive Dissonance – Progress on a Pivotal Theory in Social Psychology*, Washington, DC: American Psychological Association, pp. 25–42.

Millis, B. J. and Cottell, P. G. (1998) *Cooperative Learning for Higher Education Faculty*, Phoenix, AZ: Oryx Press.

MIT (2001) 'MIT to make nearly all course materials available free on the world wide web', available at: *http://web.mit.edu/newsoffice/2001/ocw.html* (accessed 10 July 2008).

Moll, L. C. (2005) 'Sociocultural competence in teacher education', *Journal of Teacher Education* 56(3): 242–46.

Moore, J. C. (ed.) (2002) *Elements of Quality: The Sloan-C framework*, Needham, MA: Sloan Center for Online Education.

Moore, M. G. (2003) *From Chautauqua to the Virtual University: A Century of Distance Education in the United States*, Columbus, OH: Center on Education and Training for Employment.

Moore, M. G. and Kearsley, G. (2005) *Distance Education: A Systems View* (2nd edn), Belmont, CA: Thompson Wadsworth.

Morse, K. (2003) 'Does one size fit all? Exploring asynchronous learning in a multicultural environment', *Journal of Asynchronous Learning Networks* 7(1): 37–55.

Mupinga, D. M., Nora, R. T. and Yaw, D. C. (2006) 'The learning styles, expectations, and needs of online students', *College Teaching* 54(1): 185–9.

Muppala, J. K. and Kong, C. K. (2007) 'Podcasting and its use in enhancing course content', in V. Uskov (ed.) *Proceedings of Computers and Advanced Technology in Education, Beijing, 8–10 October 2007*, Calgary, Alberta: Acta Press.

Nagel, D. (2008) 'iTunes U expands international reach', available at: *http://campustechnology.com/articles/63722/* (accessed 8 July 2008).

Naismith, L., Lonsdale, P., Vavoula, G. and Sharples, M. (2004) 'Mobile technologies and learning', available at: *http://www.futurelab.org.uk/resources/publications_reports_articles/literature_reviews/Literature_Review203/* (accessed 7 September 2008).

Neave, G. (1998) 'The evaluative state reconsidered', *European Journal of Education* 33(3): 265–84.

Neave, G. (2004) 'Higher education policy as orthodoxy: being a tale of doxological drift, political intention and changing circumstances', in P. Teixeira, B. Jongbloed, D. Dill and A. Amaral (eds) *Markets in Higher Education: Rhetoric or Reality?* Dordrecht, NL: Kluwer Academic Publishers, pp. 127–60.

Nelson, K. G. and Clark, T. D. (1994) 'Cross-cultural issues in information systems research: A research program', *Journal of Global Information Management* 2(4): 19–29.

Neumann, Y., Finaly-Neumann, E. and Reichel, A. (1990) 'Determinants and consequences of students' burnout in universities', *Journal of Higher Education* 61(1): 20–31.

New Media Consortium and the EDUCAUSE Learning Initiative (2008) 'The Horizon Report (2008 edition)', available at: *http://www.nmc.org/pdf/2008-Horizon-Report.pdf* (accessed 10 July 2008).

Ngai, P. B. (2003) 'Linking distance and international education: A strategy for developing multicultural competence among distance learners', *Journal of Studies in International Education* 7(2): 157–77.

Nielsen, J. (1997) 'Usability testing', in G. Salvendy (ed.) *Handbook of Human Factors and Ergonomics*, New York: John Wiley, pp. 1543–68.

Noam, E. (1995) 'Electronics and the dim future of the university', *Science* 270(13): 247–49.

Noddings, N. (1996) 'On community', *Educational Theory* 46(3): 245–67.

Noddings, N. (2003) *Caring: A Feminine Approach to Ethics and Moral Education* (2nd edn), Berkeley, CA: University of California Press.

Oblinger, D. G. (2003) 'Boomers, Gen-Xers, and Millennials: understanding the new students', *EDUCAUSE Review* 38(4): 37–47.

Oblinger, D. G., Barone, C. A. and Hawkins, B. L. (2001) 'Distributed education and its challenges: an overview', available at: *http://www.acenet.edu/bookstore/pdf/distributed-learning/distributed-learning-01.pdf* (accessed 15 June 2008).

Olcott, D., Jr. and Wright, S. J. (1995) 'An institutional support framework for increasing faculty participation in postsecondary distance education', *The American Journal of Distance Education* 9(3): 5–17.

Onibere, E. A., Morgan, S., Busang, E. M. and Mpoeleng, D. (2000) 'Human computer interface design issues for a multicultural multilingual English speaking country – Botswana', *The Interdisciplinary Journal of Human-Computer Interaction* 4(13): 497–512.

Organisation for Economic Cooperation and Development (2004) *Quality and Recognition in Higher Education: The Cross-Border Challenge*, Paris: OECD.

Organisation for Economic Cooperation and Development (2007) *Education at a glance: OECD indicators* 2007, Paris: OECD.

Orngreen, R. (2005) 'CaseMaker: an environment for case-based e-learning', *Electronic Journal of e-Learning* 2(1), available at: *http://www.ejel.org/volume-2/vol2-issue1/issue1-art7.htm* (accessed 31 July 2008).

Osman, M. E. and Hannafin, M. J. (1994) 'Effects of advance questioning and prior knowledge on science learning', *Journal of Education Research* 88(1): 5–13.

Owston, R. D. (1997) 'The World Wide Web: A technology to enhance teaching and learning?' *Educational Researcher* 26(2): 27–33.

Paczkowski, J. (2007) 'Web 3. Oh – God – will – this – silly – versioning – never – stop?!!', available at: *http://digitaldaily.allthingsd.com/category/web-20-20/* (accessed 7 July 2008).

Palloff, R. and Pratt, K. (1999) *Building Learning Communities in Cyberspace: Effective Strategies for the Online Classroom*, San Francisco, CA: Jossey-Bass.

Palmer, P. J. (1998) *The Courage to Teach: Exploring the Inner Landscape of a Teacher's Life*, San Francisco, CA: Jossey-Bass.

Palomba, M. and Banta, T. (1999) *Assessment Essentials: Planning, Implementing and Improving Assessment in Higher Education*, San Francisco, CA: Jossey-Bass.

Parekh, B. (1998) 'Integrating minorities', in T. Blackstone, B. Parekh and P. Sanders (eds) *Race Relations in Britain. A Developing Agenda*, London: Routledge, pp. 1–21.

Parrish, P. E. (2004) 'The trouble with learning objects', *Educational Technology, Research and Development* 52(1): 49–68.

Pascarella, E. T. and Terenzini, P. T. (1991) *How College Affects Students: Findings and Insights from Twenty Years of Research*, San Francisco, CA: Jossey Bass.

Paul, R. (1988) 'If student services are so important, then why are we cutting them back?' In D. Sewart and J. S. Daniel (eds) *Developing Distance Education. Proceedings of the 14th International Council for Distance Education World Conference, Oslo, 9–16 August 1988*, Oslo: International Council for Distance Education.

Peng, K. and Nisbett, R. E. (1999) 'Culture, dialectics, and reasoning about contradiction', *American Psychologist* 54(9): 741–54.

Perraton, H. (2000) *Open and Distance Learning in the Developing World*, London: Routledge.

Perrow, C. (1967) 'A framework for the comparative analysis of organizations', *American Sociological Review* 32(2): 194–208.

Petrina, S., Volk, K. and Soowook, K. (2004) 'Technology and rights', *International Journal of Technology and Design Education* 14(3): 181–204.

Phipps, R. A., Wellman, J. V. and Merisotis, J. P. (1998) 'Assuring quality in distance learning: a preliminary review', available at: *http://www.chea.org/events/qualityassurance/98may.html* (accessed 21 September 2008).

Picciano, A. G. (2001) *Distance Learning: Making Connections across Virtual Space and Time*, Upper Saddle River, NJ: Prentice-Hall.

Pincas, A. (2001) 'Culture, cognition and communication in global education', *Distance Education* 22(1): 30–51.

Polsani, P. R. (2003) 'Use and abuse of reusable learning objects', *Journal of Digital Information* 3(4), article no. 164 2003-02-19, available at: *http://jodi.tamu.edu/Articles/v03/i04/Polsani/* (accessed 21 October 2008).

Ponzurick, T. G., France, K. and Logar, C. M. (2000) 'Delivering graduate marketing education: an analysis of face-to-face versus distance education', *Journal of Marketing Education* 22(3): 180–7.

Postmes, T., Spears, R. and Lea, M. (1998) 'Breaching or building social boundaries? Side-effects of computer-mediated communication', *Communication Research* 25(6): 689–715.

Prince, M. and Felder, R. (2007) 'The many faces of inductive teaching and learning', *Journal of College Science Teaching* 36(5): 14–20.

Privateer, P. M. (1999) 'Academic technology and the future of higher education: strategic paths taken and not taken', *The Journal of Higher Education* 70(1): 60–79.

Prosser, M. and Trigwell, K. (1999) *Understanding Learning and Teaching: The Experience in Higher Education*, Buckingham: SHRE, Open University Press.

Putnam, R. (2000) *Bowling Alone: The Collapse and Revival of American Community*, New York: Simon and Schuster.

Rai, S. (2003) 'Rift in India leads MIT to abandon a media lab', available at: *http://query.nytimes.com/gst/fullpage.html?res=9B07E1D81F3CF 93BA35756C0A9659C8B63* (accessed 26 June 2008).

Ramsden, P. (1992) *Learning to Teach in Higher Education*, London: Routledge.

Rao, S. S. (2003) 'Copyright: its implication for electronic information', *Online Information Review* 27(4): 264–75.

Read, B. (2005) 'Lectures on the go', *The Chronicle of Higher Education* 52(10): A39.

Reeves, T. and Reeves, P. (1997) 'Effective dimensions of interactive learning on the world wide web', in B. Khan (ed.) *Web-based Instruction*, Englewood Cliffs, NJ: Educational Technology Publications, pp. 59–66.

Reigeluth, C. M. (1987) 'Lesson blueprints based on the elaboration theory of instruction', in C. M. Reigeluth (ed.) *Instructional Theories in Action: Lessons Illustrating Selected Theories and Models*, Hillsdale NJ: Erlbaum, pp. 245–88.

Reigeluth, C. M. (1997) 'Instructional theory, practitioner needs, and new directions: some reflections', *Educational Technology* 37(1): 42–47.

Reiser, R. A. (1987) 'Instructional technology: a history', in R. M. Gagne (ed.) *Instructional Technology: Foundations*, Hillsdale, NJ: Lawrence Erlbaum Associates, pp. 11–48.

Reiser, R. A. and Dempsey, J. V. (2007) *Trends and Issues in Instructional Design* (2nd edn), Upper Saddle River, NJ: Pearson Education.

Rendon, L. I. (1994) 'Validating culturally diverse students: toward a new model of learning and student development', *Innovative Higher Education* 19(1): 33–51.

Rhoades, G. (2006) 'The higher education we choose: a question of balance', *Review of Higher Education* 29(3): 381–404.

Rice, R. E. (1992) 'Task analyzability, use of new media, and effectiveness: a multi-site exploration of media richness', *Organization Science* 3(4): 475–500.

Richardson, B. (2007) 'A new realism', *Harvard International Review* 29(2): 26–32.

Robertson, H. (1998) *No More Teachers: No More Books*, Toronto: McLelland and Stewart.

Roblyer, M., Dozier-Henry, O. and Burnette, A. (1996) 'Technology and multicultural education: an uneasy alliance', *Educational Technology* 36(3): 5–12.

Rockenbach, B. and Almagno, S. (2000) 'Distance education: some of the unasked and unanswered questions', *International Information and Library Review* 32(3/4): 453–61.

Rogers, P. J. (2000) 'Program theory: not whether programs work but how they work', in D. L. Stufflebeam, G. F. Madaus and T. Kellaghan (eds) *Evaluation Models*, Boston, MA: Kluwer Academic, pp. 209–32.

Rogers, P. C., Graham, C. R. and Mayes, C. T. (2007) 'Cultural competence and instructional design: exploration research into the delivery of online instruction cross-culturally', *Educational Technology Research and Development* 55(2): 197–217.

Rovai, A. P. (2000) 'Online and traditional assessments: what is the difference?' *Internet and Higher Education* 3(3): 141–51.

Rovai, A. P. (2001) 'Building classroom community at a distance: a case study', *Educational Technology, Research and Development* 49(4): 33–48.

Rovai, A. P. (2002a) 'Sense of community, perceived cognitive learning and persistence in asynchronous learning networks', *Internet and Higher Education* 5(4): 319–32.

Rovai, A. P. (2002b) 'Development of an instrument to measure classroom community', *Internet and Higher Education* 5(3): 197–211.

Rovai, A. P. (2003a) 'In search of higher persistence rates in distance education online programs', *Internet and Higher Education* 6(1): 1–16.

Rovai, A. P. (2003b) 'A practical framework for evaluating online distance education programs', *Internet and Higher Education* 6(2): 109–24.

Rovai, A. P. (2003c) 'Discussions and classroom community in internet-based university courses', *Journal of Computing in Higher Education* 15(1): 89–107.

Rovai, A. P. (2004) 'A constructivist approach to online college learning', *Internet and Higher Education* 7(2): 79–93.

Rovai, A. P. and Petchauer, E. M. (2008) 'The digital divide and social equity', in G. D. Garson and M. Khosrow-Pour (eds) *Handbook of Research on Public Information Technology: Volume* 1, Hershey, PA: IGI Global, pp. 294–302.

Rovai, A. P., Ponton, M. K., Derrick, M. G. and Davis, J. M. (2006) 'Student evaluation of teaching in the virtual and traditional classrooms: a comparative analysis', *Internet and Higher Education* 9(1): 23–35.

Rovai, A. P., Ponton, M. K. and Baker, J. D. (2008) *Distance Learning in Higher Education: A Programmatic Approach to Planning, Design, Instruction, Evaluation, and Accreditation*, New York: Teachers College Press.

Rovai, A. P., Wighting, M. J. and Lucking, R. (2004) 'The classroom and school community inventory: development, refinement, and validation of a self-report measure for educational research', *Internet and Higher Education* 7(4): 263–80.

Rowley, D. J., Lujan, H. D. and Dolence, M. G. (1997) *Strategic Change in Colleges and Universities*, San Francisco, CA: Jossey-Bass.

Rowntree, D. (1995) 'Teaching and learning online. A correspondence education for the 21st century?' *British Journal of Educational Technology* 26(3): 205–15.

Royal, M. A. and Rossi, R. J. (1996) 'Individual-level correlates of sense of community: findings from workplace and school', *Journal of Community Psychology* 24(4): 395–416.

Rury, J. (1996) 'Inquiry in the general education curriculum', *Journal of General Education* 45(3): 175–96.

Russell, T. L. (1999) *No Significant Difference Phenomenon*, Raleigh, NC: North Carolina State University.

Ryan, J. G. (1993) 'After accreditation: how to institutionalize outcomes-based assessment', *New Directions for Community Colleges* 83(3): 75–81.

Salili, F. and Hoosain, R. (eds) (2001) *Multicultural Education Issues, Policies, and Practices*, Charlotte, NC: Information Age Publishing.

Salili, F. and Hoosain, R. (eds) (2006) *Religion in Multicultural Education*, Charlotte, NC: Information Age Publishing.

Salvatori, P. (2001) 'The history of occupational therapy assistants in Canada: a comparison with the United States', *Canadian Journal of Occupational Therapy* 68(4): 217–27.

Sanchez-Burks, J. (2002) 'Protestant relational ideology and (in) attention to relational cues in work settings', *Journal of Personality and Social Psychology* 83(4): 919–29.

Santiago, P., Tremblay, K., Basri, E. and Arnal, E. (2008) *Tertiary Education for the Knowledge Society: OECD Thematic Review of Tertiary Education: Synthesis Report*, Paris: OECD.

Savery, J. R. and Duffy, T. M. (1995) 'Problem based learning: an instructional model and its constructivist framework', *Educational Technology* 35(5): 31–8.

Schell, J. W. and Black, R. S. (1997) 'Situated learning: an inductive case study of a collaborative learning experience', *Journal of Industrial Teacher Education* 34(4): 5–28.

Scholte, J. A. (2005) *Globalization: A Critical Introduction* (2nd edn), London: Palgrave Macmillan.

Seels, B. and Glasgow, Z. (1997) *Exercises in Instructional Design* (2nd edn), Upper Saddle River, NJ: Prentice-Hall.

Seiden, P. A. (2000) 'Bridging the digital divide', *Reference and User Services Quarterly* 39(4): 329.

Seldin, P. (ed.) (2007) *Changing Practices in Evaluating Teaching: A Practical Guide to Improved Faculty Performance and Promotion/ Tenure Decisions*, San Francisco, CA: Jossey-Bass.

Sfard, A. (1998) 'On two metaphors for learning and the dangers of choosing just one', *Educational Researcher* 27(2): 4–13.

Sha, L. S. and Kaufman, D. M. (2005) 'Managing cognitive load while playing computer games', paper presented at the Annual Conference of the American Educational Research Association, Montreal, 10–14 April.

Shank, G. and Cunningham, D. (1996) 'Mediated phosphor dots', in C. Ess (ed.) *Philosophical Perspectives on Computer-Mediated Communication*, Albany, NY: State University of New York, pp. 27–45.

Shank, P. and Sitze, A. (2004) *Making Sense of Online Learning: A Guide to Beginners and the Truly Skeptical*, San Francisco, CA: Pfieffer.

Shealey, M. W. and Callins, T. (2007) 'Creating culturally responsive literacy programs in inclusive classrooms', *Intervention in School and Clinic* 42(4): 195–7.

Shoda, Y., Tiernan, S. L. and Mischel, W. (2002) 'Personality as a dynamic system: emergence of stability and distinctiveness from intra and interpersonal interactions', *Personality and Social Psychology Review* 6(4): 316–25.

Simonson, M., Smaldino, S., Albright, M. and Zvack, S. (2000) *Teaching and Learning at a Distance: Foundations of Distance Education*, Upper Saddle River, NJ: Prentice-Hall.

Sims, R. and Stork, E. (2007) 'Design for contextual learning: web-based environments that engage diverse learners', available at: *http://ausweb.scu.edu.au/aw07/papers/refereed/sims/paper.html* (accessed 30 July 2008).

Slaughter, S. and Leslie, L. L. (1997) *Academic Capitalism: Politics, Policies and the Entrepreneurial University*, Baltimore, MD: Johns Hopkins University Press.

Solorzano, D. G. and Yosso, T. J. (2001) 'From racial stereotyping and deficit discourse toward a critical race theory in teacher education', *Multicultural Education* 9(1): 2–8.

Sondergaard, M. (1994) 'Hofstede's consequences: a study of reviews, citations and replications', *Organization Studies* 15(3): 447–56.

Spencer-Oatey, H. (ed.) (2000) *Culturally Speaking: Managing Rapport through Talk Across Cultures*, London: Continuum.

Spivack, N. (2006) 'Minding the planet – The meaning and future of the semantic web', available at: *http://novaspivack.typepad.com/nova_spivacks_weblog/2006/11/minding_the_pla.html* (accessed 25 July 2008).

Spronk, B. (1998) 'Seeing the world through two pairs of eyes: staff development issues in distance/open learning programs for First Nations peoples in Canada', in C. Latchem and F. Lockwood (eds) *Staff Development in Open and Flexible Learning*, London: Routledge Falmer, pp. 127–36.

Stansfield, M., McLellan, E. and Connolly, T. (2004) 'Enhancing student performance in online learning and traditional face-to-face class delivery', *Journal of Information Technology Education* 3: 173–88, available at: *http://jite.org/documents/Vol3/v3p173-188-037.pdf* (accessed 21 October 2008).

Stead, G., Sharpe, B., Anderson, P., Cych, L. and Philpott, M. (2006) 'Emerging technologies for learning', available at: *http://partners.becta.org.uk/upload-dir/downloads/page_documents/research/emerging_technologies.pdf* (accessed 18 July 2008).

Stothart, C. (2006) 'Do the iPod shuffle, but don't miss the lecture', available at: *http://www.timeshighereducation.co.uk/story.asp?storyCode=203333&sectioncode=26* (accessed 8 July 2008).

Subramony, D. P. (2004) 'Instructional technologists' inattention to issues of cultural diversity among learners', *Educational Technology* 44(4): 19–24.

Suler, J. (2004) 'The online disinhibition effect', *CyberPsychology and Behavior* 7(3): 321–6.

Sun Certified Mobile Applications Developer Center (2005) 'Glossary', available at: *http://scmad.gayanb.com/j2me-glossary1.php* (accessed 7 September 2008).

Sweller, J. (1988) 'Cognitive load during problem solving', *Cognitive Science* 12(1): 257–85.

Tadmor, C. T. and Tetlock, P. E. (2006) 'Biculturalism: a model of the effects of second-culture exposure on acculturation and integrative complexity', *Journal of Cross-Cultural Psychology* 37(2): 173–90.

Tetlock, P. E. (2002) 'Social functionalist frameworks for judgment and choice: intuitive politicians, theologians, and prosecutors', *Psychological Review* 109(3): 451–71.

Tetlock, P. E., Peterson, R. S. and Lerner, J. S. (1996) 'Revising the value pluralism model: incorporating social content and context postulates', in C. Seligman, J. M. Olson and M. P. Zanna (eds) *The Psychology of Values: The Ontario Symposium*, Vol. 9, Mahwah, NJ: Lawrence Erlbaum, pp. 25–49.

Thamen, K. (1997) 'Considerations of culture in distance education in the Pacific Islands', in L. Rowan, L. Bartlett and T. Evans (eds) *Shifting Borders: Globalisation, Localisation and Open and Distance Education*, Geelong: Deakin University Press, pp. 23–34.

Tinto, V. (1987) *Leaving College*, Chicago, IL: University of Chicago Press.

Tinto, V. (1993) *Leaving College: Rethinking the Causes and Cures of Student Attrition*. Chicago, IL: University of Chicago Press.

Tisdell, E. J. (2001) *Spirituality in Adult and Higher Education. ERIC Digest*. Columbus OH: ERIC Clearinghouse on Adult Career and Vocational Education.

Tucker, S. Y. (2000) 'Assessing the effectiveness of distance education versus traditional on-campus education', paper presented at the Annual Meeting of the American Educational Research Association, New Orleans, LA, 24–28 April.

United Nations (1965) *International Convention on the Elimination of all Forms of Racial Discrimination*, available at: *http://www.unhchr.ch/html/menu3/b/d_icerd.htm* (accessed 25 June 2008).

United Nations Development Programme (1999) *Human Development Report 1999*, New York: Oxford University Press.

United Nations Educational, Scientific and Cultural Organization (UNESCO) (2001) *Code of Good Practice in the Provision of Transnational Education*, available at: *http://www.aic.lv/rec/Eng/leg_en/code_Tr.html* (accessed on 15 September 2008).

United Nations Educational, Scientific and Cultural Organization (UNESCO) (2005a) *Education for All: The Quality Imperative*, Paris: UNESCO.

United Nations Educational, Scientific and Cultural Organization (UNESCO) (2005b) *Guidelines for Quality Provision in Cross-Border Higher Education*, Paris: UNESCO.

US Department of Education, Office of Postsecondary Education (2006) *Evidence of Quality in Distance Education Programs Drawn from Interviews with the Accreditation Community*, Washington, DC: Government Printing Office.

Van Someren, A. (1998) *Learning with Multiple Representations*, Oxford: Elsevier Science.

•Vella, J. (2000) 'A spirited epistemology'. In L. English and M. Gillen (eds) *Addressing the Spiritual Dimensions of Adult Learning. New Directions for Adult and Continuing Education, No. 85*, San Francisco, CA: Jossey-Bass, pp. 7–16.

Verduin, J. R. and Clark, T. (1991) *Distance Education: The Foundations of Effective Practice*, San Francisco, CA: Jossey-Bass.

Vrasidas, C. and McIsaac, M. S. (2000) 'Principles of pedagogy and evaluation for web-based learning', *Educational Media International* 37(2): 105–11.

Vugt, F. von (2004) *Internationalisation and Globalization in European Higher Education*, Enschede: University of Twente.

Walther, J. B. (1996) 'Computer-mediated communication: impersonal, interpersonal, and hyperpersonal interaction', *Communication Research* 23(1): 3–43.

Wasserman, S. (1994) *Introduction to Case Method Teaching: A Guide to the Galaxy*, New York: Teachers College Press.

Waters, M. (1995) *Globalization*, London: Routledge.

Werner, W. and Case, R. (1997) 'Themes of global education', in A. Wright and A. Sears (eds) *Trends and Issues in Canadian Social Studies*, Vancouver: Pacific Educational Press, pp. 176–93.

Wiggins, G. and McTighe, J. (2005) *Understanding by Design* (2nd edn), New York: Prentice Hall.

Witkin, H. A. and Goodenough, D. R. (1981) *Cognitive Styles, Essence and Origins: Field Dependence and Field Independence*, New York: International Universities.

Witt, P. L., Wheeless, L. R. and Allen, M. (2004) 'A meta-analytical review of the relationship between teacher immediacy and student learning', *Communication Monographs* 71(2): 184–207.

Wlodkowski, R. J. and Ginsberg, M. B. (1996) 'I'm normal, you are not', *In these Times*, 5 April, pp. 29–30.

Workman, J. and Stenard, R. (1996) 'Student services for distance learners', *DEOSNEWS – The Distance Education Online Symposium* 6(3), available at: *http://www.ed.psu.edu/acsde/deos/deosnews/deosnews6_3.asp* (accessed 26 June 2008).

Zeszotarski, P. (2001) 'ERIC review: issues in global education initiatives in the community college', *Community College Review* 29(1): 65–78.

Index

Printed in the United States
218834BV00001B/3/P